INUIT YOUTH

■ A volume in the series
Adolescents in a Changing World

EDITED BY BEATRICE B. WHITING AND
JOHN W. M. WHITING

Project advisors:

Irven DeVore
Carol Gilligan
George W. Goethals
Jerome Kagan
Robert A. LeVine

Inuit Youth

Growth and Change
in the Canadian Arctic

Richard G. Condon

RUTGERS UNIVERSITY PRESS

New Brunswick and London

The Holman Settlement map (1.3) originally appeared in Richard Condon, *Inuit Behavior and Seasonal Change in the Canadian Arctic*. Chapter 1 of the present volume contains materials revised and updated from *Inuit Behavior*. This material is used by permission of UMI Research Press, Ann Arbor, Mich. Table 1.1, "Climatological Table for Holman Island," is used by permission of the Atmospheric Environment Service, Department of the Environment, Canada. The Holman Island Region map (1.2) appeared originally in Peter Usher, *Economic Basis and Resource Use of the Coppermine-Holman Region, N.W.T.,* Department of Northern Affairs and National Resources, Ottawa, 1965. This map is used by permission of the author.

Library of Congress Cataloging-in-Pubication Data
Condon, Richard G. (Richard Guy)
  Inuit youth.
  (Adolescents in a changing world ; v. 1)
  Bibliography: p.
  1. Eskimos—Northwest Territories—Youth.
2. Eskimos—Northwest Territories—Psychology.
3. Indians of North America—Northwest Territories—
Youth. 4. Indians of North America—Northwest
Territories—Psychology. 5. Holman Island (N.W.T.)—
Social conditions. I. Title. II. Series.
E99.E7C7283 1987   305.2′3′08997   86-20257
ISBN 0-8135-1212-3

8,295

British Cataloguing-in-Publication Information Available

For Margret Scott Condon
Pamela Rose Stern
and Kimberly Margret Condon

CONTENTS

.

ILLUSTRATIONS

Maps

Figures

TABLES

■ FOREWORD

to Adolescents in a Changing World series
BEATRICE B. WHITING
JOHN. W. M. WHITING

Few periods of the human life cycle have generated as much interest, or as much concern, as adolescence. The psychological, behavioral, and physical changes that occur at puberty are dramatic and have been the focus of much research by psychologists, educators, and sociologists. The study of adolescence has recently become a priority research topic among many private and government granting agencies, largely as a response to the increase in adjustment problems among American adolescents: alcohol and drug abuse, teenage suicide, juvenile delinquency, and teenage pregnancy. The study of adolescence is important not only because there is an urgent need to understand the socially destructive aspects of this life stage, but also because knowledge of this life stage can contribute greatly to a general understanding of the social, psychological, and physical aspects of human development in our own and other cultures.

Only recently have anthropologists turned their attention to the study of adolescence. Other than Margaret Mead's classic work *Coming of Age in Samoa,* few anthropologists have entered the field with the primary intention of conducting research on the adolescent experience in another society. While many ethnographies contain data on initiation rites, age grades, marriage practices, and premarital sexual behavior, all of which are important to the study of adolescence, the reporting of these topics has often been anecdotal in nature. For this reason we have organized and edited this series of volumes describing adolescence in seven different societies. These works are the product of years of fieldwork, data analysis, and writing by the staff and fellows of the Harvard Adolescence Project. These ethnographies will contribute to our knowledge of human development in other societies and perhaps stimulate similar research in other cultures on this fascinating stage of life.

Our interest in the cross-cultural study of adolescence is a natural outgrowth of our work on child development. Over the years we have had the opportunity to study the social behavior of children in a variety of cultures. Either individually or together, we have made field observations on American Indian children, the Kwoma of New Guinea, the Yoruba of Nigeria, the Kikuyu of Kenya, and preschool children in the United States. We have also directed several cross-cultural projects on child socialization, including the Six Cultures study and the socialization part of Florence and Clyde Kluckhohn's study of values in the American Southwest. Most recently, as directors of the Child Devlopment Research Unit of the University of Nairobi, we have had the opportunity to explore the patterns of family life among nine different cultural groups in Kenya.

Our involvement in these studies has provided us with a rich, cross-cultural data base on child development. We have learned that although there are many dramatic differences in the behavior of children across cultures, the common features are also striking. Some of these commonalities are particularly relevant to the study of adolescence. For example, in none of the cultures we have studied were boys and girls adequately prepared for the sudden surge of sex hormones that announce the onset of puberty. We have discovered that, in many respects, the socialization of children is counterproductive preparation for this event. Presumably as a consequence of the incest taboo, free and frank talk about sex is inhibited between parents and children. In none of the societies we have studied, nor in any other that we know of, do adults copulate in public. As a result, the sex act, from the child's perspective, is shrouded in secrecy and mystery.

Although adolescence requires many changes in the life-styles of girls and boys, the cultural scripts for social and economic behavior are more clearly formulated and more easily transmitted than those for sexual behavior. Since in late childhood same-sex companions predominate, learning appropriate heterosexual behavior and finding an appropriate mate are important tasks of adolescents. The hormonal changes that take place also require significant adjustment in self-image and emotions. Our studies focus on the changes in friendship formation, peer group relations, parent-child interactions, school achievement, self-image, and cognitive development.

In 1978, working with Robert Levine at the Laboratory of Human Development at the Harvard Graduate School of Education, we sponsored a postdoctoral fellow, Carol Worthman, to initiate a study of Kikuyu adolescence. A biological anthropologist interested in human growth, Carol Worthman conducted her research in the community of Ngeca, Kenya, a site where we had previously done fieldwork on Kikuyu children. While Worthman's study concentrated primarily upon the biological parameters of adolescent growth, it also focused upon the relationship between physical development and cognitive/behavioral changes. The success of this research proved to us the feasibility of conducting a multifactorial study of adolescence, thus laying the foundation for a larger cross-cultural investigation. In addition, our previous successes with the cross-cultural study of children convinced us that a similar design could be utilized for the study of adolescence.

In order to ensure the multidisciplinary nature of the project, we persuaded a group of our colleagues at Harvard to join us in planning the project. Clinical and personality psychology were represented by Carol Gilligan and George Goethals, child development by Jerome Kagan, biological anthropology by Peter Ellison and Irven DeVore, and psychological anthropology by Robert LeVine and the two of us. Irven DeVore agreed to accept the role of senior investigator.

We all agreed that the Harvard Adolescence Project should consist of field studies carried out in different regions of the world in cultures representing varying degrees of complexity. We also agreed that our sampling universe in each field site should consist of some bounded microcommunity, such as a band, a hamlet, or a neighborhood. We had used such a unit in our cross-cultural studies of child rearing, calling it a PSU (primary sampling unit). Briefly defined, a PSU is a small group of households (thirty to forty) which sets itself off from the larger society in such a way that it has some sort of group identification, shares frequent face-to-face interaction among its members, and possesses temporal and/or spatial stability. The PSU has the advantage of being the most appropriate social unit for using standard ethnographic research techniques, such as participant observation and informant interviewing.

Knowing that most ethnographic studies require a prolonged "settling-in" period during which the researcher learns the native language and becomes acquainted with the members of the community, we decided to select experienced field-workers who had already done extensive research in some other culture and who would be willing to return to that society to carry out a study of adolescence.

To implement the above plans, we applied for and received a post-doctoral training grant from the National Institute of Mental Health (grant number MH14066-06,07,08) that would support ten fellows for two years each. Additional support for data analysis was provided by the William T. Grant Foundation. The fellows chosen were Douglas D. and Wannie Wibulswasdi Anderson, Victoria K. Burbank, Richard G. Condon, Douglas A. and Susan Schaefer Davis, Marida C. Hollos, Phillip E. Leis, Mitchell S. Ratner, and Carol Worthman. The field sites listed from east to west included: the Inuit (Copper Eskimo) of Holman located on Victoria Island in the Central Canadian Arctic; the Australian aborigines of Mangrove located in Arnhemland, Northern Australia; the Thai Muslim of Nipa Island located on the southwestern coast of Thailand; the Kikuyu of Ngeca located in the Central Province of Kenya, twenty miles north of Nairobi; the Ijo of Ebiama and Opuware located in the central part of the Niger Delta in southern Nigeria; the Romanians of Baisoara located in the foothills of the inner Carpathian mountains; and the Moroccan Muslim of Zawiya located in North Central Morocco.

During the initial training period, a series of seminars were held in which the project's staff members and postdoctoral fellows gave presentations on topics relating to adolescent development. These seminar presentations proved helpful not only in identifying important issues in the field of adolescent development, but in assisting the project directors and fellows in developing research methods with cross-cultural applications. In addition, the information and insights provided by the research fellows on their particular field sites helped immensely in developing a research strategy that could be applied reasonably in all the research settings.

It was clear from the beginning of our discussions that no single definition of adolescence would serve all purposes. Since we were approaching adolescence from a multidisciplinary perspective, both the physiological and sociocultural definitions of adolescence were necessary to incorporate into the research methodology. Our basic assumption was that while the physiological changes that occur at adolescence are universal to all human populations, the social and cultural reactions to these physical maturational changes are not. Thus, while one culture may celebrate puberty publicly, subjecting individuals to a series of initiation rites and expecting a consequent change in the behavior of initiates, in other societies the physiological markers are a private matter.

Physiological definitions of adolescence, such as the interval between the beginning of the growth spurt and the attainment of full skeletal maturity or the interval between adrenarche and the attainment of full fecundity, could ideally be objectively measured through hormone assays in all the field sites. Theoretically, such physiological measures would provide the most valid comparison of adolescent maturation across cultures. Unfortunately, the logistical problems associated with such data collection as well as the social constraints encountered in most of the field sites prevented this type of data from being collected. (Only in Ngeca was the field-worker able to make such hormone assays.) As a result, we decided to concentrate upon the growth spurt for our physiological measure. Thus, the children at each field site were measured twice during the fieldwork period—once near the beginning and a second time near the end of the study period. From these measurements of height and weight the field-workers were able to calculate a growth rate for each child and from this determine his or her status with respect to physical maturation.

These measures of physical maturation were essential to obtain since we hoped to examine the effect the maturation process had upon such things as friendship formation, cognitive development, peer group relations, self-image, gender identity, and so forth. For example, does the young girl who has menstruated for the first time have a different self-image than the girl who is two to three years past menarche? Does the young boy who has just entered the growth spurt have a different gender identity than a boy who has attained full skeletal maturity? By combining our measures of physical maturation (as an independent variable) with other types of social and psychological data (as dependent variables) we hoped to address these questions for all the societies under investigation.

It was much more difficult, however, to operationalize a sociocultural definition of adolescence. Since we assumed that societies utilized different strategies for identifying and managing adolescence, it was not feasible to develop precise definitions that had any degree of cross-cultural comparability. In the end, we decided upon a broad definition: the transitional period between the end of childhood and the attainment of adult social status. This broad definition made it essential for our field-workers to examine local definitions of adolescence, which we assumed would vary among the seven cultures in our study. Thus, where one culture might rely upon physical maturation to mark the individual's transition into adolescence, another culture might rely solely upon chronological age as the criterion for entry into this stage. It was also theoretically possible that a society might not even recognize or name a transitional period between childhood and adulthood. As a result, the challenge to our field-workers was to remain as sensitive as possible to indigenous "folk theories" of human maturation.

To solve the practical problem of choosing a sample of subjects to be studied at each field site, we decided to select a single physiological marker that was transculturally recognized. The mean age of menarche was chosen for this purpose. For many of our field sites, an estimate of the mean age of menarche was available from previously published demographic and/or growth studies. For those field sites lacking such published estimates, the field-workers would have to collect data from postmenarcheal girls and women, which could then be averaged to produce an estimate of the mean age of menarche. This estimate could then be used as the anchor point for the selection of a study population that would include a group of preadolescents as well as a group of adolescents. Previous research on adolescent growth indicates that a ten-year interval centered on the mean age of menarche will include both the beginning of physiological adolescence for most of the early-maturing females and the end of physiological adolescence for most late-maturing females. Thus, for middle-class American girls for whom the mean age of menarche is thirteen, the catchment period would run from eight to eighteen years of age. Although there is no equivalent marker of physical maturation for males, we took advantage of the fact that males mature about a year later than females, and added a year to the interval used for females.

Ideally, we believed the sample size should range from eighty to ninety individuals. All of these individuals would be subjected to our physical measures of height and weight, while smaller subsamples would be subjected to clinical interviews, cognitive testing, behavioral observations, and a number of other structured and unstructured interviews designed to examine the social and psychological aspects of adolescence. Sample and subsample sizes would, of course, vary from one field site to the next, depending upon such things as community size and accessibility of informants. (The actual problems encountered in sample selection and informant interviewing were unique to each setting and are discussed in each of the volumes in this series.)

At the end of the training period, the staff and fellows produced a detailed field guide for the cross-cultural study of adolescence. This field guide represented the consensus of the research group concerning types of data to be collected and the manner of their collection. The document was developed in order to ensure a maximum degree of comparability among the field sites included in the study. The manual also suggested specific hypotheses to be tested and the methods for doing so. In line with the multidisciplinary focus of the project, we decided to draw upon the theories and hyotheses of a number of disciplines. The field manual included detailed discussions of research methodology (site selection, sampling procedures, geneaological and demographic data collection, psychological testing procedures, and methods for making physical measurements) as well as discussions on the substantive topics to be covered (parent-child relations, peer group formation, friendship, games and play activities, sexual activity, cognitive development, schooling, religious activities, pair-bonding, rites of passage, work, daily activities, and deviance).

With the training sessions over and the field guide complete, the researchers departed for their respective field sites, where the average stay was from nine to twelve months. The project directors and researchers maintained as much contact with one another as was possible, given the isolation of some of the field sites. In some cases, letters took several months to go halfway around the world. Nevertheless, all of us felt it important for the researchers to stay in contact with one another in order to share problems encountered and modifications made in the research design.

By February of 1983, all of the researchers reconvened at Harvard to begin the task of comparing and analyzing the extensive data that had been collected. Again, a series of seminars were held in which information was exchanged among all the project's participants. This phase of the research proved to be most exciting and stimulating as we saw the ultimate goals of the research begin to fall in place. Our research fellows returned with interesting observations and innovative ideas which were freely shared.

In the process of analyzing this extensive cross-cultural data base, all of us agreed that the first order of business should be the writing of a series of ethnographies providing detailed descriptions of the adolescent experience in each of the cultures. These would provide the necessary framework upon which later theoretical and comparative papers could be built.

Given the rapid rate of social change occurring throughout the world in general and in the field sites of the Harvard Adolescence Project in particular, we have decided to call this series Adolescents in a Changing World. With the publication of these ethnographically rich volumes by the fellows of the Harvard Adolescence Project, we hope that our cross-cultural and multidisciplinary examination of adolescence will contribute a much needed perspective to this fascinating stage of human development.

ACKNOWLEDGMENTS

This book is about adolescent development in the Central Canadian Arctic. It is the culmination of seven years of research, writing, and introspection on the Inuit community of Holman Island. In spite of having lived in this northern community for over two and a half years, I am only beginning to comprehend the marvelous complexities of Inuit culture. I offer this book not as a definitive work on Inuit youth but as a modest contribution to our understanding of adolescence from a cross-cultural perspective.

As an anthropologist I am fortunate to have had the opportunity of spending two extended field visits in Holman Island, the first during 1978–1980 and the second during 1982–1983. While my first field trip to Holman concentrated upon a different subject matter than the one discussed in this work, it helped lay the foundation for the work on Inuit adolescence initiated in 1982 as part of a cross-cultural and multidisciplinary research project sponsored by Harvard University. I now believe, more than ever, that anthropologists have much to gain by returning to their field sites to expand upon the knowledge obtained during previous visits to their "adopted" cultures.

This work would not have been possible without the support, advice, insights, and guidance of a large group of people. I owe a special debt of thanks to John and Beatrice Whiting for being a constant source of inspiration in my struggle to make sense out of an overwhelmingly large body of data. Their readings of and comments upon multiple drafts of my manuscript have helped me organize the primary themes of my research and focus upon the major perspectives of interest to the field of cross-cultural human development. I am ever grateful that I have had the opportunity to work with two such intellectual pioneers whose contributions to the fields of anthropology, psychology, and education will be permanently inscribed in the histories of those disciplines.

I would also like to thank all my postdoctoral colleagues on the Harvard Adolescence Project, including Douglas and Susan Davis, Mitchell Ratner, Vicky Burbank, Carol Worthman, Phil Leis, Marida Hollos, and Douglas and Wannie Anderson. Having the opportunity to work closely with such a varied group of scholars has aided me immensely in my own intellectual growth and greatly expanded my knowledge of other areas of the world. I will remember my time in residence at Harvard as one of the most intellectually stimulating periods of my life, largely due to contact with these persons.

I would like to single out Douglas and Susan Davis for a special note of thanks. Their moral support, encouragement, and enthusiasm have helped me keep the midnight candles burning while completing this manuscript.

The list of people in the community of Holman to whom I owe thanks is immense. Over the past seven years I have developed a number of special friendships which I hope will continue for many years to come. I thank all the residents of Holman, young and old alike, for allowing their lives to be momentarily disrupted by an inquisitive anthropologist. The Holman Hamlet Council was most supportive in granting me permission to return to Holman. I thank the council, the Government of the Northwest Territories, and the Holman Education Committee for allowing me to conduct this research. I would specifically like to thank Simon Kataoyak, David and Margaret Kanayok, Albert Elias, and Morris Nereyok for both their friendship and assistance.

I am also indebted to the principal of the Holman Island school and his wife, Peter and Ruth Murray. Not only have they helped me plan the logistics of my research but they have opened their home to me in the manner that can be expected only of true friends.

Special thanks are extended to Father Henry Tardy, who lived and worked in Holman for over thirty years. During both of my field trips, Father Tardy proved to be a valuable source of information on the community and its people. Father Tardy is a remarkable man who has given much of himself to all the residents of Holman, regardless of their religious affiliation. His contributions to the community will be remembered for many generations to come. I have found him to be a great source of inspiration and a man whose friendship I will forever value.

Other residents of Holman who I thank for assisting at various stages of my research include Gary Bristow, Jimmy Memorana, Tom Caulfield, Cheryl Christie, Harold Wright, John and Sue Rose, and Allan Sim. In addition, I owe a debt of thanks to all the young people of Holman for their cooperation in the research. Unfortunately, my concern for maintaining the anonymity of these young people prevents me from listing them here individually.

A note of appreciation is also extended to Nelson Graburn for his meticulous reading of and comments upon an earlier version of this manuscript.

Last, and most important, I am indebted to my wife and colleague, Pamela R. Stern, for providing the multiple roles of coresearcher, sounding board, editor, and proofreader. Without her assistance in the field, this research would not address the female adolescent experience in Holman and would lack the invaluable insights and perspectives that can only be provided by a woman anthropologist.

This research has been supported by a grant from the William T. Grant Foundation and by a National Research Service Award through the National Institute of Mental Health (No. 5 T32 MH14066-07). These grants are gratefully acknowledged.

A NOTE ON ORTHOGRAPHY

The spelling system of the Holman dialect of Inuktitut that appears in this text is based upon an orthography developed by the Inuvialuit Language Commission between 1981 and 1983. The Inuvialuit Language Commission (ILC) was created in May of 1981 by the Committee for Original People's Entitlement with the goal of recording, analyzing, and describing the dialects of the Western Canadian Arctic. In 1983 the work of the ILC culminated in the publication of a basic dictionary for the Holman dialect (*Kangiryuarmiut Uqauhingita Numiktittitdjutingit*) by Ronald Lowe of Laval University. Prior to the publication of this dictionary, the only writing system for the Holman dialect had been an inaccurate orthography developed by the Anglican church for use in hymnals and prayer books. The present ILC dictionary represents a more accurate and simple writing system that conforms as closely as possible to the Inuit Cultural Institute's standard orthography for all Canadian Inuit dialects.

INUIT YOUTH

■ Introduction

THE ADOLESCENTS

It is one o'clock in the morning. Under the invigorating influence of the midnight sun, a large group of children and teenagers gathers on the old airstrip that runs down the center of town. Some of these youngsters have been up for twenty-four hours or more, while others have just roused themselves from a deep sleep and ventured outdoors to take in the fresh air and warmth of the arctic summer. While the teenage boys are picking teams to play a game of baseball, a group of girls stands to the side watching the athletic bravado of their brothers, cousins, and boyfriends. Once started, the athletic event takes on an eternal quality as it continues inning after inning as though the players have lost all sense of time. There is a constant turnover of players as some boys leave briefly to grab a snack or a cup of tea at a friend's house. They are quickly replaced by others who have arrived to observe and eventually participate in the event. The score is kept by placing rocks in two circles, each circle representing the number of runs for each team. Soon even this is forgotten and no one can remember the exact score. The teenage girls who have been watching quietly to the side begin to play a game of tag and start running and giggling about the seemingly barren landscape. As they play, the tundra surface becomes illuminated by a bright orange hue as the July sun drops close to the horizon, only to start rising again on its circumferential path around the community. Some of the girls, bored with playing tag and watching the baseball game, decide to walk to the top of Uluhaktok Bluff from which they can view the small community that makes up their social and physical world. A few of the boys abandon their gloves and bats to pursue the girls up the steep grade of the bluff.

From the top of the bluff, there is a breathtaking panoramic view of the community dwarfed by the cliffs, lakes, mountains, and ocean that surround this small island of human habitation. From this perspective the settlement looks out of place, a temporary island of human activity in a timeless domain where nature is the undisputed sovereign. To the outsider, the houses, Hudson's Bay store, nursing station, community hall, and even the satellite dish used for receiving television programs all take on a transient and surrealistic quality. In the distance the boys playing baseball look like nothing more than a small herd of caribou that grazes momentarily and then moves on. The stillness of the early morning is broken periodically by exhuberant shouting from the direction of the baseball game and by the howling of a team of sled dogs chained behind their master's house.

Although it is now four o'clock in the morning, there is a great deal of activity throughout the community. A pair of motorcyclists can be seen driving full tilt along the road from the airport, stopping briefly to watch the ball game and then continuing on to one of the small houses on the opposite side of town. At one of the houses below, a man and his family get into a car, the only one in the community, and drive along the road in the direction of the game, where they stop and observe the activities while sitting comfortably in their 1976 Chevrolet.

To the immediate south of the bluff is the vast expanse of ocean still cluttered with ice floes—all that remains of the previous winter's ice cover which concealed the Amundsen Gulf with thicknesses of six to seven feet. A small boat, returning from a night of seal hunting, maneuvers its way through the narrow channels of open water. It is an inspiring view that, for most southerners, conjures feelings of desolation, isolation, and harshness. To the Inuit, however, it is a land of bounty inextricably intertwined with the rhythm of the seasons.

By eight o'clock in the morning, the game has started to disperse and groups of teenagers walk over to the co-op coffee shop for tea or coffee and a snack. As these teenagers sit in the coffee shop, talking and laughing, the adults of the community are making their ways to work. Other teenagers walk over to the Hudson's Bay store, which has just opened, to buy pop and candy. Two of them take their sodas to the coffee shop where they ask for ice-filled glasses and sit by a window overlooking the bay. A few of the teenagers decide to go fishing at Ukpilik Lake while others, exhausted after being up for thirty-six hours or more, return home to sleep before beginning another round of activities.

THE COMMUNITY

The small and isolated world of the Inuit teenagers of Holman Island is a community nestled in the midst of a vast expanse of arctic tundra on the western coast of Victoria Island. Due to the small number of buildings making up the nucleus of the settlement, it is easy to miss seeing the community altogether when flying over it for the first time.

Holman is one of more than thirty Inuit settlements spread throughout the Northwest Territories of Arctic Canada. In this sparsely populated region of the world, communities are separated by great stretches of uninhabited wilderness. Holman is a typical Inuit community insofar as its residents, only several generations ago, lived in isolated hunting and trapping camps, where they extracted a precarious livelihood from a marginal environment. The oldest members of the community remember when snowhouses and skin tents were the only shelters, when hunting by bows and arrows, harpoons, and spears was the only way to procure food, and when travel by dog team was the primary mode of transportation in a region of the world covered with snow eight months of the year. Holman is also typical in that it has experienced over the past thirty years a dramatic rate of cultural change in which residents have been exposed to the attitudes, life-styles, religion, and material goods of the "South." Adults in the community who were born in snowhouses and who spent most of the first part of their lives out on the land now watch color televisions in the comfort of heated homes equipped with running water and electricity. The elderly, who have vivid memories of starvation and frostbite, now receive government pensions to ensure their welfare and comfort. But despite these rapid social and economic changes, the residents still take great pride in being Inuit and maintaining close physical and emotional ties to the land.

Holman is distinct from most other Inuit settlements in that it is one of the smaller and more isolated communities in the Canadian North. With a population of slightly over three hundred, hunters and trappers have not yet overtaxed the wildlife of the region as has happened in other, larger Inuit settlements. Since Holman is located in a region of abundant wildlife, with ample supplies of caribou, fish, seals, and musk-ox, many residents are able to procure the bulk of their diets from the land.

My first exposure to Holman Island was in the fall of 1978 when I arrived as a graduate student to undertake a doctoral research project on the effects of extreme seasonal variation upon the social, behavioral, and physiological adaptations of the local population. One of the things that most impressed me during my first months in Holman was the overpowering influence of the arctic climate. It is impossible for an outsider to spend any length of time in an arctic community without being impressed by the pronounced seasonal changes in temperature, wind speed, light duration, and ice conditions, which affect all aspects of arctic life.

Leaving this pleasant community after eighteen months of research was difficult since I did not know if I would ever have the opportunity to return. The long hours of dissertation writing were often accompanied by longings to return to hunt and fish with friends, visit and talk over a cup of tea, or participate in a midnight baseball game. Fortunately for me, this opportunity came in the winter of 1982, when I returned to Holman as a participant in the Harvard Adolescence Research Project.

THE RESEARCH

One of the most significant events in the human life cycle, other than the obvious and definitive markers of birth and death, is the pubertal growth spurt. For girls this physiological transition involves an increase in estrogen levels, appearance of secondary sex characteristics, and the onset of menarche. For boys there is a tenfold increase in testosterone levels, growth of pubic and facial hair, and a pronounced change in voice "depth." These are irreversible and indisputable physiological changes that occur to all human beings in all cultures. As such, we can truly speak of puberty and the associated physical and behavioral changes as universal to the human condition.

Yet the term *adolescence*, which is so widely used in Western culture to refer to the transitional period between childhood and adulthood, is not a linguistic or social universal. In fact the degree of variation concerning the social recognition or nonrecognition of adolescence as a distinct life stage is perhaps more pronounced than for any other stage of the human life cycle.

The general goal of the Adolescence Project was to examine the social and psychological responses to these universal maturational changes and the nature of their incorporation into the ideological and behavioral fabric of individual societies. Thus we set out to determine whether different cultures define puberty as a separate stage of the life cycle, whether different social and behavioral expectations are placed upon "maturing" individuals, and what effect the physical changes have upon the psychological profiles of individuals experiencing the maturational process.

Inuit culture provides a fascinating social context for the examination of the questions posed by the Adolescence Project. In traditional times, before Eurocanadian contact, the transition from childhood to adulthood was rapid and unaccompanied by a prolonged period of maidenhood or bachelorhood (see Whiting, Burbank, and Ratner 1986). The attainment of social maturity and adult responsibilities roughly coincided with the attainment of physical maturity. The harsh arctic climate and scarcity of resources did not allow a prolonged period of adolescence. Children had to acquire quickly the necessary skills for survival. In addition, interactions with parents far outweighed in importance interactions with same-sex or opposite-sex peers. This was partially a consequence of a way of life in which the nuclear family was the primary social and economic unit (Damas 1969). Through intense interactions with their parents, children learned what was expected of them in later life. The extreme dispersal of the population also made it difficult for young people to obtain spouses without the intervention of parents. For the Copper Inuit, marriages were almost always arranged by parents, often when the prospective partners were infants. The scarcity and consequent difficulty of obtaining marriage partners made this a necessary social adjustment.

In the modern period, significant changes have been introduced from the outside world that have dramatically changed the natural progession of Inuit life stages. These include concentration of the population into settlements, increased economic prosperity and security, improved prenatal and postnatal health care, introduction of television and radio, increased travel to neighboring settlements, and introduction of formal schooling. All of these factors have contributed to the elaboration of a stage of life now referred to as the "teenage" years.

While traditional Copper Inuit society recognized and named a transitional period between childhood and adulthood, this period was relatively brief compared to the teenage stage of the contemporary period. Today Holman youngsters generally attend school until about fourteen to fifteen years of age, at which time the vast majority either drop out or attend only on an irregular basis. From this point until full adulthood is attained, there is a truly liminal stage in which youngsters "hang out," play games, visit other households, date members of the opposite sex, and take on casual wage employment. Since Holman remains very much of a hunting culture, boys also spend time hunting or trapping with their fathers, uncles, and other adult male relatives.

In time, and at their own pace, boys and girls gradually acquire the values and social skills that integrate them into the adult world. The transition into adulthood usually comes with the establishing of a separate household with a prospective spouse, obtaining some kind of employment, and raising children.

THE RESEARCHERS

In February of 1982 I returned to Holman after being away for two years. I was delighted to see that many of my old friends and acquaintances came out to the airstrip to greet me and shake my hand. My first few weeks in the community gave me the chance to assess the changes that had occurred since my last field trip. The most important of these involved the introduction of television and radio service. A large satellite dish that receives radio and television transmissions from the Canadian Anik-B satellite had been constructed near the center of town. I was amazed to note that every Inuit household in the community had at least one television set and that these sets remained turned on throughout much of the broadcast day. Programming on the single television station included mostly American and southern Canadian shows, along with a sprinkling of northern-oriented public affairs programs. Other changes included the construction of a new and larger nursing station, a communal walk-in freezer, and fourteen new three- and four-bedroom housing units equipped with running water and flush toilets.

The research project officially started a month after I disembarked from the plane. I set up my residence (and office) in the Roman Catholic mission's guest house, which was generously offered to me by Father Henry Tardy, an Oblate missionary with whom I had established a close friendship during my last trip. I proceeded to organize my files in the hopes that they would soon be overflowing with information about various aspects of adolescent life. An eighteen-year-old teenage boy, Johnny Apiuk, was hired as a field assistant. Johnny assisted with the initial household census, the drawing of a detailed settlement map, and the collection of spot observations. In addition to providing much valuable ethnographic information on adolescent life in Holman, Johnny participated in a large number of interviews on moral development, friendship formation, gender ambivalence, ethnic identity, sexual activity, parent-child relations, and so forth. This enabled me to pretest and subsequently revise a number of structured and unstructured interviewing instruments that I eventually administered to a large number of Holman teenagers.

During this initial stage of the research, I began a series of other data collection strategies, including informal interviewing of parents and adolescents, examination of medical and health records at the nursing station, collection of height and weight data, as well as the time-tested technique of participant observation. Also, throughout the research period children and teenagers were encouraged to visit whenever and as often as they liked—to talk, play games, or just enjoy a cup of tea. As more and more of these youngsters visited me and began to feel comfortable in my presence, I started formal interviewing with those who agreed to participate in the research.

Several months into the research, however, it became apparent that a male researcher alone could not complete an adequate investigation of adolescent development. Since adolescent girls in Holman are remarkably shy, much more so than teenage girls in our own society, attempts to establish contact and interview these young girls were unsuccessful. Fortunately, a colleague from graduate school (Pamela Stern) had already expressed interest in the research project and arrangements were made to have her fly in during the first week in June. When Stern arrived, the research picked up momentum as large numbers of adolescent girls were contacted and agreed to be interviewed. As weeks went by, visits from these adolescent girls became increasingly common. Adolescent boys also continued their visits, but always to visit me, while the adolescent girls came to visit Stern, who remained in Holman through the end of October. In response to the shyness of these adolescent girls, which was amplified in my presence, I would often disappear under the pretext of visiting someone or working outside the house. It was relatively easy for me to find outdoor chores to perform such as painting, cutting meat, or repairing the project snowmobile, which had an unfortunate tendency to break down frequently. In the cold of early winter, only my committment to the research project could rationalize my taking leave of a warm and brightly lit house to ensure the privacy of my female research assistant and her adolescent visitors.

One of the more interesting consequences of Stern's arrival was that many teenagers expressed curiosity concerning our relationship with one another. After an initial period of shyness and reticence, we were inundated with all kinds of subtle questions about our relationship—were we married, living together, or what. These questions provided a marvelous opportunity to explore adolescents' perceptions of marriage, interpersonal relationships, and sex. In Holman, formal marriage ceremonies mean very little since most young couples live together for two to four years and have one or two children before undergoing a formal marriage ceremony. Because we were sharing the same house, it was automatically assumed by most members of the community that we were husband and wife. From their perspective, what other arrangement could be possible?

There was also an interesting change in the nature of our interactions with adults. Married couples now started visiting with greater frequency than was the case when I had been living alone, almost as though the presence of a female provided me with a degree of respectability that had hitherto been lacking. Similarly, it was more acceptable for us to visit certain households as a couple than it had been previously for me to visit as a lone male.

In time, the assistance of the school principal was sought in order to obtain permission to conduct interviews at the school on a larger sample of adolescents. The principal was enthusiastic about the research project and arranged a meeting with the Holman Education Committee, at which time I explained the project's goals and methods in detail. The committee also expressed interest in the project, and permission was granted to conduct interviews on school grounds immediately after school hours. While we had hoped to conduct interviews and observations during school hours, the regional superintendent of education, who was also consulted, felt that such research techniques would be unnecessarily disruptive. Since school attendance in Holman was already the lowest in the Central Arctic region, it was felt that taking these students out of class for even brief interviews would monopolize too much classroom time.

Formal interviewing in the school began in early September, after we came to the school and described the research to the senior grades (7 through 9). Teenagers who were interested in the research put their names on a sign-up sheet and interview times were allotted to each youngster. As an incentive, students were offered a small fee for their participation. Interviews lasting forty-five to sixty minutes each were conducted in the kitchen/workshop area of the school, with Stern interviewing the girls in the kitchen and me interviewing the boys in the workshop. This division of settings was felt to be appropriate due to the girls' greater familiarity with the kitchen area, where sewing and home economics classes are held, and the boys' familiarity with the workshop area, where carving and woodworking are taught. In two months we managed to interview at least once a total of twenty-two girls and twenty-one boys between eleven and nineteen years of age. Unfortunately, not all of these youngsters were interviewed at the school. Since many older children and teenagers attend school irregularly or not at all (either because they have graduated or dropped out), it was necessary for us to track down these potential informants on an individual basis and schedule interviews at our house. Such efforts turned out to be extremely time-consuming, but well worth the effort since we wanted to include as many non–school attenders as possible. While we hoped to get a slightly larger sample, a number of youngsters expressed no interest at all in the research and could not be coerced into interviews.

The school interviews had the advantage of isolating a number of boys and girls who agreed to participate in further interviews, which we conducted at our home. Total interview time with these youngsters ranged from four to thirty hours each and provided a wealth of data beyond what we were able to obtain during our school interview sessions.

At the same time that the adolescents were being interviewed, we conducted formal and informal interviews with parents and young adults. Most of these conversations transpired during evening visits, which we made on a regular basis to households in the community. In addition, we sought out the non-Inuit teachers in order to take advantage of their knowledge of the community and the children.

THE SAMPLE POPULATIONS

Due to the small size of Holman, it was unnecessary to isolate a sub-sample of the community to be the focus of the research investigation. Since the settlement is both spatially isolated and socially homogeneous, the primary sampling unit (see Whiting et al. 1953; Whiting et al. 1966) encompassed all families and households in Holman.

Three different sample populations were isolated for various stages of the project. The first population included all children and teenagers between the ages of eight and twenty. For this group of 111 individuals, data were obtained on height and weight, age at menarche for the girls, and general medical history. This population also served as the target group for the behavioral observations conducted throughout the fieldwork period.

Within this "physical measures" population, a smaller group of youngsters was isolated for cognitive testing and interviews on such topics as friendship formation, parent-child relationships, aspirations, activities, household sleeping arrangements, acculturative influences, and gender identity. To keep this survey sample down to a manageable level, we concentrated upon youngsters between 11 and 19 years of age. This age distribution was also selected because it included individuals who categorized themselves as children (roughly 11 to 13 years of age) as well as youngsters who labeled themselves as teenagers (roughly 14 to 19 years of age). As previously mentioned, most of these interviews were conducted at the school, while a smaller number were conducted at our residence. Every attempt was made to interview an equal number of males and females evenly distributed across the age spectrum. While we were able to accomplish this with the 11-to-16 age-groups, we encountered numerous problems contacting and interviewing older teenage girls from 17 to 19. This group proved to be the most difficult with which to establish rapport since they were often busy working at the craft shop or caring for younger siblings. Teenage boys in the 17-to-19 age category were much easier to contact and interview since they were more outgoing and seemed to have more free time on their hands. The final size of this survey sample included twenty-one boys between 11 and 19 years of age and twenty-two girls between 11 and 16. It should be emphasized, however, that the survey sample does not constitute a random sample of older children and teenagers. The youngsters interviewed included only those who expressed an interest in the project and a willingness to participate. A number of young people whom we had targeted as potential informants did not want anything to do with the project.

The last and smallest sample included six boys (11 to 18) and four girls (11 to 16) who made up the clinical sample of the research. These individuals cooperated in intensive interviews on a large number of topics, many quite personal, relating to their experiences in growing up in a small and isolated Inuit community. Total interviewing time ranged from fifteen to eighty hours per individual, depending upon the stamina of both researcher and clinical informant. All clinical interviews were open-ended, and every attempt was made to recruit clinical informants who felt comfortable with both the interviewer and the interview situation. As would be expected, some of these informants were much more open and talkative than others. While we were able to obtain some very revealing information from the older adolescent boys, all but one of the girls were very hesitant to reveal much of a personal nature. (Because these clinical informants are quoted extensively in various sections of this work, brief biographical sketches are provided for each youngster in Appendix A. All clinical informants, as well as all other youths referred to or quoted in this work, have been given pseudonyms to ensure confidentiality.)

By the end of January we had managed to collect an impressive amount of data from these various sample groups, including intensive interviews with our eleven clinical informants, survey interviews with forty-three older children and adolescents, 467 spot observations, height and weight measurements on all youngsters between eight and twenty years of age, as well as general ethnographic information obtained through standard participant-observation techniques.

THE BOOK

This book reports the major findings of our research. It is organized around several themes essential to an understanding of adolescent life in Holman Island. The first and most important is the extremely rapid rate of social change, which has catapulted the Inuit of Holman into the modern world in a matter of decades. While all the cultures included in the Harvard Adolescence Project are experiencing varying degrees of social and economic change, Holman is in the forefront of these rapidly changing societies. The adolescents of Holman constitute a generation caught between the traditional culture and life-style of their ancestors and the more materialistic and competitive way of life recently introduced from the outside world.

Chapter 1 begins with a brief historical survey of the settlement, emphasizing both material changes in the infrastructure of the community as well as modifications in traditional social and political organization. Paramount among these is the gradual transition from economic cooperation to occupational individuation. In the not too distant past, cooperation between families and individuals was essential if people were to survive in this marginal environment. Such cooperation was most vividly expressed in group hunting and meat distribution. It was inconceivable that anyone could survive without relying heavily upon the social graces and obligations of one's fellows. With the introduction of trapping, rifles, snowmobiles, wage labor, canned goods from the store, pensions, and welfare, many of the adaptive features of intense cooperation ceased to be necessary. The margin of survival has been dramatically extended so that cooperative labor has become an artifact of a passing era. Ironically, however, the same items that have enabled individuals to assert their independence from their neighbors have made these same people increasingly dependent upon the material goods and services of outside world.

The second theme deals with the overpowering influence of seasonal variation in the arctic ecosystem, which largely regulates all aspects of local social and economic life. Regardless of the number of modern conveniences introduced into the community from the outside world, Holman residents are still closely tied to the land through hunting, trapping, and fishing. While Inuit adolescents play hockey, baseball, and football and learn how to dance to disco music, they are still taught the fundamental skills that enable them to hunt, travel, and survive on the land. These seasonal changes in temperature, light intensity and duration, wind conditions, and ice movement give rise to a unique "rhythm" of human social and economic activity unlike that seen anywhere else in the world. The impact that seasonal variation has upon both adults and adolescents is detailed in chapter 3, "The Seasons of Adolescence."

The third theme, which permeates all aspects of adolescent social interaction and behavior, is the high degree of autonomy that Inuit youngsters have in organizing their own lives. In many respects, autonomy is what adolescence is all about in any culture. Adolescence is that stage of identity formation when the young person first begins to assert his or her independence as a unique individual, often doing so in ways that can lead to parent-child conflict when the wants and desires of the maturing individual no longer coincide with the expectations of parents. Societies vary significantly in the degree to which such adolescent autonomy is tolerated. In American society, varying degrees of adolescent assertiveness and rebellion are interpreted as the road signs of this gradual development to adulthood and are tolerated to a limited degree. In other societies, the adolescent's desire to achieve autonomy may be significantly constrained by high degrees of parental control and surveillance. The existence of age-grades, puberty rites, and compulsory schooling are all cultural devices that function to constrain, totally or in part, the adolescent quest for self-determination.

As discussed throughout this work, autonomy is one of the most salient features of adolescent life in Holman. In comparison to the other societies included in the Harvard Adolescence Project, the degree of freedom Holman youngsters have to organize their own lives is unprecedented. Recent social and economic changes have given rise to circumstances in which Inuit youngsters spend more time with friends and peers than with parents. With the concentration of the population into the settlement has come an increased emphasis upon the adolescent peer group, the activities of which take youngsters away from the socializing influence of parents and other adults. How this situation compares to the traditional period of Inuit society is one of the underlying goals of this work as we seek a deeper understanding of what it means to be an adolescent in this isolated region of the world.

■ 1
The Community

GEOGRAPHY AND CLIMATE

The settlement of Holman Island is located on the western coast of Victoria Island in the Northwest Territories of Canada. Holman is among the northernmost of the Canadian Inuit communities, with a latitudinal position of 70° 44′ N, placing it approximately 325 miles north of the Arctic Circle and 275 miles above the tree line in an area of continuous permafrost (see maps 1.1 and 1.2). Victoria Island is the second largest island in the Canadian Archipelago with a total surface area of 79,000 square miles and is characterized by a harsh and highly seasonal arctic climate. The three bodies of water having the greatest impact upon the regional ecology are Prince Albert Sound to the east, Minto Inlet to the north, and the Amundsen Gulf to the south and southwest.

The physiography of Victoria Island is characterized by lowlands in the east and hills and plateaus in the west. The plateau region is extremely rugged, with numerous cliff faces that rise hundreds of feet in height. Because of the abundance of rocks and cliff faces, travel through this area is extremely difficult and is restricted by the natural contour of the terrain. To the immediate northwest of Holman lies an area of drift uplands that rise gradually from the coast to undulating

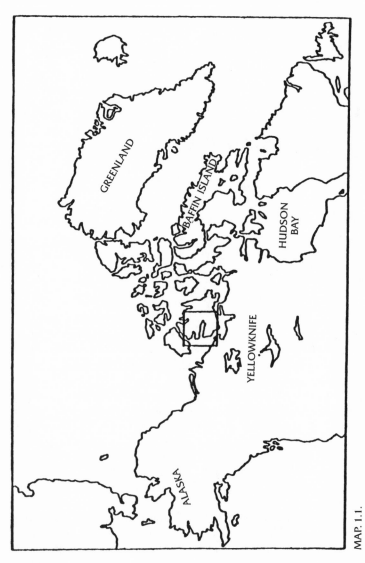

MAP. 1.1.
Holman region in relation to northern Canada.

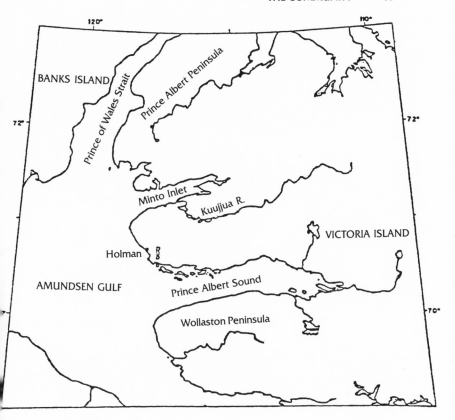

MAP. 1.2.
Holman Island region. *Source:* Usher 1965.

hills. Travel through this region is much easier and less restrictive than in the rocky scarp region.

Ponds and lakes are numerous throughout the Holman region, as they are throughout most of Victoria Island. Many of these provide excellent fishing sites in the spring and fall. Most of these meltwater lakes are covered by thick ice for eight to nine months of the year. Consequently, water runoff is limited to the summer months when the ice cover melts and the rivers and streams start to break up. The longest river in the area is the Kuujjua which is located approximately 50 miles north of the settlement. The Kuujjua originates in the Shaler Mountains in the northcentral part of the island and is approximately 150 miles in length, draining into a series of large lakes before emptying into Minto Inlet. The last of these large lakes, Fish Lake (Tahiq) is abundant with arctic char and is the primary fall fishing site for Holman residents.

The climate of Victoria Island is severe and characterized by pronounced seasonal variation in temperature, wind conditions, and light duration (see table 1.1). Summers are extremely mild and short in duration. While temperatures occasionally reach highs of 70° F (21° C) during the summer months, the daily mean of the warmest month of the year (July) is a mere 45.3° F(7.4° C). Temperatures generally drop below freezing by the middle of September and remain there through the month of May. On average, there are only seventy-one frost-free days throughout the year. By far the coldest month is February, with a daily mean of −23.7° F (−30.9° C) and a monthly minimum mean of −43° F (−41.6° C). The ocean tends to have a moderating influence along the coastal areas, while temperatures inland are more extreme.

Perhaps a more important feature than temperature variation, and one that has a significant impact upon the local hunting ecology, is the seasonal variation in wind speed and wind direction. The prevailing winds in the Holman region are from the east along Prince Albert Sound and from the west and northwest across Amundsen Gulf. Throughout the year, the cold east winds tend to be of higher velocity, picking up speed as they travel down the sound and drop into the settlement from an escarpment located a mile east of town. Westerly winds, on the other hand, while not as severe, frequently bring rain in summer and snow in winter. Of particular interest, however, is the fact that the coldest months of the year are fortunately not the windiest. The months of December through April have a greater percentage of calm days with lower wind speeds than do the summer and fall months. Despite

TABLE 1.1
Climatological Table for Holman Island

Month	Daily Mean	AIR TEMPERATURE (F) Mean of Daily max	min	Mean of Monthly max	min	Absolute Extremes hi	lo	Pressure MSL	PRECIPITATION Mean Total	Mean Snowfall	NO. DAYS with Frost	% OF TIME Clear sky <2/10	Overcast >8/10
Jan.	−19.2	−13.1	−25.2	5	−40	20	−48	1021	0.25	2.5	31	50	31
Feb.	−23.7	−17.1	−30.2	2	−43	25	−50	1020	0.24	2.4	28	55	27
Mar.	−14.8	− 7.9	−21.7	12	−38	24	−48	1021	0.29	2.9	31	58	25
Apr.	0.5	7.7	− 6.8	27	−27	40	−35	1021	0.35	3.5	30	40	38
May	21.2	26.8	15.5	42	− 3	54	−18	1021	0.33	2.9	30	26	56
June	38.7	44.6	32.7	60	20	71	12	1016	0.29	0.8	15	19	56
July	45.3	52.2	38.3	68	30	78	26	1012	0.80	0.1	7	19	52
Aug.	44.0	49.8	38.2	64	29	75	23	1012	1.04	0.8	7	18	57
Sept.	32.8	36.8	28.8	48	16	63	5	1014	0.79	3.2	24	12	68
Oct.	16.1	20.7	11.4	34	− 6	42	−15	1012	0.68	6.4	30	21	64
Nov.	− 3.9	1.3	− 9.0	19	−25	28	−38	1017	0.33	3.3	30	41	47
Dec.	−13.5	− 8.1	−18.9	9	−34	19	−48	1017	0.22	2.2	31	47	38
Mean	10.3	16.1	4.4					1017				34	47

SOURCE: Atmospheric Environment Service, Department of the Environment, Canada, 1941–1967.

the relative calm of the winter months, wind chill remains a significant environmental constraint. Wind chill factors will frequently lower temperatures to -80° and -90° F (-62° to -68° C). September and October, in particular, are the stormiest months of the year, with significantly fewer calm days and higher wind velocities than the other months of the year.

Precipitation throughout the region is minimal. The mean annual snowfall for the Holman area has been recorded at 31.0 inches, while the mean annual precipitation expressed in liquid terms is a meager 5.61 inches (Canada, Department of Transport 1970, 48). Due to constant cold temperatures, however, precipitation in the form of snow accumulates over an eight-month period. Contrary to popular belief, the Arctic is not totally covered by a blanket of snow during the winter months. Incessant wind activity blows the snow into drifts and packs it down into a hard layer. Consequently, large expanses of tundra will be clear of snow throughout much of the winter, while drifts six to twelve feet in depth will appear in areas where the snow has been caught by a rock, dwelling, or the unfortunate snowmobile.

Perhaps the most popularized, but least understood, aspect of the arctic environment is the seasonal fluctuation in sunlight, or photoperiod. Due to the angle of the earth's rotation around the sun, most nonequatorial regions experience varying degrees of photoperiod change throughout the year, increasing at higher latitudes north and south of the equator. In the Arctic, human populations have had to adapt to dramatic seasonal changes in light intensity and light duration. The northernmost Inuit group, the Polar Inuit of northern Greenland, experiences four months of constant daylight during the summer and three and one-half months of alternating twilight and darkness in winter (Weyer 1932, 16). The Holman Inuit experience similar, although not quite as extreme, photoperiod changes. Direct sunlight becomes markedly curtailed during November. By the middle of the month there are only one to two hours of direct sunlight per day, with the sun disappearing altogether by the end of the month. The duration of midday twilight gradually diminishes until the winter solstice, when there are only a few hours of very dim twilight at the middle of the day. After the solstice, twilight slowly increases in duration and intensity until the sun reappears above the horizon toward the end of January. Often, however, the sun may not be seen for several days or even weeks after its return above the horizon due to visual obstruction from landforms and cloud cover. The remainder of January is still characterized primarily by darkness and twilight, even as periods of direct sunlight increase in duration.

"Normal" photoperiod returns in February and extends to the beginning of April. By the end of April there is daylight nearly twenty-four hours a day, with the sun dropping below the horizon for several hours during the middle of the night. From the middle of May through July, the sun circles above the horizon constantly. In August the sun begins to creep below the horizon for increasing periods of time as the cycle begins anew.

In addition to pronounced seasonal variation in temperature and photoperiod, ice conditions in the Holman region are also cyclical. Wind, temperature, and current all contribute to the formation, movement, and breakup of ocean ice throughout the Canadian Archipelago. Not only is there significant seasonal variation in the behavior of sea ice, but marked fluctuation from one year to the next in freeze-up and breakup. Generally, the bays and coastal areas around Holman will freeze around the end of October. Nevertheless, open water will persist beyond the newly formed landfast ice, several miles into Amundsen Gulf. Freeze-up of the gulf itself varies from one year to the next, depending upon temperature and wind conditions. When low temperatures are combined with relative calm, the gulf may freeze over by the end of November. Other years, complete freeze-up may be delayed until January or February.

Once freeze-up occurs, ice thickness increases throughout the winter until depths of six to seven feet are attained in the early spring. Breakup of the ocean ice also varies slightly from one year to the next. Due to the extreme thickness of the ice and the small amounts of heat energy absorbed by the surface, ocean ice melts very little except along coastlines and areas where there are strong currents. More important than melting is the combined action of winds and currents which break up and disperse the ice during July and early August. Generally the ocean ice remains solid through June, when it is still safe for travel, although some care must be taken to avoid cracks and areas of thin ice where there are strong currents. By the beginning of July the ice begins to break up, permitting towards the end of the month some boat travel through the ice floes. At this time of year, seal hunters and other boaters must pay strict attention to wind direction since it is not uncommon for ice to be blown back against the shore, blocking return passage to the settlement. By the first week in August, the ocean is usually completely cleared of ice.

Holman is situated in a fairly abundant wildlife area compared to other communities in the Canadian Arctic. Consequently, hunting, fishing, and trapping remain an essential part of the local economy. Land mammals that are actively hunted include musk-ox, arctic hare, arctic wolf, and the Peary caribou. The most important of these is the Peary caribou, which is found in great numbers in the inland areas to the north of the settlement. Unique to the Canadian Archipelago, the Peary caribou is a small, white-colored species of caribou distinct from the larger barren ground caribou to the south. Fortunately for local Inuit hunters, the Peary caribou is a year-round resident of Victoria Island. Little is known concerning the population and migratory behavior of the Peary caribou herds on Victoria Island. It appears, however, that their numbers are increasing. Inuit hunters in the region uniformly comment that there are many more caribou now than twenty years ago and that they are coming much closer to the settlement during the winter months, when they migrate southward from the foothills in the northcentral part of the island.

Marine mammals common to the oceans around Holman include ringed seals, bearded seals, and polar bears. The ringed seal, or *nattiq* as it is referred to by the Inuit, is the most abundant marine mammal in Canadian Arctic waters (Smith 1973, 118). Traditionally, the ringed seal constituted a major source of food, clothing, fuel, and shelter. These days, the ringed seal does not play as crucial a role in the Inuit diet, although it is still a major food source during the summer months when caribou are scarce. Ringed seals are also hunted for their skins, which are sold for cash or used locally for boots, mitts, and parkas. In addition to seals, polar bears are actively hunted on the ocean ice during the winter months. Hunting polar bears is now strictly regulated by the Northwest Territories (N.W.T.) Wildlife Department, and Holman hunters are allowed to kill only a limited number, generally from fifteen to twenty, each year.

Of the various species of birds found in the region, only the ptarmigan, the raven, and the snowy owl are year-round residents. Migratory birds include ducks, geese, cranes, swans, loons, and seagulls. Of these, only ducks and geese are of any importance as a food source for local residents. Migrations of king eiders, common eiders, oldsquaws, and brants reach the Holman region around the beginning of June and last for about a two-week period.

The two most important fish in the Holman area are the arctic char and the lake trout, both of which inhabit the numerous lakes around the settlement. These are actively fished during fall, spring, and summer using nets and jigging hooks.

Since the introduction of trapping to the Holman region in the 1920s and 1930s, the arctic fox has become a vital resource in the Inuit cash economy. The arctic fox feeds off mice and lemmings in summer and scavenges from the remains of seal carcasses left by polar bears and Inuit hunters in winter. Fox populations tend to follow a cyclical pattern, one inextricably linked to fluctuations in mice and lemming populations. Thus the Inuit trapper must contend with both the rise and fall of prices on the southern fur market and the natural cyclical fluctuations of the fox population. In addition to the arctic fox, the red or colored fox is also found in the Holman area, albeit in smaller numbers.

HISTORICAL BACKGROUND

To fully understand the nature of contemporary settlement life in Holman, a brief overview of changes in Copper Inuit culture since Eurocanadian contact is necessary. The Holman Inuit have experienced dramatic social, material, and economic changes during the last five to six decades. As a result, the Holman Inuit have gone from a precarious, nomadic existence to a sedentary and secure one within a modern settlement equipped with medical facilities, government housing, electricity, televisions, and radios.

Traditional Copper Inuit culture is representative of the Central Arctic Inuit area, which encompassed most of the Canadian Arctic and included the Netsilingmiut and Iglulingmiut groups to the immediate east. In winter, large numbers of Copper Inuit families gathered in snowhouse settlements on the ocean ice to engage in breathing-hole (*mauliqtoq*) sealing. Summers were generally spent in smaller nuclear or extended family units engaged in inland caribou hunting and fishing. In the fall these families, which had been separated for most of the summer, would begin to congregate along the coasts to wait for freeze-up, when cooperative breathing-hole sealing would once again commence. The designation *Copper Eskimo* was conferred upon the inhabitants of the area because they used native copper, which was mined by hand from the surface and cold hammered into knives, chisels, and harpoons.

Traditionally the Copper Inuit lived in numerous geographically defined subgroups that were extremely flexible in composition and structure. These groups differed little in language or culture, as frequent movement between one regional group and another was a common feature of Copper Inuit life. These groups have been described in varying detail in the works of Rasmussen (1932), Stefansson (1913), and Jenness (1922). Rasmussen (1932), Jenness (1922), and Oswalt (1979) estimated the entire Copper Inuit population at about eight hundred individuals spread from Stapylton Bay in the west to King William Island in the east. The Copper Inuit of the Holman region referred to themselves as the Kangiryuarmiut of Prince Albert Sound and the Kangiryuatjagmiut of Minto Inlet. Together these comprised the northernmost extension of Copper Inuit culture. Stefansson (1913) estimated the population of these two groups to be around 176. Exact population counts for each group, however, were difficult to obtain due to the frequent population exchange between the two regions. Generally the Kangiryuarmiut spent their winters sealing on the ice in the middle of Prince Albert Sound, while their northern neighbors spent the winter months on the ocean ice between Minto Inlet and Banks Island. Members of the northern group occasionally spent the summers traveling and hunting on Banks Island.

The very first European explorer to enter Copper Inuit territory was Samuel Hearne. By order of the governor of Fort Prince of Wales, Hearne was directed to explore the region about the Coppermine River and find the fabled copper mines believed to be abundant in the area (Hearne 1958). Hearne and his Indian guides reached the Coppermine River in 1771, where his Indian companions massacred a group of Inuit at a location now referred to as Bloody Falls. The expedition failed to find the copper reserves sought after, and European exploration of the area ceased for nearly half a century. Between 1820 and 1853, a number of expeditions entered the area, including the Franklin expeditions of 1821 and 1825 (Franklin 1828). The latter expedition mapped the arctic coastline from the Mackenzie River to the Coppermine River and was also the first expedition to sight Victoria Island. Exploration into the Holman region was delayed, however, until the early 1850s when Robert McClure and Richard Collinson set out in two boats and charted the coastline of northwestern Victoria Island from Prince Albert Sound to Wynniat Bay. These two parties were also the first to establish contact with the Copper Inuit of the area. In fact, one Kangiryuarmiut informant later told Stefansson that the Inuit who once inhabited the region north of Minto Inlet had been exterminated by one of these parties in revenge for murders perpetrated by some local individuals (Stefansson 1919, 29). While there is no documentary or physical evidence for such an occurrence, it is possible that a number of Inuit may have died from diseases contracted from Collinson's expedition when it wintered north of Minto in 1851–1852 (McGhee 1972, 128).

The initial exploratory period was followed by a fifty-year interval during which the region was left to itself. Although fairly extensive whaling activities were being carried out in the Beaufort Sea to the west, the large marine mammals did not travel as far as Victoria Island in any great numbers; hence the Copper Inuit were not disturbed by any intrusive whaling activities.

Despite the lack of intense direct contact between the Copper Inuit and Eurocanadian society, which was slowly encroaching upon the Inuit of other areas, the inhabitants of this region experienced some indirect changes. Although only a few Inuit had had any first-hand contact with whites, the presence of this strange race was universally known among the various regional groups, and some individuals had even obtained certain valued objects from the expeditions that had crisscrossed the area in the first half of the nineteenth century. Trade with neighboring groups brought in a small number of metal objects such as knives and files. Southern diseases also began to take their toll on the residents of the area. In fact when Jenness studied the Copper Inuit between 1914 and 1916, there was evidence that population reduction and redistribution had already occurred, although it was much less pronounced than in the Mackenzie Delta to the west (Jenness 1922, 42). More significant population changes occurred in the mid to late 1920s when a wave of epidemics swept through the territory of the Copper Inuit, leaving scars upon the population structure that were still visible in the 1960s.

Direct contact between the Copper Inuit and representatives of the outside world did not resume until the beginning of the twentieth century. Oddly enough, it was believed by many explorers and government administrators that the Victoria Island Inuit seen by McClure and Collinson in the middle of the preceding century had all migrated east to Hudson Bay in order to trade with whalers. In 1906 the Canadian government issued a map that marked Victoria Island as "uninhabited" (Stefansson 1913, 12). At the time it was not yet known that an independent trader named Christian Klengenberg had sailed to Victoria Island the previous year and had established contact with the Kangiryuarmiut (Klengenberg 1932). Six years later Vilhjalmur

Stefansson, the famous explorer and ethnographer, also established contact with the people of Prince Albert Sound and made a number of subsequent visits to the area. Between 1914 and 1916 the Southern Party of the Canadian Arctic Expedition carried out geological, biological, and ethnographic work in the Coronation Gulf area. The ethnographic work of Diamond Jenness produced from this expedition remains the definitive work concerning the traditional culture of the Copper Inuit (Jenness 1922).

Although some sporadic trade was carried out during the opening years of the twentieth century, the first permanent trading post in the area was not established until 1916 when the Hudson's Bay Company opened a store at Bernard Harbor on the mainland side of Dolphin and Union Strait. Due to its remote location from the Kangiryuarmiut, this trading post had no direct impact upon the residents of either Prince Albert Sound or Minto Inlet. The first trading post in the Holman region was established in 1923 on the north shore of Prince Albert Sound at a location called Alaervik. This post was closed five years later and relocated to Fort Collinson on Walker Bay to the immediate north of Minto Inlet. Two other companies opened stores at Walker Bay, but by 1939 all three had closed down. In 1939 the settlement of Holman was established when the Hudson's Bay Company moved its Fort Collinson store to the east shore of a deep water bay designated King's Bay. The name *Holman* was applied to the new settlement due to its close proximity to Holman Island, the nearest geographical reference point to the newly established post. In the same year that the Hudson's Bay Company established its Holman Island store, an Oblate missionary named Father R. P. Buliard, who had come to the area by dog team two years before, began construction of a Roman Catholic mission at the same location (Buliard 1951, 128).

Throughout the early twentieth century, the local Inuit population became increasingly dependent upon the trading posts to supply them with foods and material possessions that they had previously done without. Although introduced later than in other areas of the Arctic, fur trapping was encouraged by traders, who frequently paid unsuspecting trappers extremely low prices for their skins. Beginning in the 1920s and 1930s, the Holman Inuit gradually made the transition from a traditional, subsistence-oriented economy to a cash-oriented economy. The introduction of trapping as an economic pursuit also had a significant impact upon social organization. No longer were families able to gather in large groups on the ocean ice during the winter to cooperate in breathing-hole sealing; instead they spent the winters in isolated family groups engaged in trapping activities. Large social gatherings became limited to Christmas and Easter ingatherings when families came to the settlement from outlying camps to trade their skins for supplies.

Oddly enough, the original Inuit residents of the settlement were not Copper Inuit but Alaskan Inuit from the Mackenzie Delta who came to Holman to work for either the mission or the Hudson's Bay Company. These families built makeshift houses from scrap wood, cardboard, canvas, and other materials found about the settlement. While some mild hostility was felt between the "westerners" living in Holman and the Copper Inuit who were still living out on the land, these rivalries gradually dissipated through intermarriage and prolonged contact.

The year 1960 roughly marks the beginning of a new period in the Holman region, when the federal government started to play a more active role in the administration of the area. That year the government embarked upon a program designed to concentrate the regional population into the settlement in order to provide adequate schooling, housing, and medical care. Between 1962 and 1963, a federal day school was constructed approximately one-half mile west of the settlement on the north shore of a neighboring bay called Queen's Bay. This coincided with a government plan to relocate the settlement around Queen's Bay. This new location provided a smooth, gravelly, and gently sloping surface with excellent drainage. Since population increase was inevitable, the new site provided greater room for expansion as well as a better surface for the construction of roads and buildings.

In 1960 the government shipped three "matchbox" housing units to Holman, followed by four additional one-room units in 1961. By 1963 the settlement consisted of seven prefabricated matchbox units, six scrap houses, four plywood shelters, and one frame house (Usher 1965). With the relocation of the settlement around Queen's Bay in the mid-1960s, the government embarked upon a more extensive building project. As more housing became available, families that had previously lived out on the land were attracted to the greater security of the settlement. The first Copper Inuit to become residents were the old and infirm who were no longer able to support themselves by hunting and trapping. Government subsidies made it possible for these individuals to take advantage of the new housing facilities. Throughout the 1960s, more and more families took up either year-round or part-time residence in the newly formed community. In 1967 the very last family to remain out on the land full time moved into Holman from Berkeley Point. Despite the movement into the community, many families continued to spend at least the spring and summer months at seal hunting camps in Prince Albert Sound and Minto Inlet.

With the concentration of the population complete, the expansion and modernization of the community proceeded at full speed. In 1972 a nursing station was built in the center of town in order to minister to the health needs of the local population. A full-time nurse was employed by Health and Welfare Canada to operate the public health programs and clinics at the new facility. In 1982 a much larger and more modern nursing station was constructed.

Prior to 1978, airplanes flying into Holman would land on the ocean ice in winter or on a landing strip, which ran down the center of town, in summer. The summer landing strip was deemed a public safety hazard by the Department of Transport, so a new airstrip complete with an airport building was constructed between 1976 and 1978. This new airport, located two miles to the west of town, was completed in the fall of 1978. A local entrepreneur bought a used car, had it shipped up by barge, and started Holman's first taxi service between the airport and the community.

Other innovations and modern conveniences that have made their mark upon the community over the past few decades include snowmobiles, telephones, electricity, radio, television, running water, trucks, and motorcycles.

Prior to the early 1970s, all land-based hunting and trapping were carried out by dog team. In 1972 the first snowmobile arrived in Holman, and by 1974 snowmobiles had become the primary mode of winter transportation. Due to their greater speed and ability to pull heavy sled loads, snowmobiles have allowed Inuit hunters to exploit a much larger hunting area than was previously possible. Nevertheless, the numerous and often-mentioned disadvantages of the snowmobile include high initial purchase cost, high breakdown rates, high maintenance costs, and unpalatability. (The latter is important only insofar as it was possible for a hunter to eat his dogs if he was stuck out in a blizzard and starving to death.) While snowmobiles are now the paramount form of winter transportation in the settlement, a number of hunters and trappers have started running dog teams again, primarily for guiding sports hunters who fly in each February and March to hunt polar bears.

The most dramatic recent change in Holman has been the introduction of television service. In the fall of 1980 a satellite dish was erected near the center of town. This dish provides one-channel television and radio service for the entire community. Within several weeks after its construction, almost every household had a television set with which to view the satellite offerings. These include U.S. and southern Canadian programs as well as a limited number of northern special interest broadcasts. While in the past it was often necessary to wait for several weeks to get news from the outside world, it is now possible for local residents to keep pace with world events. Despite the culturally disruptive influence that television has had in the community (which is discussed in later chapters), it has nevertheless resulted in a dramatic increase in the ability of local residents to understand and interpret previously incomprehensible world events.

Although a number of traditional religious beliefs persist, primarily among the older residents of the settlement, traditional religious observances and ceremonies have been replaced by attendance at one of the three local churches. Over time, the Inuit's reliance upon shamans (*angakoks*) as religious practitioners diminished as more and more people were converted to and baptized in the Christian faith. At present there are no practicing shamans in the community, although a few of the older residents are purported to have once been powerful shamans. Oddly enough, many of these shamans were among the first to be converted to the new faith brought north by Anglican and Roman Catholic missionaries. The Roman Catholic mission, constructed in 1939, was the first to begin active missionary work among the local Inuit population. Although an Anglican minister made periodic trips to Holman from the neighboring community of Coppermine, the first Anglican church in Holman was not established until 1959. Several years later a mission house was built and a permanent minister arrived to attend to the religious needs of the Anglican congregation. The third church in Holman was built in the mid-1970s at the invitation of several residents. It is largely Pentecostal in form and content, and services tend to be highly emotional by Inuit standards, with emphasis upon singing, speaking in tongues, and confession of sins.

Since the Roman Catholic mission was the first religious organization to be established in Holman, it quickly became a focal point of settlement life. The mission building was used frequently as a community hall for dances and other community celebrations. In addition, the Catholic missionaries, who were Oblate fathers from France, were in-

TABLE 1.2

Chronology of Social Change in Holman, 1930–1982

1930s	Introduction of trapping and cash economy. Gradual increasing reliance upon southern-made foods and material goods.
1939	Construction of Hudson's Bay Company store on east shore of King's Bay, followed by construction of Roman Catholic mission.
1939–1967	Gradual process of population concentration within newly formed settlement.
1960	First prefabricated matchbox houses arrive in the community.
1962	Construction of federal day school at new settlement location on Queen's Bay. Schooling in English language instituted.
	Establishment of Holman Eskimo Co-operative.
1965	Government starts moving buildings from old King's Bay settlement site to new community location on Queen's Bay and begins construction of newer and larger government-subsidized housing.
1967	Last family moves into town off of the land.
1970s	Electricity introduced into government-subsidized housing units.
1972	Nursing station constructed. Full-time nurse becomes resident in community.
1973	Snowmobiles supplant dog teams as primary mode of travel.
1977	Long-distance telephone service installed.
1978	Completion of new airport.
	Arrival of first privately owned car.
	Completion of ten new housing units. First to have running water and flush toilets.
	New, larger nursing station constructed.
1979	Co-op builds new hotel.
1980	New Hudson's Bay store constructed (complete with piped in "musak").
	Television and radio service installed.
1982	Co-op celebrates twentieth anniversary and doubles hotel beds to eight.

strumental in helping establish the Holman Eskimo Co-operative in 1962.

Another change was the transition from Inuktitut (the Inuit language) to English as the dominant language. During the formative years of the settlement, Inuktitut remained the primary language of interaction. With the introduction of the federal day school in 1962, instruction in English was instituted. Since 1980 the use of English has received additional reinforcement from television and radio. At present the primary language of children, teenagers, and young adults is English. While middle-aged adults tend to be proficient in both languages, only the elderly are monolingual Inuktitut speakers. This has given rise to a linguistic situation in which many parents speak to their children in Inuktitut, while children respond in English. While each generation has a passive understanding of the other's language, parents and children are often unable or unwilling to speak in the language of the other. It is also common for young children to be completely unable to communicate effectively with older adults and grandparents. Needless to say, many adults lament the fact that the younger people in the settlement are no longer able to speak the language of their ancestors.

The chronology of recent changes in the Holman region is provided in table 1.2, beginning with the introduction of trapping in the 1930s.

COMPOSITION OF THE POPULATION

Holman Island remains one of the smaller Inuit communities in the Central Canadian Arctic, with a population of 310. This figure includes the small Eurocanadian (white) population, who occupy various government and administrative positions within the community. While a few of these whites have become permanent residents of Holman, the vast majority are transient and leave the community after one to four years of service. During 1982 the non-Inuit population fluctuated between 20 and 30. The Inuit population, however, remained at a fairly stable 286 throughout the 1982–1983 field season.

The demographic structure of the community has changed dramatically over the past twenty-five years. In 1963 the population of the Holman region was 135, with 115 persons residing in the community and 20 in isolated hunting and trapping camps (Usher 1965, 72). Since then the Holman population has more than doubled. By 1982 children and teenagers comprised more than 55 percent of the popula-

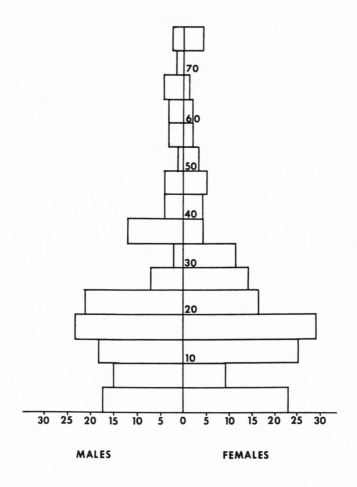

FIG. 1.1.
Population pyramid for Holman Island, 1982.

tion (see fig. 1.1). Interestingly, the largest age cohort at present is made up of adolescents between the ages of fifteen and nineteen. Not only is adolescence a newly created stage of life in Inuit society, but significantly more individuals occupy its ranks than ever before.

Several factors have contributed to the rapid population growth since the early 1960s. Perhaps the most important was the introduction of bottle-feeding in the late 1950s and early 1960s which functioned to shorten birth intervals. Prior to the introduction of bottle-feeding, Inuit mothers breast-fed their offspring for three or four years, and even up to five (Jenness 1922, 165; Graburn 1969, 61; Schaefer n.d.). Recent studies have established the relationship between lactation and amenorrhea, indicating that frequent and unrestricted suckling contributes to prolonged postpartum infertility (Delvoye, Delogne-Desnoeck, and Robyn 1976; Kippley and Kippley 1977). For the Inuit, as well as other hunting and gathering societies, postpartum infertility provided an ideal system of population regulation whereby prolonged birth intervals maximized each offspring's chances for survival. With the introduction of bottle-feeding, however, these traditional birth-spacing techniques have become significantly altered, resulting in both a shortening of birth intervals and an acceleration in the live-birth rate. Similar increases in live births have been documented for other Inuit communities in which bottle-feeding was encouraged by public health officials (Schaefer 1959, 1973; McAlpine and Simpson 1975; Hildes and Schaefer 1973; Blackwood 1981; Berman, Hansen, and Hellman 1972).

Fertility data collected from obstetrical history files at the Holman nursing station indicate a dramatic drop in the mean birth interval for the decade 1960–1969, accompanied by an increase in the total number of births (see table 1.3). This trend reversed in the 1970s with the

TABLE 1.3
Fertility Figures for Holman Island, 1982

DECADES	1940–49	1950–59	1960–69	1970–79	1980–82
No. recorded births	23	45	87	64	23
No. recorded intervals	16	35	76	44	14
Mean interval in months	33.5	35.5	26.8	40.9	46.3
Mean age of primiparous mothers	18.9 ($n = 7$)	18.8 ($n = 9$)	17.9 ($n = 11$)	20.2 ($n = 21$)	18.6 ($n = 9$)

introduction of contraceptives and a return to breast-feeding, both encouraged by Northern Medical Services. This resulted in an increase in the mean birth interval from 26.8 months to 40.9 months. Despite this increase in mean birth intervals, the birth rate in the community is steadily rising, presumably because the younger and more numerous members of the community are now reaching reproductive maturity. Similar increases can be seen throughout the Canadian Arctic, where the Inuit live-birth rate remains twice that of the national average: 33.9 per 1,000 versus 15.5 per 1,000 as of 1977 (*Canada Yearbook 1980–1981*).

Another factor contributing to the rapid population growth of Holman and other Inuit communities is the improvement in prenatal and postnatal health programs, which has reduced the Inuit infant mortality rate, once the highest in Canada. In 1962, for example, the Inuit infant mortality rate was 194 per 1,000 compared to 27 per 1,000 for all Canada (Abrahamson et. al. 1963, 22). By 1967 this mortality rate had been reduced to 84 per 1,000 births (*Report on Health Conditions in the N.W.T.* 1978, 10). The devastating effects of tuberculosis were also controlled through a massive TB program, which became most effective following the introduction of streptomycin in 1945. This contributed to an overall decrease in mortality, especially for infants, in a population with a high fertility potential (Milan 1978, 17).

The combination of bottle-feeding, improved medical services, and increased economic security has led to an overall increase in family size, not only in Holman, but throughout the Canadian Arctic. The availability of government subsidized housing, wage employment, government assistance, and child allowances now permits families to provide for a larger number of offspring than was ever possible in the pre-settlement era. The practice of infanticide during periods of famine has, thus, become a thing of the distant past.

Physical Structure of the Community

The physical structure of the settlement has also expanded substantially since the first housing units were moved from King's Bay to the new community site in the early 1960s (see map 1.3). In 1982 there were sixty-eight government-subsidized housing units which were leased to residents through the Housing Corporation of the N.W.T. Seven additional housing units were maintained by the territorial gov-

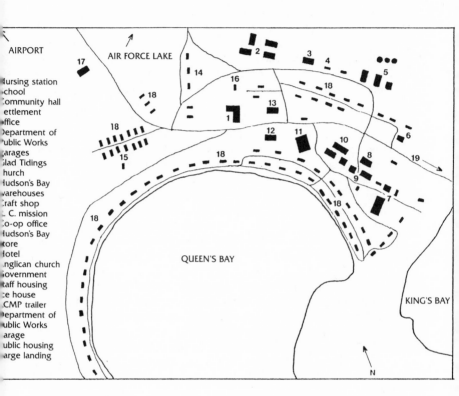

AIRPORT

AIR FORCE LAKE

Nursing station
School
Community hall
Settlement
office
Department of
Public Works
Garages
Glad Tidings
Church
Hudson's Bay
warehouses
Craft shop
R. C. mission
Co-op office
Hudson's Bay
store
Hotel
Anglican church
Government
Staff housing
Ice house
RCMP trailer
Department of
Public Works
garage
Public housing
Barge landing

QUEEN'S BAY

KING'S BAY

N

MAP. 1.3.
Holman settlement.

ernment to house teachers, administrators, and other personnel employed by the government. Rents for the sixty-eight public housing units are adjusted according to the family's income and include the cost of heating oil, electricity, water delivery, and sewage disposal.

Overall housing conditions in the settlement have improved dramatically in recent years. Prior to 1978, none of the houses were equipped with running water or flush toilets. Water was delivered by truck to a large water tank maintained in each house, while sewage was disposed of using the "honey bucket" method. Honey buckets are large pails equipped with toilet seats into which a plastic bag is inserted. When full, the plastic bag is tied at the top and placed outside for removal to the local dump. Between 1978 and 1982, however, the Housing Corporation constructed twenty-seven newer and larger units that have both running water and flush toilets. Due to continuous underground permafrost, it is impossible for water and sewage lines to run underground. As a result, these houses all have self-contained water and sewage systems. Water is still delivered by truck to a large holding tank located in the utility room of each house. Rather than draining water out of the tank by hand, which is still the standard procedure in the forty-one older housing units, residents of these newer houses procure water through faucets in the kitchen and bathroom. Sewage from these new units is collected in large holding tanks and pumped clean once a week by a special sewage truck that, when full, spreads the waste at the dump. In addition, these newer units have baths and showers, which are lacking altogether in the older public houses. Residents of older houses must either bathe from a bucket or visit a friend or relative residing in a newer unit. In 1982 the N.W.T. Housing Corporation began to install running water and flush toilets in a number of the older houses, with the ultimate goal of eliminating altogether the honey bucket method of waste disposal in the community.

All of the houses in the settlement now have electricity and are heated by thermostatically controlled, forced-air oil furnaces. Only a few of the older "matchbox" units retain their original oil-burning cooking stoves. Although the Housing Corporation has been trying to phase out the matchbox homes, the supply of houses is unable to keep up with the demand; thus the matchboxes remain occupied, usually by single individuals or young couples.

The interiors of the new homes stand in marked contrast to the squalor that so often prevailed in the older housing units. Now that families are spending more time in the settlement and less time at hunting, trapping, and fishing camps, many people have begun to furnish their homes according to southern standards. Thus many households are comfortably furnished with carpets, sofas, chairs, coffee tables, televisions, and other furnishings purchased from the Bay store or through the Simpson-Sears mail order catalog. Kitchens are virtually indistinguishable from those in the South and are equipped with electric stoves, refrigerators, toasters, and coffee makers. Often, the only marker identifying these kitchens as Inuit is the raw-frozen fish or caribou meat placed atop a piece of plywood on the floor or strips of dried caribou meat hanging from a rack on the ceiling. Almost all households have some kind of washing machine, making hand washing of clothes a thing of the past. As unusual as it may sound, most households are equipped with large freezers in which substantial amounts of fish, caribou, duck, and rabbit can be stored over the summer months.

In addition to residential units, major buildings in Holman include the nursing station, mission buildings, the Uluhaktok school, Hudson's Bay Company store, settlement office, community hall, and buildings owned by the Holman Eskimo Co-operative. The co-op is one of the dominant social and economic institutions in the community, operating a hotel, craft shop, art shop, and hardware store. In the northern part of town are located the Department of Public Works garages, where all service vehicles for the settlement are maintained. These include the water truck, sewage truck, tractor, bulldozer, and grader. Gasoline and oil storage tanks are located immediately behind these garages.

Approximately one mile to the north of the settlement lies a freshwater lake that is the source of the community's water supply. A gravel road has been cut through the tundra connecting the lake with town, and water is transported to local buildings by truck.

Due to the relative isolation of Holman, access to the settlement is limited to air transportation, with scheduled flights arriving two times a week from the territorial capital of Yellowknife. The only other form of transport into the community is the summer barge that arrives immediately following breakup, bringing with it a yearly supply of nonperishable grocery items, gasoline, heating oil, snowmobiles, and building supplies.

ECONOMIC ADAPTATIONS

The rapid rate of change in the material and economic spheres of Inuit life throughout the Arctic has been staggering. Due to the comparative isolation of the Holman area, the local Copper Inuit have been relative latecomers in experiencing the impact of these social, political, and economic alterations. Trapping as a renewable source of income was introduced to the Holman region later than its initial introduction in the Mackenzie Delta area, and at a point when fur prices were dropping considerably on the international fur market.

In contrast to the relative affluence of contemporary settlement life, the early period of settlement existence was marked by extreme poverty, malnutrition, overcrowded housing conditions, and widespread disease. In the 1960s an increase in sealskin prices added another abundant renewable resource to the impoverished Copper Inuit economy, and many people resumed active seal hunting for both subsistence and trading purposes. Largely through the efforts of the Roman Catholic missionary, Father Henri Tardy, the Holman Eskimo Cooperative was founded to organize the production and sale of native handicraft items. With the increase in government services in the mid-1960s and the gradual expansion of the co-op as a successful business venture, more opportunities for wage employment became available. Although full-time wage-labor jobs are still limited, the economic sector in Holman is experiencing a degree of affluence that was unthinkable fifteen to twenty years ago.

In discussing the economy of Holman, the concept of flexibility as an economic strategy cannot be overemphasized. Flexibility and opportunism have always been essential elements in the traditional resource strategy of the Inuit people. The Inuit hunter of the past had to be prepared to adjust his seasonal movement, his resource utilization skills, and even his social organization to the seemingly capricious availability of food. This flexibility was also evidenced by his willingness to adopt new technologies and even social practices introduced to the North by whites.

Currently the Holman economy consists of five overlapping sectors which are continually evolving: subsistence hunting, trading of renewable resources, local wage employment, industrial wage employment, and a cottage industry that includes carving and sewing.

Despite the increasing reliance upon imported foodstuffs, subsistence hunting still plays a major role in the economic sphere. The notion of a traditional hunter-trapper who stands apart from the more acculturated wage earner is something of a misnomer, since all adult males, a large number of adolescent boys, and a few adult women in the settlement engage in varying degrees of subsistence hunting. Although wage-earning households generate income that can be used to purchase southern foods at the Bay store, there is nevertheless a preference for fresh "land" foods over expensive canned goods and frozen meats. In fact, some of the most active subsistence hunters in the settlement are wage earners who must limit their hunting trips to weekends and vacations.

In addition to its functional aspects, subsistence hunting has an expressive dimension that should not be overlooked. While many families could live adequately without engaging in subsistence hunting, many hunt for the pleasure they derive from the activity itself. In a small, isolated settlement where there is little entertainment, getting out of town and hunting as one's ancestors did provides a pleasant as well as a functional distraction. As we will see in later chapters, such expressive and functional hunting is also carried out by older adolescent boys, both in groups and with parents, and provides one mechanism whereby parents can impart traditional knowledge and skills to their children.

Only recently has the trading of renewable resources become an inextricable part of the northern economy. Today such trade finds its expression in the trapping of foxes and the hunting of seals, polar bears, and musk-oxen for pelts. Such trade is a major source of income for many residents. In 1981, for example, Holman residents received a total of $116,345 for fox pelts and $110,591 for sealskins.

The trapping season extends from November through April, and trappers are free to set their traplines in any area they desire. In general, trappers maintain the same trapping areas from year to year due to their greater familiarity with particular areas. Full-time trappers may often run several traplines in different areas and spend three to four days checking each line. Trappers who run relatively long traplines that are located at some distance from the settlement usually travel with a trapping partner in case of a snowmobile breakdown or other emergency. These trapping partnerships may be based upon kinship as well as informal friendship ties. Older trappers frequently travel with their adolescent sons (and in one case a teenage daughter) in order to train these young people in trapping techniques.

As in subsistence hunting, the exploitation and trading of renewable resources are not limited to one group of people. Even wage earners in the settlement spend some of their free time maintaining fox traps in winter or hunting seals in the spring, summer, and fall. The difference, however, lies in the amount of time and energy invested in such activities. While full-time trappers set several traplines that can run up to one hundred miles in length, wage earners rarely set more than twenty to thirty traps in the immediate vicinity of the community. Wage earners' commitment to other employment activities effectively limits the amount of time and energy they can devote to trapping and seal hunting. Wage earners also have much less need to generate income from such activities than do full-time hunters and trappers.

To assist hunters and trappers in exploiting renewable resources, the territorial government has instituted an outpost program whereby government funds are made available to families who desire to establish permanent hunting and trapping camps away from the settlement. The initial grant for these camps covers the cost of building supplies, transportation, heating oil, gasoline, and food. Money spent on food must eventually be repaid by the recipients of the grant. Subsequent funds cover only the cost of heating oil and gasoline. The only requirement is that the grant's recipients spend at least six months of the year with their families at the camp. The Holman region currently has two camps, each one supporting two families. The first of these camps, Alaervik, is located approximately one hundred miles east on the north shore of Prince Albert Sound; the second, Omingmagiuk, is situated on the north shore of Minto Inlet. In general this outpost program has been very successful. One trapper indicated that he is able to maintain closer contact with his children out at his camp than he is able to do in the settlement. He also feels that it is a more effective environment for teaching his children about the Inuit way of life.

In addition to subsistence hunting and trapping, a limited number of possibilities exist within the settlement for local wage employment. Table 1.4 gives a breakdown of permanent and casual wage employment by sex and ethnic affiliation. The largest employers in the settlement are the government and the Holman Eskimo Co-operative. Most co-op employment is in the craft shop where a variety of handicraft items are produced. Craft shop positions are held mostly by women and older teenage girls and are characterized by a high turnover rate, which is, in part, seasonally related. The craft shop may employ as few as four individuals and as many as twenty-five, depending upon the time of year. In addition, the co-op supports a cottage craft industry

TABLE 1.4

Local Sources of Permanent and Casual Employment for Holman Island, 1982

	WHITES		INUIT	
	M	F	M	F
Government				
School	2	2	1	2
Nursing station	0	1	1	1
Settlement office	1	0	0	1
Department of Public Works garage	1	0	0	0
Municipal services	0	0	(3)	0
Road maintenance	0	0	(3*)	0
Airport communicator	0	0	1	0
Post office	0	0	0	(1*)
Housing	1	0	2	0
Fish and wildlife	(1*)	0	0	0
Holman Eskimo Co-operative				
Hotel/coffee shop	0	0	1	3
Office/art shop	2	0	3	4
Craft shop	0	0	0	(4–15)
Hardware shop	0	0	2	0
Fuel truck	1	0	0	0
Hudson's Bay Store	2	0	(1*)	2
Local private enterprise (all part time or seasonal)				
Taxi	0	0	1*	0
Trucking	0	0	2*	0
Construction	0	0	2*	0
Other				
Northern Canada Power	0	0	1*	0
Canadian National telephone	0	0	1*	0
Airline agent	1*	0	0	0
Cope	0	0	2*	1*
Kitikmeot Inuit Association	0	0	2*	0
TOTAL	12	3	29	19–30

NOTES: Parentheses indicate high turnover; asterisk indicates part time.

whereby sewing, carvings, drawings, and other handicraft items made by people at home are purchased for sale. Other co-op employment may be found at the hotel, coffee shop, print shop, and hardware store.

Other possibilities for casual wage employment exist outside of the co-op, primarily in the area of construction and maintenance. These jobs peak in the summer and fall months, especially after the arrival of the barge. One activity that generates a fair amount of income for local residents is the outfitting and guiding of sports hunters who come in the spring to hunt polar bears and musk-oxen. The hunt is organized and sponsored by the local hunters and trappers association with the aid of an outfitter in Yellowknife. During the 1982 season, six sports hunters paid approximately $16,000 each for the opportunity to shoot a bear.

Although there is pronounced variation in income between households, the small size and cultural homogeneity of the settlement have prevented the development of social and spatial class divisions. Only a few of the permanent, wage-labor jobs require skills contingent upon advanced educational training. Such high-paying jobs as settlement manager, housing manager, and assistant manager of the co-op require fluency in written and spoken English and some knowledge of accounting and bookkeeping, and hence are closed to most Holman residents. In general, the overall educational background of most wage earners is slightly higher than that of most active trappers, due primarily to the younger age of the former. The majority of casual and permanent wage-labor jobs, however, are open to anyone who is willing to abide by a daily work schedule.

A dominant ethic in the community is that wealth shoud be distributed in an equitable fashion based upon need rather than skill. This is most evident in the manner in which the settlement council awards jobs to applicants. In most cases a decision will be made to give the job to the applicant whose family needs the money rather than to the person who might be the most qualified. This admirable ethic ensures that everyone is taken care of in much the same way that traditional meat-sharing systems ensured the equitable distribution of food.

Despite the number of employment prospects within the community, unemployment remains a significant problem. The high turnover associated with most wage-earning jobs ensures that a larger number of people are able to partake of the advantages of regular employment. Nevertheless, as the population has grown, the employment sector has been unable to keep up with the total number of available workers. This is primarily felt by many older adolescents and young adults who would like employment, at least on a part-time basis, but are unable to find work locally.

Finally, industrial employment has not had as great an impact upon Holman as it has had upon more populated arctic settlements such as Tuktoyaktuk, Inuvik, and Frobisher Bay. Although some mineral exploration has been carried out on Victoria Island, no industrial employment exists in the immediate vicinity of the community. Nevertheless, Holman residents are able to take advantage of the industrial opportunities available in other areas. Perhaps the most profitable of these opportunities is seasonal employment with Canadian Marine Drilling Ltd. (Canmar), which is engaged in oil exploration in the Beaufort Sea. Wages are high and, although work hours are long, employees are given one week off for every two to three weeks of work. In addition, transportation to and from the employee's settlement is arranged free of charge. Over the past five years, Canmar has employed approximately twenty-five Holman residents, mostly young adult males. Despite high wages, Canmar has had some trouble persuading native employees to stay on the job for any length of time. Many report feeling ill at ease in strange working environments and lonely so far away from home. However, a young man or woman willing to put up with long hours and an unfamiliar work situation can earn enough money in a two-to-three month period to provide himself or herself with enough cash for an entire year.

Other opportunities for industrial employment are made possible through the territorial government's vocational training program at Fort Smith, which offers courses in a variety of fields such as heavy-duty mechanics, heavy equipment operation, carpentry, electronics, welding, and so forth. Applicants who meet the necessary requirements can get free tuition and accommodation as well as a living stipend from the Department of Manpower and Immigration. After completion of the training program, graduates are placed in appropriate jobs. Unfortunately, due to limited employment prospects in many of the smaller communities, graduates must be willing to relocate to larger communities to live and work.

SOCIAL STRUCTURE

At the time of initial contact with Eurocanadian society, the Copper Inuit displayed extremely flexible kinship and political networks. The basic social and economic unit was the nuclear family, although kin relations were recognized well beyond the immediate family (Damas 1969, 48). During the summer the nuclear family units of the Copper Inuit would disperse throughout the tundra in search of game. Occasionally families would travel together for all or part of the summer, but these unions were only of a temporary nature and could be formed with kinsmen and nonkinsmen alike. During the winter, regional groups would gather together in large snowhouse communities on the ocean ice, where seal hunting could be carried out. The majority of inhabitants in these temporary communities were *nuatakattait*, that is, related by either blood or marriage (Jenness 1922, 86). Due to the lack of any unilineal descent ideology in Copper Inuit society, these winter groups were bilateral with perhaps a prevalence of male relevant ties (Damas 1969, 48). Copper Inuit society was also replete with various alliance mechanisms acting to unite individuals and families that were either unrelated or only distantly related. Leadership in these large winter communities was ephemeral, and cooperation was maintained through bilateral kin ties, alliance mechanisms, as well as by economic necessity.

At present, social organization is not too dissimilar from the situation found by the earliest explorers, missionaries, and anthropologists. Although the population has been residing in the settlement for a number of years, very little formal organization of an indigenous nature acts to unite the various family groups. Bilateral kin networks and informal alliances such as friendships and trapping partnerships still function to unite individuals and families. What little overriding political structure there is in the community, such as the settlement council, has been introduced from the outside.

The composition of households is very much constrained by the availability of housing units in the settlement. Until recently, the supply of government housing has been unable to keep up with the natural expansion of the population. When housing units were first introduced to Holman, it was typical for several families to share one dwelling. Consequently, extended households were much more common in the recent past. As more houses became available, there was a tendency for extended and joint families to divide into smaller units. Changing expectations also make it desirable for young couples to set up households independent of parents. Since all housing is subsidized by the Housing Corporation of the N.W.T., there are few financial constraints placed upon young couples who wish to establish their own households. The only real constraint is the availability of housing units.

The introduction of permanent household structures has also led to significant alterations in the spatial organization of Inuit social life.

In the distant past, when people still resided in tents and snowhouses, individual families could decide where they wanted to live and who they wanted as neighbors. Thus several families could decide to put up their tents or snowhouses in close proximity to one another; since these shelters were not permanent structures, people could relocate at will. Today, however, this is no longer feasible. Families are now assigned housing units on the basis of need and family size, and it is no longer possible for individuals to decide who their neighbors will be. Consequently, closely related families are now spread throughout the settlement, where previously they would have set up households next to one another.

A breakdown of household types is given in table 1.5. The most prevalent household type is the nuclear family, accounting for 56.7 percent of all households. Only one nuclear family household without children was counted during the research period. This household was made up of a young couple who recently moved in together. Due to the heavy cultural emphasis placed upon bearing children, it is unlikely that this couple will remain childless for long. (In general, however, it is common practice for a young couple to begin having children before they have established a separate household. In the rare event that a

TABLE 1.5
Household Composition in Holman Island, 1982

	MEAN SIZE	NO. HOUSE-HOLDS	% OF HOUSE-HOLDS	NO. INDIVI-DUALS	% INDIVI-DUALS
Nuclear with children	5.10	34	56.7%	174	60.2%
Nuclear, no children	2.00	1	1.7%	2	0.7%
Extended	5.93	15	25.0%	89	30.8%
Single men	1.00	3	5.0%	3	1.0%
Widowers and widows with children	2.50	4	6.7%	10	3.5%
Unmarried women with children	2.50	2	3.3%	5	1.7%
Sibling core	6.00	1	1.7%	6	2.1%
TOTAL		60	100.0%	289	100.0%

couple is infertile, children will be adopted.) Those nuclear families with children had a mean number of 3.1 offspring still residing at home.

Extended families were of four different types: (1) nuclear families with one or more bilateral kin (usually a sibling of the husband or wife), (2) nuclear families with an attached grandparent, (3) older nuclear families with an unmarried daughter and her offspring, and (4) older nuclear families, including one or more offspring living with a girlfriend or boyfriend. These four types of extended families made up 25 percent of all households in the community, with a mean size of 5.93 persons per household. The first two extended family types tended to be made up of younger couples and their offspring who have enough room in their home to accommodate a grandparent or unmarried sibling. The latter extended family types, however, are older families with a large number of offspring plus grandchildren and/or live-in girlfriends or boyfriends. These older extended households tended to be the largest in the community, having a mean size of 7.6 and a mean number of 5.3 offspring residing at home.

Single individual households accounted for only three housing units. These were occupied by older men who had no wives or children. Only one sibling core household was identified in the settlement; it was composed of the offspring of a recently deceased woman. Other household types included four households made up of widowers or widows plus children and two households made up of unmarried women and their children. The biological fathers of this latter group of children tend to be men residing in the settlement, although a few have been fathered by men from neighboring communities. In a number of cases, the exact paternity is not known and may be attributed to several "possibilities."

At this point it is necessary to briefly note the nature of biological and social kin relations in the settlement. The amount of crosscutting of kin ties is staggering, and it takes years for an outsider to develop the same knowledge of kin relations taken for granted by residents. Inuit society is not visibly sexually promiscuous; however, premarital and extramarital sexual liaisons are common and are more openly accepted than in our own culture. Even though the traditional practice of spouse exchange is no longer active, many of the traditional attitudes toward sexuality persist. In many cases, for example, an individual's social father may be a different person from his recognized biological father, and thus he will have a large number of half brothers and half sisters spread throughout the community.

POLITICAL ORGANIZATION

The formal political organization that exists in the community has been introduced by the Government of the N.W.T.. The primary political body of the settlement is the Holman Settlement Council, made up of delegates who are elected for two-year terms. The settlement council maintains roads, municipal services, the airport, recreational facilities, and other community services with the financial and advisory support of the territorial government. The settlement council, however, may not generate any of its own funds from taxes, but receives its funding from the Government of the N.W.T., which specifies exactly how these monies are to be spent.[1] The settlement council also has no direct control over such things as education, town planning, economic development, health care, or welfare, but is occasionally consulted for recommendations in these areas. The council is also expected to work with other community organizations such as the housing association, recreation committee, education committee, hunters and trappers association, and health committee.

In many respects, the settlement council in Holman is an artificial phenomenon, not only because it is a form of organization introduced from the outside, but because the operation of the council, as established by the Department of Local Government (Canada, Department of Local Government 1971), is antithetical to traditional methods of consensual decision making. Although the structure of settlement council meetings is similar to that of any southern town meeting, many traditional values and behaviors permeate these sessions. Council meetings tend to be extremely long and drawn out, with lengthy periods of silence between comments and discussions. Even though the council will make formal decisions through majority voting, there is a preference for discussing items until consensus is attained.

Political activity is not limited to the settlement council. Many residents are actively involved in regional and national Inuit organizations formed to address a variety of topics. The most salient of these topics at present are the issues of land claims, economic development, and native rights. Organizations such as COPE (Committee for Original People's Entitlement) and Kitikmeot Inuit Association are actively involved in pursuing these concerns. Men and women from Holman are elected to the governing boards and committees of these organizations to represent the concerns of the community.

In sum, Holman Island remains a relatively small and kin-based community that continues to maintain close ties to the land in the form of hunting, trapping, and fishing. Residents are extremely fortunate to live in a region abundant in wildlife. The combination of abundant renewable resources with increasing wage-employment opportunities and small community size gives Holman a reputation as one of the more desirable northern communities in which to reside. This is recognized by most residents, including adolescents, who are quick to point out that their community is one of the safest and friendliest in the Canadian Arctic. This may also account for the low degree of out-migration to other communities and towns. Yet despite the small size and isolation, Holman is a community that is coming into increasing contact with the outside world via television, radio, mail order catalogs, school trips to the South, and political involvement with regional and national Inuit organizations. In short, Holman is a community rapidly becoming integrated with the social, political, and economic institutions of the outside world. It is from this perspective that we approach our investigation of adolescent development.

■ 2
Life Stages
and Cycles

Kids become teenagers at around fourteen to fifteen. At thirteen, they still seem too young. Teenagers start drinking, dating, stop running around at dances. The girls' bodies start to change. Teenage girls start to wear make-up, stay cleaner, and take care of themselves. . . . Teenagers become adults when they get shacked up I guess, when they stop roaming around, and when girls get babies. Adults become old men and women when they don't walk around as much or hunt. Maybe also when they get false teeth.
—Johnny Apiuk, eighteen-year-old research assistant, 1982

One of the basic premises of the Harvard Adolescence Project is that adolescence, at least as a physical-maturational event, can be studied using standard anthropological methods in all human societies. At first, project members were somewhat hesitant to apply such a specifically Western construct to other cultures where adolescence possibly was not recognized as a separate stage of human development. It was conceivable, some of us postulated, that other cultures do not recognize a stage of life similar to the one we have labeled *adolescence* in our own society. These criticisms were verbalized, alerting all of us to the pitfalls of applying certain Western constructs in settings where they might not be appropriate. They also sensitized us to the importance of examining local terms used to describe various stages of the human life cycle. In the final analysis, we agreed that our cross-cultural investigation of adolescent development would have to take into consideration two separate dimensions: physical growth and sociocultural maturation.

From a biological point of view, adolescence is a human universal. All human beings must go from infancy to adulthood, and along the way pass through puberty. They must grow taller, develop secondary sex characteristics, complete long-bone growth, and in the case of girls attain menarche. This transition is no mean feat, and it is hard to imagine that its occurrence would go unnoticed by either the individual undergoing the change or by the adult members of the society. The only remaining questions are whether the transition is recognized linguistically, ritually, behaviorally, or attitudinally by the society as a whole and how closely sociocultural maturation coincides with physical maturation. In short, do people react to puberty as a major life event? It is this reaction to puberty that constitutes the second, and undoubtedly more challenging, dimension of our research investigation. While it can be readily concluded that all human beings experience puberty, it is not so obvious that this stage of life is a source of cultural elaboration or even recognition in all societies.

PHYSIOLOGICAL MATURATION OF HOLMAN ADOLESCENTS

Height and weight measurements were obtained for 111 youngsters between nine and nineteen years of age. From this group we were able to gather reliable repeated measures for eighteen girls and nineteen boys. This final physical-measures sample, therefore, constituted approximately 33 percent of the total target population. These data were obtained with the cooperation of the nurse and through detailed examination of medical files, some of which contained measures of height and weight repeated over several years. The primary goal was to calculate height and weight velocity by comparing the two most recent height and weight measurements for each individual. A large number of individuals had to be excluded either because we were unable to obtain a second reliable measurement or because medical files were incomplete.

We had originally entered the community with the intention of obtaining Tanner ratings of secondary sex characteristics (Tanner 1978, 60–77) as well, however the extreme modesty of the adolescents led us to conclude that such a procedure would interfere with other aspects of the research. Even the community nurse, who was approached to perform the ratings, expressed discomfort with such an examination. The nurse was able, however, to gather data on age of menarche for 34 postpubescent girls and young women.

In Holman the mean age of menarche for girls was calculated at 13.4 years with a range from 12 to 15, based upon the self-reports of young women and postmenarcheal girls. While this figure is low in comparison to the other cultures included in the Adolescence Project, it coincides with similar findings for the Inuit of North Alaska, for whom the average age of menarche was 13.68 ± 0.79 years (Milan 1978, 227). As in the traditional period, the onset of menarche is unmarked by any social ceremony. All of the girls interviewed indicated that they had received no preparation from their mothers prior to their first menstruation. In addition, many of these girls received little information about menstruation or reproductive physiology even after they had menstruated. Many stated that their mothers told them simply that it meant they were growing up. Girls begin the growth spurt at 10 to 11 years of age, reach peak height acceleration at 11 to 13 years, and attain adult stature at 16 to 17. The mean age of the fastest growing girls in this sample ($n = 6$) was 11.5 years.[1] The greatest range in absolute heights for any one age category was 141 to 156 cm for thirteen-year-olds. The data on weight velocity indicates approximately the same pattern as that for height velocity, with the mean age of the six fastest-weight-gaining girls being 11.9 years.

As expected, the growth spurt appears one to two years later for males. Boys enter the growth spurt at 11 to 13, reach peak height velocity at 12 to 14, and attain adult stature at 17 to 19 years of age. The mean age of the fastest growing boys in our sample ($n = 6$) was 12.6 years. As with girls, there was substantial variation in absolute height within age categories. The greatest range appeared with two seventeen-year-old boys, one of whom measured a towering 179 cm while the other measured 149 cm. Finally, the peak of weight velocity also appeared much later for boys than girls, with the mean age of the six fastest-weight-gaining boys being 13.3 years.

The data on height, weight, and menarche indicate that physiological adolescence in Holman begins at around 10 to 11 years of age for girls and continues until the individual has attained physiological maturity at about 16 to 17 years of age. For boys, physiological adolescence begins slightly later at 11 to 13 and extends to 18 or 19 years of age.

SOCIAL MATURATION OF HOLMAN ADOLESCENTS

Physical changes that occur at puberty are only a small part of the adolescent experience. While these changes have an obvious effect upon the individual, they also serve notice to parents and other adults that the young child is about to undergo significant alterations in physical appearance and behavior. The manner in which a society recognizes and manages these physical changes largely determines the nature of the adolescent experience as well as the gradual process by which the individual becomes integrated as an adult member of society.

An examination of contemporary life-stage designations in Holman indicates that Holman residents recognize a transitional stage of life between childhood and adulthood, a stage now referred to as the teenage years. Entrance into this new life stage is generally defined not only by the maturational processes described above, but by a host of accompanying behaviors that are more clearly adultlike in character.

Before embarking upon a detailed description of contemporary life stages in Holman, I provide a brief reconstruction of the traditional Inuit life cycle and the manner in which the physical maturation of individuals was recognized and handled. The reconstruction will give the reader a greater appreciation for the changes that have occurred since the creation of the settlement and the introduction of schooling, wage employment, television, and other social and material innovations from the outside world.

Traditional Life Stages

The term *inuhaaq* was used to describe young people making the transition from childhood (*nutaraq*) to adulthood (*inirniq*). *Inuhaaq* roughly translates as "becoming a person," based upon the root word *inu(k)*, "a person," + *haaq*, "just" or "becoming." Rasmussen (1932, 304–305) notes the use of a similar term, *inojak*, for the eastern Copper Inuit, which translates as "doll" but is actually used to describe "something that resembles a human being." Both terms, *inuhaaq* and *inojak*, imply a stage in which a young person is making the transition into adulthood but is not yet considered fully mature.

Although *inuhaaq* is now translated "teenager," it was used traditionally as a maturational marker for young people entering puberty, beginning at ten to 13 years of age. At this point in the life cycle, sex distinctions took on greater significance, and young people were called either *inuuhuktuq* (boys) or *arnaruhiq* (girls). In the previous stage, *nutaraq*, sex distinctions were not made. Entry into the *inuhaaq* stage was also dependent upon a host of behavioral changes that were the natural consequence of physical maturation. According to one of our older informants, when a boy was mature enough to hunt his first small game (e.g., a rabbit or ptarmigan), he was referred to as *inuuhuktuq*. For girls the *arnaruhiq* stage was reached when she started performing more household chores and doing some of her own sewing. While boys and girls at this stage were not mature enough to be self-sufficient, they did start to develop the skills of adulthood.

For the neighboring Netsilik Inuit, Balikci (1970, 105–109) notes that significant changes in the behavior and parental expectations of young people occurred by age ten to eleven. At this age a young boy developed a more intense relationship with his father and, in effect, became his helper, accompanying him on hunting trips and performing light but useful chores. In winter young boys from twelve to thirteen years of age went breathing-hole sealing on a regular basis with the adult men. At this period in the life cycle of Inuit boys, "the authority of the father remained very strong and the boy undertook no hunting trips on his own or without the father's approval" (Balikci 1970, 105). In general, girls had much less freedom than boys. By seven to eight years of age, a girl was expected to interrupt her play activities to assist her mother with such tasks as cutting fresh ice, getting water, and gathering moss (Balikci 1970, 107). By ten to eleven, girls were required to help their mothers with a greater variety of household chores, thereby creating a close working relationship with the mother similar to that established between fathers and sons. For both sexes, the learning of appropriate sex roles and adult responsibilities commenced at an early age.

The adult stage of Copper Inuit life was referred to as *inirniq*. Rasmussen (1932, 304) translates this term as "fully grown," implying the attainment of physical (and reproductive) maturity. According to one of our older informants, this stage was reached when a young man started growing a beard and began hunting large game alone. Young women reached adulthood when they developed fully mature breasts and had their first mensus. As in the previous stage, males and females were distinguished from one another, but with different terms: *angun* for males and *arnaq* for females.

The onset of puberty was unmarked by any ceremony or ritual for either boys or girls. A girl's first menstrual period was a sign that she had attained adulthood. Generally there was no preparation or training for this event. While a girl's mother would provide instruction on how to deal with the monthly bleeding, there were no taboos or ceremonies related to menstruation.

The most significant event for a boy entering adulthood was the killing of his first large game, usually a caribou or seal. If a caribou was his first kill, the boy's mother would make herself a pair of trousers out of the skin. In the case of a seal, all the meat would be distributed among the members of the community. In both circumstances, the parents were able to serve notice, in an informal sense, that their son had come of age and was now mature enough to support a wife (Jenness 1922, 158). Thus, for males especially, the transition into full adulthood was dependent not only upon the attainment of sexual maturity, but also upon the proven ability to engage in adult subsistence activities.

In the traditional period, marriage occurred much earlier than is the case today.[2] While it was common for marriages to be arranged by parents at an early age, sometimes even before a child's birth, there was much flexibility in such contracts. A mother who had promised her daughter to a particular man could change her mind a week later and make another arrangement. In addition, a daughter who did not agree with her parents' choice could refuse to marry her betrothed. As in all other aspects of Inuit life, there were no rules that could not be modified or occasionally broken. Nevertheless, arranged marriages were functional since, given the sparse distribution of the population, a young man or woman might have trouble finding an appropriate partner upon reaching a marriageable age. Today arranged marriages are no longer functional given the concentration of the population in the settlement. Young people can now make their own selection from a much larger pool of prospective partners without parental assistance.

While girls would often marry at or just prior to menarche and begin bearing children three to four years later, boys did not marry until after they had proven themselves capable as hunters. Thus until a boy could develop the skills and strength necessary to build a snowhouse or hunt large game unassisted, he was not considered old enough to take a wife. In chronological terms, this was probably not until he was at least seventeen or eighteen years of age. Since women's tasks, other than childbearing, were less related to maturation and shear physical strength, females were able to marry before the onset of puberty. While a female could marry at any age, and still have time to grow into her adult role, the male had to prove beforehand that he was capable of supporting himself and his future family. From a survival perspective, the negative consequences of a male marrying too soon were much greater than of a female marrying too soon. For both sexes, however, chronological age was unimportant in marking the young person's entry into adult society.

Marriage occurred with little or no ceremony. Usually a period of bride service was expected during which a young man would join his future father-in-law's household while his betrothed was still pre-pubescent. The young man worked with his father-in-law until both partners were considered adults and allowed to set up a neolocal residence (Damas 1972, 42). At that point the marriage was recognized. If, on the other hand, the young man planned to take his future wife to another area without providing a period of bride service, a small bride price was paid to the young woman's parents, who reciprocated with a small farewell feast (Jenness 1922, 159). In both cases, the first years of such a union were viewed as a trial period, as the couple got to know and adjust to one another. Separations during this period were not uncommon, but extremely rare after the couple started to produce offspring.

Contemporary Life Stages

The traditional life cycle of the Copper Inuit stands in marked contrast with that of the contemporary period. The social and economic changes that have occurred over the past thirty to forty years have led to significant alterations in the timing of life stages and the expectations placed upon maturing individuals. In addition, since the dominant language in the community is now English, traditional designations have dropped out of use in favor of the English terms *babies, kids, teenagers,* and *adults.*

Today the birth of an Inuit child is an event greeted with great joy and excitement by all members of the community. Expectant mothers may give birth either in the Yellowknife Hospital located in the territorial capital or at the local nursing station assisted by the resident nurse. Prior to the construction of the nursing station in 1972, childbirth took place either at the mother's home or at a hunting camp, with assistance provided by older and more knowledgeable women. Today the vast majority of women prefer to give birth at the nursing station rather than remain in Yellowknife for two to three weeks prior to the birth of the child. Generally, only women pregnant with their first child or those with a history of birth complications are encouraged to fly to Yellowknife where better obstetrical and neonatal care is available.

Infants up to the age of three or four are now referred to simply as babies. An infant may also be addressed in "Eskimoized" terms such as "babiq" and "dadiq." Because infants are new additions to the community, they are the center of attention wherever they go. Newborns often have a large number of caretakers, including grandmothers, older siblings, and unmarried aunts and cousins. Teenage girls related to the mother frequently spend a great deal of time visiting those households with new infants. Consequently, the mother of a newborn rarely has any trouble finding a baby-sitter when she must attend to other business. Thus households that have recently acquired a new member often experience a significant increase in visitors, as friends and relatives drop by to play with and help care for the newborn.

Children are named immediately after birth. While the child is given an English first name, he or she is also given the Inuit surname of the father, a practice only recently introduced from the South. In addition, a child is given one or more Inuit personal names, usually bestowed by an older female relative. Thus, a young Inuk will have an English first name, one or more Inuit middle names, and an Inuit surname.

Unlike their Eurocanadian counterparts, Inuit infants are rarely left alone for any length of time. Newborns are never given a room apart from other family members, and the first years of the infant's life are usually spent sleeping in the same bed as the parents. During the day, the large number of visitors to newborn households provides adequate distraction for the child, and rarely is the child set aside to entertain itself. Infants also spend much of their sleeping and waking hours packed on the mother's back. Packing is accomplished by placing the child ventrally on the mother's back under a loose-fitting shirt or jacket, held in place with a belt tied under the child's buttocks. Packing has a number of adaptive functions. It enables the mother to perform household chores when there are no other caretakers available to attend to the child. It is also the only safe and efficient mode for transporting the child when the mother leaves the house to visit or run errands. The close body contact between mother and child under the mother's outer parka provides ample protection from the extreme cold of winter. Mothers are not the only ones who pack children, and it is common to see a parental surrogate packing a younger sibling or the child of a sister or cousin. While males frequently pick up and carry infants in their arms, packing is almost exclusively a female activity. Packing also accomplishes many of the same functions as crib rocking in southern culture. A crying infant is placed on the mother's back and rocked up and down while the mother gently pats the infant on the buttocks to calm it down. While packing becomes less common as the child gets older, children as old as three to four years are still carried on the mother's back in cold or windy weather.

Breast-feeding is currently the prevalent mode of infant feeding and is practiced except in cases where a child has been adopted.[3] The duration of breast-feeding varies, depending upon the mother and the spacing between children. As the infant gets older, breast milk is supplemented with powdered milk and fruit juices. Although becoming less common, it is not unusual to see three- and four-year-olds nurse occasionally. In the first years of life, the crying of an infant usually brings an immediate response on the part of the mother, and breast-feeding takes place on demand. Leaving a child crying by itself is unacceptable by Inuit standards.

In sum, the first years of a child's life are characterized by a high degree of security, freedom from want, constant attention from household members and visitors, and a high degree of tactile stimulation. The intense interaction that occurs between infants and caretakers helps prepare children for the cultural emphasis placed upon the interdependence and close interpersonal relations that are an integral part of Inuit life.

By four to five years of age, a child is no longer considered a baby, but has reached the stage of life where he or she is called a kid. *Kid* generally refers to both the early and late childhood years, beginning with the start of schooling and ending with entrance into the teenage years. Sex distinctions are rarely made during this stage of life, and little girls and little boys are almost always referred to in the same manner. Occasionally, individuals will distinguish older children from younger children with the terms *little kids* and *big kids*. Mixed-sex play groups are also much more common at this stage than they are in the teenage years, primarily because the play activities and interests of male and female children have not yet diverged to any significant degree.

Children in this age category display an increase in physical mobility around the settlement. While babies and toddlers are always accompanied by a caretaker, either the mother or an older sibling, kids begin ranging farther from home. Kids also begin visiting other households, at first those located fairly close to home and later extending to all the homes in the community. While parents actively discourage their children from wandering too far from the settlement, there are no pronounced differences in the ranges of male and female children. Both sexes freely wander about the community, and there are no households or public settings that are considered off-limits.

By southern standards, Inuit children have a great deal of freedom to go where they want and do what they please. As the child matures and becomes increasingly mobile, the social world expands beyond the child's immediate household to the households of friends and relatives. As the mother has subsequent newborns to care for, the child receives less and less attention from adults. When misbehaving, a child will be briefly chastised or teased by adults, but physical punishment and menacing verbal reprimands are rarely used.[4] If a child ignores initial reprimands and continues misbehaving, parents will often ignore the child altogether, even when the child becomes so exasperated that he or she starts swearing at or hitting the parents. Inuit adults generally regard such impulsive, childish behavior as unworthy of response. Misbehavior that is totally ignored is, in effect, negatively reinforced, and the child gradually learns the importance of patience and self-restraint through the example of tolerant adults.

The function of such restrained child-rearing practices is to instill culturally valued behaviors in children by example. These behviors include emotional inhibition, self-restraint, nonaggressiveness, and responsibility. Undoubtedly the average Inuit adult tolerates a great deal more misbehavior and abuse from children than most Eurocanadian parents. The techniques of being patient and ignoring childish behavior serve as efficient modeling devices for children to learn culturally acceptable behavior. In fact, the style and content of modern child-rearing and socialization practices appear to have changed little from the traditional techniques observed by Jenness (1922, 169–170):

Eskimo children show little respect for their elders in the manner to which we are accustomed. They address them as equals, and join in any conversation that may be taking place, not hesitating to interrupt or even correcting their parents. . . . Boys are more apt to be spoiled than girls, probably because they are more errant and come less directly under their parent's influence. . . . Generally speaking, boys and girls grow up like wild plants, without much care or attention from the time they can run about till they approach puberty.

Adults and teenagers tend to describe the behavior of kids in similar terms. Kids are considered to be extremely bossy. Since they have not yet incorporated the culturally valued norms of patience, generosity, and self-restraint, kids often make excessive demands of others and become greatly upset if these are not forthcoming. Children are also viewed as being overly aggressive, stingy, and exhibitionist, all behaviors viewed as antithetical to ideal behavioral norms. A sixteen-year-old girl described kids as "always touching stuff that isn't theirs, fighting with one another, and taking things that don't belong to them."

Children are also much more talkative than adults and tend to ask many, often inappropriate, questions. As Minnie Aodla Freeman (1978, 21) notes in her autobiography:

In my [Inuit] culture, children are encouraged to speak. As they grow older, questioning becomes a boring habit; they [children] have not gained wisdom and eventually become more intelligent. The more intelligent they become, the quieter they are. That is the reason Inuit children are allowed to be children.

One of the consequences of noninterventive child-rearing practices is that parents are unable to exert direct control over children, a phenomenon aggravated by collective living in the settlement. In the presettlement era, when the child's social environment consisted primarily of immediate family members, interaction between parents and children was necessarily much more intense, and children benefited more from direct modeling of parental behavior. In the modern settlement, however, child socialization practices remain largely unchanged despite significant alterations in the social and economic spheres of life. Children spend much more time interacting with other children than they do with their parents. Also, in the settlement there are opportunities for groups of children to get into mischief, which were absent in the presettlement era.

As children become older, they gradually accept more responsibilities in helping around the house. Household chores tend to be delegated to girls at an earlier age than to boys. By late childhood (ages nine to fourteen) young girls, especially first borns, are expected to help their mothers with sewing, cleaning, taking out the honey bucket, and caring for younger siblings. Young boys, in line with the division of labor between the sexes, are more likely to be taken hunting and trapping with their fathers. Instruction in these skills, as in most areas of cultural transmission, tends to be a nonverbal process. Parents rarely verbally instruct their children at such tasks, but expect them to learn through observation. In fact, the persistent asking of questions is regarded as "childish."

The most significant behavioral change occurs with the individual's transition from kid to teenager. At this stage distinctions are made between the sexes, through the use of the terms *boys* and *girls*. It is important to emphasize that kids are never referred to as being either boys or girls. Rather these distinctions are reserved for the teenage years, when sex differences first appear.

Our informants initially defined the teenage years in chronological terms, that is, anyone between thirteen and nineteen years of age. This chronological orientation is probably related to the introduction of schooling and television programming. On closer examination, however, certain behavioral attributes are associated with teenagers, such that a fourteen- or fifteen-year-old can "be a teenager" in chronological terms but still be accused of "acting like a kid" if his or her behavior is not commensurate with age-mates.

The behavioral changes among teenage girls are the most obvious. As kids, females are physically active. They run around, engage adults in frequent conversation, and call attention to themselves. When they become teenagers, this behavior ceases and they become quiet, reserved, and exceedingly shy, exhibiting behaviors more characteristic of adult females. These behavioral changes undoubtedly coincide, for many young girls, with the onset of menarche. While these maturing girls do not appear ashamed of their bodies, the awareness of new bodily functions and developing secondary sex characteristics result in an increase in modesty not seen in prepubescent girls.

One fascinating behavioral change we observed was something we decided to call the parka syndrome. This syndrome was characteristic of all teenagers, but tended to be most pronounced in post-pubescent teenage girls. The parka syndrome simply refers to the unwillingness of young girls to take off or even unzip their parkas in public settings. In all probability, it is the onset of menarche and the growth of breasts that make these young people exceptionally modest regarding the exposure of body parts. While kids will frequently throw off their parkas once they have entered someone's home to visit, teenage girls will invariably keep their parkas on.

When my colleague on this project (Pamela Stern) began interviewing the adolescent girls, she was impressed that the girls appeared more comfortable keeping their parkas on, even if the temperature in the room was quite high. After a time, however, presumably when the girls got used to her and started feeling comfortable in her presence, they would unzip their parkas and then take them off altogether if they were planning a long visit. Such unzipping occured only if I was absent. On several occasions, I entered the room briefly while an interview was underway, and the young girl present quickly zipped up her parka. On another occasion, two girls were visiting Stern and had taken their parkas off to play a game. As soon as they heard me enter the house, they jumped up and threw on their parkas. By the time I entered the room, they were completely covered and zipped.

Not surprisingly, such modesty is also displayed at school. According to the female teacher of the senior grades, the teenage girls leave their parkas on at all times if there is a single male student present. However, on those days when all the boys are absent or during home economics classes when only girls are present, the girls will feel comfortable enough to take off their parkas.

The distinction between the behavior of kids and the behavior of adults and teenagers is most vividly seen at social functions held at the community hall. Kids attending such functions are invariably running across the floor, yelling, screaming, and roughhousing. In contrast, adults and teenagers enter quietly and seat themselves on the benches that line the outside wall of the building. Conversations transpire in muted tones, and often in whispers for the adolescent girls. The general tendency is to avoid calling attention to oneself. Kids, on the other hand, behave in a manner diametrically opposed to that of adults: the kids run around the hall, throw objects, play tag, and yell at the top of their voices. In these social contexts, the behavior of teenagers is more similar to that of adults. Perhaps, for this reason, one sixteen-year-old girl claimed that there were no differences between adults and teens other than age.

Interestingly, adults and teenagers can readily discern in whom "childish" behavior is acceptable. On several occasions I witnessed a thirteen-year-old boy being chastised by older teenagers (ages seventeen to nineteen) for running around the hall and playing with the younger children. One of these critics attempted to embarrass the youth by telling him that "he wasn't a kid anymore."

The teenage life stage generally lasts until the individual reaches the early twenties. Different criteria are used to mark the transition into full adulthood, including the attainment of economic responsibility, marriage, the production of children, and in some cases simply chronological age.

One of the procedures we used to identify these criteria was asking our teenage informants to assign life stage terms to a list of individuals residing in the community and explain why these people were placed into this category. All individuals living with a spouse, married or unmarried, in a separate household were considered adults, especially if they had started producing offspring. Those individuals living with a boyfriend or girlfriend in their parents' household were categorized as adults only if they were beyond their chronological teens. For example, one seventeen-year-old boy whose girlfriend had just moved into his room was still considered a teenager due to his generally irresponsible behavior *and* his young age. Had the boy displayed more responsibility by getting a job, he would most likely have been placed in a transitional category between teenager and adult. By and large, individuals who have established permanent pair-bonds, by setting up house with a prospective spouse, tend to be older in chronological years. Of the nine young couples who established separate households between 1980 and 1982, the mean age for the males was 21.1, while the mean age for the females was 19.6. All of these individuals were indisputably labeled adults.

Young unmarried men in their early to midtwenties posed the greatest problem of categorization. Many of our teenage informants hesitatingly labeled these young men as adults due to their age, but admitted that they were not as mature as young men living with spouses in separate households. The adults we interviewed, however, had no problem categorizing these individuals. From their perspective, these young unmarried men were more like teenagers than adults simply because they had not yet taken on the obligations and responsibilities of supporting a spouse and maintaining a household.

Young unwed mothers also provided an interesting case. Many of these young mothers were considered adults because they had children. A few, however, were still labeled teenagers because of their young age (fifteen to seventeen). An adolescent boy described one of these girls as still a teenager because she had not lost her "teenage touch." In this particular case, degree of mobility was an important measure of "teenagerness." Unwed mothers who keep irregular schedules and roam around with other youths continue to be regarded as teenagers, while those who become more sedentary after the birth of their child are considered more adultlike.

From the perspective of teenagers, mobility and activity, in addition to chronological age, are important features that distinguish teenage boys and girls from adult men and women. Teenagers spend more time roaming around town ("running around" as it is commonly called), visiting households at all hours of the day and night, and playing team sports such as hockey, baseball, and football. Adults, on the other hand, are viewed as less active, despite the fact that they may be hardworking and actively involved in subsistence activities. One young informant, when queried about the difference between adults and teenagers, actually created a new category which he called "active adults." Active adults were those individuals, usually young adults in their early twenties, who were married with children, but who nevertheless participated a great deal in teenage sports. Such individuals were described as "adults, but active like teenagers." Nevertheless, as family and work obligations make increasing demands upon their time, most of these young men cease their participation in teenage sports by their mid-twenties.

Becoming an adult is a gradual process for Inuit teenagers, and for many there is a period of time when they are precariously balanced between the two social domains. When individuals finally receive the social recognition of adulthood, they are likely to spend more time at home with spouses, less time roaming around with peers, more time visiting other households with their spouse, and less time playing games with the teenagers. In local parlance, adults are referred to as men and women. One of the most noticeable changes occurring at adulthood is that the individual's active social networks expand to include a much greater age range. Thus while teenagers spend much of their time only with other teenagers of approximately the same age, young adults begin associating and visiting adults of all ages. This is especially true if a young couple has children, in which case they spend more time visiting parents, grandparents, and other relatives with their offspring.

Cultural distinctions between adults and teenagers are vividly portrayed at the community hall when indoor team games are played at Easter or Christmas. These games involve relay races such as balloon popping, three-legged races, wheelbarrow races, and so forth. When a new game is to be played, the director of these activities will ask for kids to come up and play first. Since kids rarely make any displays of modesty, false or otherwise, there is always a vast movement of kids to the front of the hall to play. After the kids have finished and a group of winners is announced, the director will ask for "older people" to come up and play. Since teenagers and adults are a little more restrained and inhibited, it takes a fair amount of cajoling to get people to participate. Often the master of ceremonies will visually scan the room and ask for particular individuals to come up. Once a sufficient number of men, women, teenage boys, and teenage girls have gathered at the front of the hall, participants will naturally divide themselves up into teams based upon sex and age differences. Thus, one team will be made up of "girls," another made up of "boys," another made up of "men," and yet another made up of "women." (During my first field trip I was often placed with the teenage boys five to ten years my junior, while during my second field trip I was invariably placed with the men. While most individuals seem locked into a particular category, a few individuals, by nature of their transitional status, are able to alternate age categories. One, for example, was an unmarried twenty-year-old who seemed equally accepted in either age group.)

Most of the individual's life is spent in the adult age category. The final stage of old man or old woman is reached when the individual no longer follows an active life of hunting, trapping, wage labor, and child rearing. While old age certainly limits the degree of strenuous activity in which an individual can engage, the elderly do not have to resign themselves to an unproductive existence. Some of the older women in the settlement are among the best and most productive seamstresses in town and generate substantial incomes by sewing for the co-op. Older men will often continue hunting and trapping with sons and grandsons until infirmity confines them to the settlement.

Older individuals rarely live by themselves, but frequently reside with married or unmarried sons and daughters. Because older adults often have a number of offspring, they have many households through-out the community that they can visit. Older people also spend time visiting one another. By and large, old age is relatively comfortable and secure. In addition to generating income by working for the co-op, the elderly frequently receive an old-age pension from the federal government as well as gifts of fresh meat and fish from sons, daughters, in-laws, and grandchildren.

Due to the small size of the population, death is a relatively infrequent phenomenon. The death of a member of the community, whether it be from old age, disease, or a hunting accident, has a significant emotional impact upon all residents. A southern church ceremony, attended by most community members, marks the funeral, and the loved one is interred in the community cemetery.

As is typical of other areas of Inuit life, death is met with emotional restraint. Open display of sorrow in public rarely accompanies the loss of a loved one, even one as close as a parent, spouse, son, or daughter. Although the sorrow of such occasions is hidden by a facade of stoicism, there is no doubt that the loss is felt deeply and intensely by those left behind.

The average Inuk spends his or her entire life in close contact with fellow members of the society. Social and emotional integration with friends and family has been reinforced by close social and economic cooperation in all spheres of life. The individual who has married, produced offspring, proven his or her value as a provider, and successfully lived to old age, in spite of the many hazards of arctic life, has lived a full and meaningful existence, leaving behind many friends and relatives to mourn the passing.

CHANGING ADOLESCENCE

This brief overview of traditional and contemporary life stages has outlined the changes that have occurred in the Inuit life cycle since contact with Eurocanadian society. In the past, young people made a rapid transition from childhood to adulthood. As Graburn (1969, 62) notes, "children learned little else than their respective roles and by 10–12 could be useful, although not fully self-supporting members of the community." For girls, the transition to adulthood was especially rapid since they would often be married and performing many adult roles even before reaching sexual maturity. For boys, marriage was delayed slightly because they had to prove their capabilities for fulfilling the duties and obligations of adulthood. Not all was hard work and regimentation, however. Young people were allowed a high degree of freedom to play games, stay up all night, wander off by themselves, and engage in sexual intercourse if a suitable partner were available. Ultimately, however, social maturity was expected at a much earlier age than is the case today. The marginal and precarious adaptation to the harsh arctic ecosystem simply did not allow for the frivolity and nonproductiveness which is so characteristic of modern-day teenagers.

The freedom and autonomy experienced by young people in the traditional period pales in comparison to that of today's youth, who have a longer period of time before taking on the responsibilities of adulthood. If, then, it can be assumed that the prolongation of the transitional stage between childhood and adulthood is a recent phenomenon, the question must be posed as to how this came about. Presumably, an important factor has been the increased security of modern settlement life, wherein local residents are no longer precariously balanced on the edge of survival. The availability of wage employment, social assistance, and child allowances now makes it possible for parents to support nonproductive offspring for an indefinite period of time. Parents no longer have to worry about their families perishing from famine if their sons and daughters fail to take on adult responsibilities at an early age. Another important contributing factor is undoubtedly the introduction of schooling, which has helped create a whole category of individuals who, although physically mature, are chronologically labeled as children or teenagers rather than adults.

Finally, the recent impact of television and radio programming has probably contributed a great deal to the formulation of a teenage age set. In fact, the term *teenager* was not widely used in the community until after the introduction of television, with its abundant offerings of teenage-oriented programs. In sum, adolescence (or more appropriately "teenagerness") is a recent import into the community, along with television, radio, schooling, snowmobiles, and stereos.

■ 3
The Seasons
of Adolescence

■ Daily Routine Interview

JOHNNY APIUK, (AGE EIGHTEEN), MAY 15, 1982

3:00 P.M. Woke up and went into the kitchen to put some water on to boil. Nobody else was in the house, so I put on the TV for a while and had a breakfast of instant oatmeal and coffee.

4:30 P.M. Went out for a drive on my ski-doo [snowmobile], but had to turn back right away because I had problems with my fan belt which had broken. The fan was also worn out.

6:00 P.M. Worked on my machine for about an hour and then went into the house to watch more TV.

8:00 P.M. Went outside to work on my snowmobile again, but quit right away because I realized that I would need some more parts from the Bay store.

8:30 P.M. Stayed in the house for a while and watched TV. Only my parents were in the house with me.

12:00 MIDNIGHT. Borrowed my brother's ski-doo and drove over to Father's Lake to watch the other boys play hockey. A little while later I decided to get my skates. When I came back, I played hockey until about 2:00 A.M.

2:00 A.M. Went home, washed up, and watched the ending of

the late movie which was about terrorists. Only my brother Allen was still up.

3:00 A.M. Went over to my friend Eddie's house and went out walking around town with him and his sister Molly. We didn't stay out very long because it was getting pretty cold. After we walked around for a while, we went back to Eddie's house and stayed in until about 7:00 A.M. During that time, we talked around and had some coffee.

7:00 A.M. I went home and washed my hair. Everybody else was asleep. I had some caribou soup which had been made the day before.

8:30 A.M. Woke up my sisters for school and then went out to the co-op coffee shop. Some of my friends were already waiting outside for it to open.

9:00 A.M. The hotel opened at 9:00 and we all went in. I had two egg sandwiches and a glass of orange juice. After eating, we just sat there and talked around. We made plans to go out ice fishing later on.

10:00 A.M. Came over here [the anthropologists' house] to work.

This daily routine is an actual report made by our primary field assistant, Johnny Apiuk, who also functioned as a clinical informant. Johnny provided us with seventeen such daily routines throughout the course of the fieldwork. Additional daily routines were collected from our other clinical informants. These routines provided a wealth of data pertaining to the activities and daily schedules of Holman teenagers. The daily routines were quite varied, indicating the diversity of adolescent activities in a community that has little to offer in the form of recreational activities and behavior settings. They also indicate that Holman adolescents are not necessarily confined to a regular and predictable schedule of activities, which may be more characteristic of their age-mates in other cultures, where schooling and parentally-imposed duties and schedules are more pervasive.

Johnny Apiuk is fairly typical of Holman adolescents in the sixteen-to-twenty age-group. Generally this age group is made up of youngsters who are no longer attending school. Few of these older teenagers have actually graduated from the ninth grade, the highest grade offered at the local school. Johnny is one adolescent who did successfully complete the ninth grade and then went to Yellowknife for high school. After several months of attending Sir John Franklin High School and living in the school dormitory, Johnny became homesick and returned to Holman. His parents, who are very traditional, encouraged him to leave Yellowknife. Neither parent could see any value in having their son spend so much time away from home in a strange town where he might get into trouble. Consequently, Johnny has spent the past year and a half hanging out around town, helping his father hunt and trap, playing hockey and football with his friends, and taking on temporary employment about town. Johnny talks about attending vocational school at Fort Smith to learn a trade such as electrical work or carpentry, but as yet, has not committed himself to any long-range plans. For this reason Johnny, along with many of his same-age friends, passes much of his time doing whatever he pleases. Johnny's father would like his son to follow in his footsteps as a hunter and trapper, but the ultimate decision, as Johnny says, will be made by himself alone. Johnny also claims that his parents have not placed any undue pressure upon him to make a decision one way or the other. Since he is still young, he has plenty of time to make up his mind.

In examining the daily routines of Johnny and other teenagers, it is immediately apparent that adolescent activities change dramatically with the seasons. Just as the hunting, trapping, fishing, and wage-employment activities of parents are determined by seasonal changes in temperature, photoperiod, ice conditions, and food availability, the activities of adolescents are also affected by seasonal variation. This chapter describes both adult and adolescent activities as they alter from one season to the next. I use the Inuit demarcations for seasons since these more effectively elaborate upon seasonally based social and economic activities. Individual daily routines provided by our adolescent informants exemplify the extent to which activities and settings change with the seasons.

EARLY FALL (*Ukiahaaq*)

The Inuit designation *Ukiahaaq* refers to the transitional period between summer (*Auyaq*) and fall (*Ukiaq*). *Ukiahaaq* generally begins around the end of August when increasing darkness and deteriorating weather conditions herald the end of the pleasant and all-too-short summer season.

By the end of August most families have returned to the community from summer hunting and fishing camps. September is generally accompanied by an increase in casual wage employment for adults and teenagers alike. Since the barge usually arrives in mid-August with building materials and other supplies, a fair amount of work is available on construction and maintenance projects. The Hudson's Bay store hires a large number of adolescent boys to help unload supplies from the barge and store them in warehouses. Wage labor at this time of year is frequently intense and employs large numbers of workers due to the necessity of completing most projects before the arrival of winter. During September of 1982, for example, three teenage boys between sixteen and eighteen years of age were hired by the Northern Canada Power Company to help erect power poles throughout the community. They worked twelve-hour days for approximately three months at an astounding $13 an hour. When finished, one of the boys had earned enough money to buy a brand new snowmobile. Other boys secured temporary employment through the settlement council, which hired them to haul gravel for the roads; several girls were hired by the co-op to assist in organizing and storing supplies in the craft shop.

Subsistence activities at this time of year are limited to seal hunting on the ocean and rabbit hunting on the land. The latter is extremely productive since the arctic hares are beginning to turn white and consequently are easy to spot on the snow-free landscape. Many boys go rabbit hunting near the community with friends. Older boys, aged seventeen to nineteen, are also permitted to borrow their parents' boats in order to hunt seals on the ocean.

By local standards, September is a relatively unpleasant month since weather conditions restrict mobility in and out of the settlement. The movement of cold air from the north results in extremely rough ocean conditions, making travel by boat both unpleasant and dangerous. In addition, travel by snowmobile is delayed until the first permanent snowfall, usually in the first or second week of October. September is thus frequently wet, windy, cold, and overcast, which may explain why people look forward to the first snows which will enable them to go fishing and caribou hunting. The lack of mobility and subsequent boredom of being confined to the settlement, as well as the increased availability of cash from wage labor, result in an increase in alcohol consumption. While alcohol use and abuse tends to be more pronounced among adults, adolescents have limited access to liquor. Since there are no liquor outlets in Holman and all alcohol must be ordered air freight from Yellowknife, it is difficult for teenagers to obtain. Occasionally a young adult couple will have a drinking party to which some of the older adolescent boys and girls will be invited. Under these rare circumstances, teenage drinking does occur. Some teenagers are also able to convince an older friend or relative to order alcohol on their behalf.

School is in session throughout September, having started in the second week of August. Students who are good attenders spend their days in school, while those who have quit school take advantage of the increased wage employment opportunities. Toward the end of the month, children and teenagers begin ice skating on the small ponds around the community. Boys begin playing hockey, first on the smaller ponds and then on the larger lakes as the ice reaches a safe thickness.

Organized teenage dances at the community hall are another activity that commences in the fall, having been temporarily suspended during the summer months. These dances, which are primarily teenage affairs and take place with no parental supervision, are organized by older adolescent boys and young unmarried men. Music is provided either by a record player or, more rarely, by a group of young people who have organized themselves into a rock and roll band. Dances start anytime between midnight and two in the morning, often continuing into the early morning hours. Although these affairs are organized primarily for teens and young adults, it is common for both young children and some older adults to attend.

▪ Daily Routine Interview
JACK ULIKTUAQ, AGE FIFTEEN, SEPTEMBER 28, 1982

9:30 A.M. Got up and made breakfast of egg, toast, and tea. My parents were up, Peter [older brother] was asleep, and everybody else was at school. I got dressed, washed myself, put on my boots and jacket, and went to school. I arrived at 10:30, just in time for recess. Went to Bay and bought soda pop and potato chips. Then went to the hotel to eat them. Went back to school.

12:00 NOON. Went home from school and had lunch of frozen caribou meat. Everybody else was home having lunch. Listened to the radio for a while, then got ready to take some scrap wood apart for a storage shed.

1:00 P.M. Went outside and started breaking up some large, wooden shipping crates.

3:30 P.M. Went to the Bay and bought a coke and some chocolate. Went home, put some music on, and ate them. Then went to the washroom and then back to work on the shipping crates. After work, I went home and ate supper. I made chicken soup for myself, and then put on my hockey equipment.

5:30 P.M. Went down to the ponds to play hockey. After hockey, I put my boots back on and walked back to town with Willy. Went home, watched TV, and ate potato chips. Everybody else was home. At 9:00, I came over here to work.

FALL (*Ukiaq*)

By the first or second week in October, snow has fallen and snow-mobiles are evident everywhere, speeding throughout the community. Many of these speeders are teenagers playing follow the leader or hide-and-seek on snowmobiles. The older boys are spending more time play-ing hockey, usually beginning in late afternoons and extending until darkness hampers the players' ability to chase the hockey puck. The hockey rink has now been moved to a larger lake about a half mile from town, and snowmobiles can always be spotted ferrying players and spectators to and from the playing rink. Hockey playing is fre-quently hampered by blowing wind, which covers the ice with a hard layer of packed snow. When this occurs, the boys will either plow off the rink with snow shovels or move to a nearby lake that has not been covered. On occasion the snow cover may be such that the boys will have to wait until the next "blow," which will naturally clear one of the lakes in the vicinity of town. Kids and girls continue to skate, but gen-erally on the small ponds closer to town.

Although the days are becoming shorter and are often character-ized by overcast skies, travel conditions on the land are fairly good. Once snow has fallen, rabbits are much harder to spot during the day, so many boys and young men begin hunting rabbits at night using their snowmobile headlights to blind their prey. Often late at night one can see groups of snowmobile headlights bobbing up and down near the top of Uluhaktok Bluff as young snowmobilers hunt these animals.

Around the second week in October, people begin traveling to Fish Lake, located fifty miles north of Holman, to set nets under the newly formed ice. The trip to Fish Lake is undoubtedly one of the major events of settlement life and is anticipated by young and old alike with great excitement. The fishing period usually lasts several weeks, with some people spending the entire period camped by the lake. Others, usually adults committed to wage employment in town, make periodic trips to and from town. Although Fish Lake is predominantly a male excursion, it is becoming increasingly common for wives to accompany their husbands. Many parents decide to take their children out of school for a short period so that they too can help with the fishing. Older teenagers, mostly boys who are no longer attending school, also come along to assist.

The journey to Fish Lake also marks the beginning of caribou hunting season. Since caribou are scarce during the spring and summer, there is much excitement at the prospect of obtaining fresh caribou meat. In October the caribou begin moving southward from their summer feeding grounds, and hunters travel from the Fish Lake camp to intercept the herds. Hunting trips may last one to two days, and a hunter may have to travel up to one hundred miles before caribou are sighted. While these prolonged hunting trips are made exclusively by men, older boys (fifteen to twenty years of age) frequently accompany their fathers, usually driving a separate snowmobile and sled. By this age, boys have often become fairly experienced hunters and snowmobile repairers in their own right, and are usually an asset on long hunting trips.

Around the middle of the month, freeze-up of the bays and coastal areas around Holman occurs, and soon afterward the ice is safe for travel. The newly formed ice provides an excellent surface for the frequent snowmobile races that teenagers engage in at all hours of the day and night. Braver, and perhaps more reckless, individuals drive across the bay at high speeds even before the ice is totally safe.

■ Daily Routine Interview

SARAH KITIGAT, AGE THIRTEEN, OCTOBER 10, 1982

8:30 A.M. Got up to get ready for school. Everybody else was up except my brother Ricky who was sleeping in. Had tea and bannock [fried bread] and walked to school with my older sister and younger brother.

9:00 A.M. Spent the rest of the morning at school except for recess when Nancy [a friend] and I walked over to the Bay store to buy candy and pop. We then went over to the coffee shop and sat with my older sister until it was time to go back to school.

12:00 NOON. Went home for lunch. Had tea, bannock, dried fish. Everybody else was home. I played with Leslie [my infant brother] while my mother was making lunch. After lunch, I cleaned the table and did the dishes.

1:00 P.M. Went back to school. In the afternoon, we had sewing class and I did some beadwork.

3:30 P.M. Came home right after school and went shopping at the Bay store with my Mom and Ruby [older sister]. When we came back home, I got my skates and went down to the lakes to go skating. There were a lot of kids down there skating around. I stayed down there for a couple of hours skating with some friends.

6:00 P.M. Came back home. Everybody was home except Ricky who was out skating. Watched TV for a while and had dinner of tea and caribou stew. Ricky came back from skating and asked if he could borrow my Dad's snowmobile. He and and my other brother went out to drive around.

8:00 P.M. Went out visiting. Went over to Judy's house, but she wasn't home. Then went over to Roberta's. She was watching TV with her family. She and I decided to go out for a while. We went over to my grandparent's place where we stayed and played with Bobby [grandparent's adopted infant].

9:00 P.M. Went back home. My parents were playing cards and watching TV with some friends. I had some tea and bannock, and then cleaned the kitchen. I watched TV for a while and played with Leslie.

12:00 MIDNIGHT. My mother told me to take out the garbage and then I went to bed.

WINTER (*Ukiuq*)

Ukiuq refers to the coldest and darkest period of the year and roughly coincides with the noticeable dimunition of daylight in November until the arrival of warmer and brighter weather conditions in mid-March.

November officially opens the trapping season, and trappers busy themselves with the setting and checking of traps. Young and older adolescent boys also participate in trapping activities. Younger boys may set a limited number of fox traps close to the community, while older adolescent boys may set traplines slightly longer and more numerous. Also many older boys go out with fathers or other relatives to help check and reset longer traplines. Trips may last two to three days depending upon the length and productivity of the trapline. Trapping is predominantly a male activity, although a number of unmarried adult women set short traplines close to home.

Seal hunting at the ice edge also begins in November. Although the bays and most of the coastline around Holman have frozen solid, there is generally open water beyond the landfast ice. A seal hunter travels by snowmobile over the ocean ice to the edge of the open water. There he tries to locate a section of ice that is firm enough for him to launch a small open-water boat (*wiinikhiut*) he has carried on his sled. Once a seal has surfaced within firing range, the hunter shoots and, if the shot has hit its mark, retrieves the seal by rowing out to it in his small boat.

By the middle of November there are only two to three hours of direct sunlight, and the sun disappears altogether by the last week of the month. Trapping and caribou hunting continue throughout November, although the increasing darkness makes travel difficult. The presence of headlights on snowmobiles makes it much easier, however, to continue these activities even as days get shorter. Caribou begin moving closer to town, so hunting expeditions can generally be accomplished in a single day.

Adolescents in town continue attending school, skating, and playing hockey during daylight hours. Skating and hockey, especially, are restricted due to increasingly cold temperatures and diminishing daylight. Many kids and teenagers begin playing "street hockey" under one of the town's two streetlights. The hard-packed snow surface on the road makes it possible for would-be hockey stars to pass a puck back and forth between two makeshift goals, but not hard enough to do so wearing skates. Older boys can often be seen playing this game in the early hours of the morning, almost as though they are completely resistant to the cold temperatures. Street hockey as well as regular ice hockey are primarily male activities, and girls limit their participation to spectating.

Adolescent girls at this time of year spend significantly less time out of doors than boys of the same age. While girls can often be seen skating on the smaller ponds or skating around the outside margins of the boy's hockey rink, they do not seem as obsessed with outdoor sports as are teenage boys. As the weather gets colder and darker, the focus of female activities moves indoors where teenage girls visit one another to talk, watch television, play cards, perform household chores, and assist in the care of younger siblings.

Hunting and trapping activities continue through December, but are somewhat curtailed later in the month due to darkness. Although the darkness and cold act to limit mobility, this immobility is not as marked as it was during September. Snowmobiles are still driven freely in and around the settlement. Some rabbit hunting continues, and individuals who have set traps around the settlement check them during the brief period of twilight that occurs around the middle of the day. Caribou hunting also continues but is limited to brief day trips since the caribou are much closer to the settlement.

By and large, the increasing cold and darkness of mid-December result in a temporary lull in trapping, subsistence hunting, and other outdoor activities. Ice hockey almost ceases altogether and is replaced by street hockey. Throughout most of the month, only one to two hours of very dim twilight appear at midday. For this reason, skating and ice hockey on the lakes and ponds around town are suspended until the return of the sun in January. Increasingly more time is spent indoors watching television and visiting friends and neighbors.

Any confinement stress generated during this month is significantly reduced by the Christmas holiday celebrations, which coincide with the height of the dark period. Christmas vacation marks the time when all but the most essential services, such as water delivery and sewage pickup, are temporarily suspended. Both the school and co-op close for a two-week period, and hunting and trapping activities are momentarily halted. Because of the constant darkness, residents begin to get "turned around" in their activity rhythms. This alteration of activity rhythms is most pronounced with the adolescents and young adults who begin to stay up later into the night and sleep during the day. Young and old congregate at the community hall to dance and play games. Often these activities do not get underway until one or two o'clock in the morning and extend until eight or nine. Adults as well may become disoriented as they stay up a little later each evening. Adolescents spend their time visiting one another, going to the hall to watch and play games, and occasionally waiting for the adults to tire themselves from square dancing so they can start a teenage "disco" dance.

During the Christmas of 1982, many of the adults started leaving the hall at three or four o'clock in the morning, at which time the teenage band would set up their equipment for a disco dance. The dances lasted until eight or nine in the morning, followed by street hockey under the streetlight located in front of the Bay store. When the Bay opened, large numbers of these young people went in to buy soda, candy, and potato chips, after which most returned home to sleep until the following evening.

Settlement activities gradually resume during the month of January. Most adults have so exhausted themselves during the holidays that they are glad to get back to a normal routine. Many of the kids and teenagers, even those attending school during the day, remain significantly altered in their activity rhythms. The effect these altered activity rhythms have upon school attendance is particularly fascinating. One would expect school attendance to be quite low with the beginning of the new year because many young people are still sleeping during the day and staying up all night; the reverse is actually true. School normally resumes the first week of the new year with attendance levels at an all-time high. Field-note entries for the years 1979 and 1980 respectively elaborate:

> January 2 [1979]—Today was the first day of school after the Christmas break. The teachers report unusually good attendance for all grades. The number of children who reported staying up all night is also quite high. For grades 2 and 3, 4 out of 14 students stayed up all night, 4 out of 17 for grades 4 and 5, and 16 out of 24 for the senior grades. Even for beginners and grade 1, 1 child out of 6 attenders reported staying up all night. Particularly interesting is the fact that many of these school attenders are children who rarely, if ever, come to school the rest of the year.
>
> January 8 [1979]—By the end of the week, most of the younger children have reverted to a somewhat normal schedule. While not staying up all night, many are still staying up very late in the evenings and coming to school with little sleep. Students in the senior grades, however, are still hanging on to a "dark period schedule." The typical pattern as reported by many of these young people is to go to bed immediately after school, sleep through the early evening, and get up at midnight to go out visiting until the start of school.
>
> January 3 [1980]—School has resumed after the Christmas holidays. In the senior grades, twenty-two teenagers were in attendance, the highest figure yet for the 1979–1980 school year. Fourteen of those in attendance reported staying up all night and were nodding off to sleep at their desks. Despite their exhaustion, all of these students returned for the afternoon session, in body at least. The middle grades also had excellent attendance, with eleven students having stayed up all night. While the younger grades had excellent attendance, only one child reported staying up all night.
>
> January 7 [1980]—Fewer children are staying up all night as in the beginning of the week. In the older grades, however, a large number of children are going to bed right after school, rising between midnight and 3:00 A.M., and staying up until school opens. The teachers still notice a high degree of weariness among their students.

Although it was not possible to obtain more precise data on children's activity rhythms, the indication is clear that kids and teenagers, more so than adults, resist returning to a normal routine. Much of this resistance seems to be voluntary. As with children and adolescents everywhere, there may be a certain degree of excitement associated with staying up all night or getting up in the early hours of the morning when most adults are asleep. These teenagers spend the early morning hours visiting, playing cards, and playing street hockey when weather permits. The excellent attendance during the first few weeks of January may be explained by the fact that when school time finally rolls around, nonattenders tag along with good attenders simply because there is nothing else to do. Ironically, this good attendance causes no end of pain to teachers who suddenly find themselves confronted with hordes of exhausted and nonattentive students.

Although the sun returns in the third week of January, periods of twilight and darkness still dominate the arctic landscape until the middle of February. By the end of February the days have become noticeably longer and brighter. Nevertheless, February is the coldest month of the year, with temperatures rarely rising above -30 degrees F (-34 degrees C). Hunting and trapping activities gradually resume with the brighter weather, and in town hardy groups of boys return to nearby lakes and ponds to indulge themselves in hockey. Periods of play tend to be a bit shorter due to the extreme cold, and skaters often complain that the subzero temperatures make the lake surface so hard that even sharpened skates have difficulty cutting into the ice. By February most kids and teenagers have returned to somewhat "normal" activity patterns.

▪ Daily Routine Interview
PETER NILGAK, AGE EIGHTEEN, DECEMBER 29, 1982

10:00 P.M. Woke up and had breakfast of tea and bannock. Everyone was home except my Mom who was out visiting her brother. My sister was making bannock in the kitchen and my older brother was in his room listening to music. My sister and I talked around and she asked me what I had done the night before.

11:00 P.M. Watched the news on television with my brothers and sisters.

12:00 A.M. Went out to visit Johnny [Apiuk] and I talked with him and his older brother. Both of his parents were home talking and having tea with some visitors. We watched the late movie on TV and had some tea and caribou stew.

1:30 A.M. Johnny and I went out driving around on his snow-mobile. We drove out to the lakes just outside of town where we met some other boys who were driving around. We all decided to drive up to the bluffs to see if we could catch any rabbits.

2:00 A.M. Drove over to the hall to see what was happening. A lot of people were there playing different kinds of games. We walked in and sat with some friends. Johnny and I played some games and then left.

3:30 A.M. Went over to Allen's house and visited for a while. He was fixing his snowmobile engine which he had all apart on the floor. He asked what was going on up at the hall and we told him that there were a lot of people up there. We watched him fix his engine and then had tea and some bannock.

4:30 A.M. The three of us decided to go back to the hall. When we walked in, most of the people [adults] were leaving, and the band was setting up for a disco dance.

5:00 A.M. The dance got started and I danced with a lot of different girls.

8:00 A.M. The dance ended and everybody started to leave. Johnny and I went back to my place with Rosie and Milly [two teenage girls]. My sister was the only person at home. Everybody else was either asleep or out. We all sat around and had tea and talked. Johnny, Rosie, Milly, and I decided to go out and see if anybody was playing street hockey in front of the Bay store. We got there and there was a large group of boys playing. A group of girls was watching and playing tag.

9:30 A.M. We played until the store opened and then went inside. I got a can of pop and a bunch of us went over to the coffee shop where we sat and talked. I ordered two egg sandwiches and ate them.

11:00 A.M. Went back home. My brother was just waking up from a nap. We made tea and talked around while we watched TV.

12:30 P.M. Went into my room and read a Zane Grey book that I bought the other day at the store. I got really tired and went to bed.

EARLY SPRING (*Upin'ngakhaaq*)

With the months of March and April come the first sure signs of spring, even though temperatures are still well below freezing. The sun is climbing higher into the sky and staying up most of the day. Temperatures during daylight hours are noticeably warmer than temperatures at night. Caribou hunting continues, even as the herds are beginning to move farther from the settlement. The warmer weather makes trapping, which officially ends April 30, more productive since foxes are moving about more than during the midwinter dark period. April is generally regarded as the best month of the year for traveling on the land and on the ocean ice.

On weekends the settlement is often deserted since most families go ice fishing on nearby lakes. Ice fishing is particularly enjoyable in April and May since it affords an opportunity for families to get out of the settlement together. Not surprisingly, many teenagers prefer staying in town when their parents go out ice fishing with younger siblings. This allows many of them to have friends over in the early morning hours or even to arrange clandestine meetings with members of the opposite sex.

Teenagers do not limit their activities to town, and many will go caribou hunting and ice fishing. While kids and younger teens are more likely to accompany parents, older teenagers will strike out on their own in groups. One favorite activity is for several teenage couples to go ice fishing and camping. Again, this provides the opportunity for sexual activity, which might be more difficult to arrange in town.

In town, boys and young men begin playing hockey with a vengeance. With the warmer and brighter weather, hockey appears to be played on an almost continual basis. Around the beginning of April teenage boys convince the settlement council to plow open a hockey rink on the snow-covered ice in the middle of Queen's Bay. This area is then filled with fresh water, using the water delivery truck, providing a nice smooth skating surface. Because the rink is located on Queen's Bay right in front of the community, it is easily reached by all community members. In the late afternoon and early evening, large groups of kids and girls can be seen skating around the edges of the new rink while boys dominate the center. The rink also becomes the site of informal gatherings of adults, who sit and talk with one another as they watch the boys display their athletic prowess.

Easter festivities are also a characteristic feature of April. As during the Christmas holidays, the school and co-op close for a two-week period, during which there are numerous outdoor and indoor games. A communal supper is held at the community hall early Easter morning, and most adults, teenagers, and kids stay up all night dancing and playing games. Outdoor games include snowmobile races, snowhouse building, rifle shooting, dog team races, and other competitions.

By the end of April there is nearly continual daylight, with a brief period around midnight when the sun dips below the horizon. Because of the continuous light, it is not uncommon to see children playing outside most of the night. Although school does not end until the first week of June, many schoolchildren attend with much less frequency as the weather gets nicer and as they start getting "turned around," once again, in their sleep-activity cycles.

Another event at this time of year, which has only recently been established in the community, is the annual school trip. The first of these school trips occurred in 1980, when a group of Holman students in the senior grades went to Toronto to visit students there. These exchange trips are funded by the YWCA and provide an opportunity for Indian and Inuit youngsters in the Northwest Territories to visit and live briefly with families in the South, after which the southern students fly north for a week-long visit. The 1980 trip to Toronto was the first time many Holman students had been out of the community to a large southern city; most were awed by elevators, escalators, fast-food restaurants, bowling alleys, roller skating rinks, and shopping malls. Now that many Holman youngsters have been on two or three of these exchanges, they are beginning to have a much more worldly outlook than many adults.

■ Daily Routine Interview
ROBERT NILGAK, AGE FIFTEEN, APRIL 27, 1982

5:30 P.M. Got up from bed. I had been up all night playing hockey and didn't get to bed until 8:30 A.M. Had breakfast and washed my face. I watched TV for a while and then went down to the skating rink where Peter, Walter, and Albert were practicing hockey. I talked around with them for a while and then shot the puck around. Peter and Walter didn't have their skates on so they left to get them. Albert and I shot the puck around for a few more minutes and then left for home.

7:00 P.M. Came back home and watched TV. Then I had some tea and caribou meat. I don't remember who else was home.

8:00 P.M. Went over to Peter's house and we talked about his getting a new organ from Radio Shack to use for the band. I then walked over to my Mom's house.[Robert was adopted by his aunt and uncle and lives in a separate household from his natural mother. See appendix for biographical information.] My brother and two sisters were there. We talked for a while about Mom. I stayed for a couple of hours.

10:00 P.M. Returned home. Most everybody was home. I had some tea, talked with the family, and watched "The National," "The Journal," the regional news, and sports.

12:45 A.M. Went down to the hockey rink to see what was going on. A group of boys was down there playing hockey. I didn't have my skates with me so somebody gave me a ride on their ski-doo back to my place so I could pick them up. I joined them and played for a couple of hours.

3:00 A.M. The wind started to blow so Allen and I went back to his place. We had tea and bannock and talked around for a while.

4:00 A.M. Came home and went to bed.

SPRING (*Upin'ngak*)

Upin'ngak stretches from the melting of snow on the land to the gradual breakup of the ocean ice in Prince Albert Sound and Amundsen Gulf. In May the snow on the land gradually disappears, first by evaporation and then by melting. Although May is still fairly cold, with a daily mean temperature of 21 degrees F (−6.1 degrees C), temperatures during midday begin to rise above the freezing mark for the first time in seven months. By the end of the month, warm daytime temperatures begin to melt the snow in and around the community, forming large puddles in poorly drained areas. May is characterized by wet, blowing snow often turning to slush. Ice fishing on inland lakes continues, although the gradual diminution of snow cover makes it increasingly difficult to travel by snowmobile and sled. Caribou hunting ceases altogether because the herds have moved north to their spring calving grounds.

Tents begin to mushroom in and around town as the warm weather heralds the onset of more amenable weather. Some tents are set up right next to homes, while others are placed within walking distance of town. With the invigorating weather of spring, people want to be outside as much as possible.

The high point of this season is the arrival in early June of thousands of ducks and geese which migrate northward along the coastline. Since Holman is located along a migratory flyway, families usually wait until after the migration to go out to summer seal hunting camps. The annual spring flight of these ducks and geese takes them down the Mackenzie corridor, up to and across Banks Island, and down the west coast of Victoria Island into Prince Albert Sound. By June a large crack has formed in the ice that runs parallel to the coastline. Due to wind and current action, this crack forms in the same place every year. Since the migrating ducks travel and feed along this crack, duck hunters position themselves along the crack in areas where pressure ridges provide natural blinds.

Young and old alike enjoy the excitement associated with duck hunting season, and the crack is often dotted with individuals and groups waiting for flocks to fly overhead. Teenage boys and girls go out hunting in groups, although it is almost always the boys who wield the guns.

The ocean ice remains solid through June, usually five-to-six feet thick, but the melting of the snow and ice on the surface makes travel wet and unpleasant. Since most of the snow on the land has melted, travel by snowmobile is limited to the ocean ice. Toward the end of June, the melting of the ice along the shore makes it necessary for hunters to leave their snowmobiles and sleds on the ice and travel to and from the shore in small boats.

School officially ends by the first week in June. By this time, kids and teenagers, as well as many adults, display noticeably altered activity rhythms. A brief excerpt from my field notes elaborates upon this disorientation in Johnny Apiuk and another eighteen-year-old:

Tuesday, June 1 (1:30 P.M.)—Met Johnny Apiuk and Albert Kagyut at the Bay store. It was the first time that I had talked to Johnny in about two weeks since he has not shown up lately to work for me. He said that he was not able to come to work because he was sleeping at odd hours and getting up early in the morning to play baseball and fool around with the girls. Johnny said that he had been up all night and wanted to stay up until five or six in the afternoon so he could then go to bed and get up at 3:00 A.M. He complained that it was very boring with nothing to do and that he was having trouble staying awake. I indicated that I did not understand and inquired why Johnny just didn't go to bed right now. Albert laughed and said that if Johnny went to bed now, he would probably wake up between 11:00 P.M. and midnight, but that he didn't really want to get up until 3:00 in the morning.

Adolescent activities become increasingly concentrated outdoors. Baseball and touch football games are organized and played spontaneously in the early morning hours. Hikes and fishing trips are also favored activities. One can often spot groups of girls picking flowers along the bluffs to the east of town. With the total disappearance of the snow, boys and young men can be seen careening around town at all hours on their motorcycles. Occasionally some vandalism occurs in the early morning, but it is almost always directed at public buildings such as the co-op, school, and Bay store rather than private homes. Such cases of vandalism and breaking and entering, while rare, appear to be limited to the spring when teenagers are beginning to stay up all night outdoors. Since there are no organized games or dances at the community hall, as at Christmastime, many young people end up getting into mischief.

A trip to the Bay or coffee shop first thing in the morning often reveals large aggregations of boys and girls. In all cases, these youngsters have been up all night. This stands in marked contrast to other times of year when both locations are completely deserted, save for employees, in the early morning hours. As Johnny Apiuk told me in February, "when spring comes along, you're going to see lots of teenagers hanging out at the coffee shop and the Bay first thing in the morning." He was right, of course, but he failed to mention that there are also a lot of kids (ages 10–14) who stay up all night and descend upon the Bay and coffee shop before returning home for a "good day's sleep."

Possibly one of the most noticeable changes in adolescent behavior during spring is a dramatic intensification of interest in the opposite sex. Based on my observations of two springs in the Arctic (1979 and 1982), I can say unequivocally that there is no spring fever like arctic spring fever. Adolescent conversation suddenly turns to an obsession with the opposite sex as boys and girls talk about who they are going out with or who they would like to go out with. When asked what they did the night before, boys invariably mention that they were chasing girls:

June 29 (1:30 P.M.)—Made a trip to the Bay and had the following interchange with Jack Uliktuaq, who was walking around the store in a state of total exhaustion:

R.C.: *You look awfully tired.*
JACK: *Yeh, I'm really tired.*
R.C.: *Up all night?*
JACK: *Yeh, I was up all night.*
R.C.: *What were you doing?*
JACK: *(Big smile) Chasing girls.*
R.C.: *Why do the girls always run away from you?*
JACK: *I'm too slow I guess.*
R.C.: *Probably because you stay up all night and get too tired.*
JACK: *Yeh, must be.*

Two other boys, again Johnny Apiuk and Albert Kagyut, were a little more graphic in describing their activities at this time of year:

June 1 (3:00 P.M.)—Met Johnny Apiuk and Albert Kagyut in front of the Bay. I asked why neither of them had come around to visit me for a while. Johnny said that he was busy staying up all night playing baseball, scrabble, and playing with girls. He indicated that this was what all the other teenagers were doing and that there was a lot of "screwing" going on in the early and late morning hours while most parents were asleep. When I commented that there would probably be a lot of babies born nine months from now, he agreed but claimed that none of them would be his since he was always very careful about such matters. I told both of them that they were lucky that there were no such things as "shotgun weddings" in the Arctic. They have never heard of such a thing and when I explained it to them, they thought that such a thing was really sick.

The fact that both boys had never heard of shotgun weddings or any other forms of coerced marriage indicates the relatively open nature of adolescent sexuality. Consequently, the thought that parents might force a young couple to get married simply because their sexual activities had resulted in pregnancy was anathema to them.

This obsession with the opposite sex is also characteristic of adolescent girls, although they tend to be more discrete in discussing the boys they are going out with. More so than at other times of the year, mixed groups of boys and girls can be seen walking around town, hiking out on the land, or watching the early morning football or baseball games. Many youngsters reported that this is the time when couples will sneak out of town and find a secluded place to engage in either sexual intercourse or heavy petting.

Interestingly, this obsession with the opposite sex lasts only two to three months and appears to subside just as quickly as it develops. Certainly sexual liaisons are established throughout the rest of the year, but with neither the same intensity nor frequency. My own observations indicate that by the fall, boys cease to talk as frequently about sexual matters, prefering discussions about their favorite hockey, baseball, or football teams.

▪ Daily Routine Interview
ANNIE APIUK, AGE ELEVEN, JUNE 30, 1982

1:00 P.M. Woke up. My brother Johnny and my Dad were both at home. Ate breakfast of bread, jelly, and milk.

1:15 P.M. Went over to the Bay and talked with Annie Ukpilik [a relative who works at the check-out counter]. I bought three suckers and one Bubble Burger. Then I went to the post office to mail a C.O.D. order. At the post office, I talked with Janet Memogana [the postal clerk] for a while.

1:30 P.M. Went to visit Pam Stern. Richard was there too but went out to work on his snowmobile. Pam and I worked until 2:45 P.M. Lillian came over to visit just when we finished. We ate cookies and played.

4:00 P.M. Went home and watched "Edge of Night." I then went outside and watched my older brother fix his motorcycle for a while. Then went inside to watch the "Beachcombers."

6:00 P.M. Went outside and played baseball with Brenda [a neighbor]. We then walked toward the school and picked flowers along the way. We watched the boys play baseball.

9:00 P.M. Went with Brenda to visit Pam and Richard. Clara came over also.

10:00 P.M. Went back to watch the baseball game and played around with some friends who were there too.

1:00 A.M. Went home to have a snack and then went back to the baseball game and talked with Ida.

1:30 A.M. Went over to Bessie Noakadlak's house.

1:45 A.M. Went to visit Betty Kagyut. She was in her tent next to her house. We went inside and had some tea. Betty and I went out to pick flowers with Betty's baby sister, Susan.

2:00 A.M. Walked over to the baseball game and watched for a while.

3:15 A.M. Went home to sleep and woke up at 2:30 P.M.

SUMMER (*Auyaq*)

Auyaq refers to the brief summer season, which begins with the final clearing of ice off the ocean and ends with the onset of colder and windier weather at the end of August. This period roughly coincides with the months of July and August.

During July the ocean ice begins to rot and breakup, thus preventing snowmobile travel. Most snowmobiles have to be taken off the ice and placed on the shore by the second week of the month. Snowmobilers will generally do so by driving along the coast until they find a protected place where the ice still connects to the land. Another technique, generally reserved for the more adventurous, is to drive the snowmobile off the ice at high speed and then hydroplane across the water until "touching down" on the beach.

As more open water appears in the bays and along the coast, boats are prepared for the summer season and placed in the water. Seal hunting resumes in July once the adult seals have grown new coats of fur. There is a one-to-two week period when travel on the ocean is curtailed as the transition is made from snowmobile travel on firm ice to boat travel in open water. As the ice gradually breaks up, it is easier to maneuver boats through the ice floes that generally remain in the area until a strong wind blows them farther out into the gulf. By the latter part of July, there is usually enough open water to make seal hunting by boat easier. This is also the time of year when seal hunting is the most productive. As long as the ice flows remain in the vicinity of Holman, the water stays calm, making it easier to spot and shoot seals. Hunters pull their boats out of the water onto an ice pan, where they wait for seals to pop up within firing range. Once the sea is completely cleared of ice, which varies from year to year, seal hunting is done completely by boat. Teenage boys also participate in such seal hunting. Younger boys tend to accompany their fathers, while older boys may be allowed to go out on their own accompanied by a friend. The seals they shoot are skinned and flensed by either a mother or sister, and the boy takes the prepared skin to the Bay or co-op to be sold for cash. The skinning and flensing of seals is also a source of cash for some teenage girls, who may be allowed to keep part of the money for their labors.

At the beginning of the month, many families leave the community for seal hunting camps located along Prince Albert Sound and Minto Inlet. Here these families set up camp and spend the rest of the summer hunting seals and netting fish. While kids and some younger teenagers often accompany their parents to these camps, the older adolescents prefer the freedom afforded them by staying in town while their parents are away.

As long as the weather remains bright and warm, adolescent activity rhythms and sexual activities remain similar to that described for spring. However, spring and summer disorientation in activity rhythms is slightly different from the disorientation of the midwinter dark period. While the constant darkness of the winter months makes it arduous to rise in the morning, the constant daylight of summer makes it difficult to go to bed at night. Although black plastic bags taped to bedroom windows function as efficient insulators of sunlight, one frequently wants to stay up as long as possible.

The constant daylight of summer also has a pervasive influence upon settlement residents. Individuals who reported having little difficulty maintaining normal schedules during the dark period find themselves disoriented as the temptation to stay up for long periods of time hunting and fishing becomes increasingly powerful. Families that spend time out at camp will stay up for extended periods between sleeping. Weather and hunting conditions become the primary determinants of activity rhythms. Periods of poor weather, when it is too rough to go out by boat, may be spent sleeping until better weather breaks. If weather is good and hunting productive, a hunter may stay up for twenty-four hours or longer. Similar effects may be seen in kids, teenagers and adults who spend most of the summer in town. One teenager, for example, reported sleeping for twenty-two hours after he had stayed up for an extended period of time hunting with his father. After another long period of activity, the same boy reported sleeping for sixteen hours, and so on through the summer.

One of the more exciting events of August is the arrival of the barge, which brings the settlement's yearly supplies of food, gasoline, oil, construction materials, snowmobiles, and so forth. Once the barge arrives there is an increase in casual wage employment. Unloading the barge takes several days, during which the settlement is a beehive of activity as crates are unloaded, broken open, and the contents stored in their proper locations. For many teenagers, this provides an ideal opportunity to earn extra cash by assisting in the unloading. ·

The school resumes operation in August, but attendance often remains poor as long as weather is nice. While many kids and teenagers still keep irregular activity rhythms, most of the adults in the settlement have returned to normal schedules, aided by the increase in darkness toward the end of the month. Weather at the end of August begins to worsen, with windy, wet, and cold days becoming more and more common. By the end of the month, most families have returned to the settlement, resigning themselves to the end of the short and pleasant summer.

■ Daily Routine Interview
EMMA MIKITOK, AGE FOURTEEN, JULY 27, 1982
1:50 A.M. Got up and had breakfast of tea and bread.

2:00 A.M. My mother gave me a candy bar and some black candy.

She then told me to go down to the shore to check the boat since it might blow away from the wind.

2:45 A.M. I went to check the boat which was alright. I then met Lena on the road who was walking home with her sister. I went with them and visited for a while. Lena's husband was outside fixing his Honda which he had just bought this morning.

4:00 A.M. I went over to Walter and Joanne's [a young married couple] house to watch a tape on TV. A group of people were there and we all watched a Bruce Lee movie. I ate tea and dried fish. After the movie, I went outside and met a group of boys and girls who were playing tag. I joined in with them.

5:00 A.M. We all walked over to the hotel and sat on the front steps. The boys started to play softball. We played with them for a while. Molly [a friend] and I then sat and watched them play.

9:30 A.M. Walked over to the Bay when it opened and talked around with some people we met there. Then went over to Molly's house to visit.

9:45 A.M. Went over to my older sister's house and babysat my niece for a while. I had some soup.

10:45 A.M. Came over to visit Pam and Richard [the anthropologists] and started to work.

■ 4
The Family Life
of Adolescents

Due to the small size of the community, Holman residents rarely have an opportunity to interact with people outside the sphere of family, friends, or close acquaintances. The average resident of Holman can claim at least half of the community as kin and knows everyone else on a first-name basis. What is immediately evident is the pronounced sense of belonging, of being integrated into a social network where people are accepted as individuals rather than as the occupants of a particular social status or role. When a teenager enters the community hall during some community event, he enters a room full of aunts, uncles, grandparents, cousins, siblings, friends, and more distant relatives. This is, perhaps, one of the most characteristic features of settlement social life and one that ensures the individual's sense of identity and belonging.

THE SIZE AND SPATIAL ORGANIZATION OF
ADOLESCENT FAMILIES

The typical adolescent's family in Holman is made up of from four to five siblings living at home, with at least one older, married sibling living in another household within the community. Of the 21 households which were the source of our adolescent survey sample of 21 boys and 22 girls, the mean household size was 6.6 persons. This figure included parents, grandparents, nieces, nephews, and all other individuals residing in the household at the time of the survey. The mean number of full siblings still living at home was 3.8, while 1.14 full siblings were married and living in other houses in the community. We also counted a substantial number of half siblings ($n = 18$) who were living either in the same household or another household within the community. Adoption figures were also fairly high, with 11 children having been adopted from other households.

Essential to the discussion of interpersonal relations on the family level is the question of who shares sleeping quarters and how these sleeping arrangements are determined. In Holman, household composition and sleeping arrangements are determined by the availability of space within the house as well as by conscious decisions among household residents. There is a fair amount of variation within the community regarding size of housing units and number of available rooms. While most of the older houses are limited to one or two bedrooms, many of the newer units have as many as three or four separate sleeping rooms. When interviewing the survey sample of adolescents, we asked our informants to draw floor plans of their homes and describe where household members slept. Using this procedure, we obtained 21 floor plans. Two additional floor plans were obtained from adolescents not included in the survey sample. The 23 floor plans we obtained accounted for 71 preadolescents and adolescents between ten and twenty years of age.

The results are surprising when compared to the sleeping arrangements of the other cultures included in the Adolescence Project, specifically Morocco and Romania, where there is much less space available in households, and where household members frequently must share both beds and bedrooms. In the Holman sample, 58 youths (82 percent) had their own beds while only 13 (18 percent) shared a bed with a sibling. Of the 13 sharing a bed, only three were cross-sex bed mates, while 10 were same-sex bed mates. Of the three cross-sex bed mates, one was a sixteen-year-old girl sharing a bed with a six-year-old brother, and two were an eleven-year-old girl and her eleven-year-old adopted brother sharing a single bed.

The most salient finding from the floor plan data was that older teenagers tended to have their own bedrooms. This was true even for larger families in which parents shared both bed and bedroom with several children. In one household, for example, the parents shared their bedroom with three younger children, while their two oldest adolescent children, ages nineteen and twenty-one, had their own rooms. Of the 23 children having their own rooms, the average age was 16.2, while the average age of the 48 children sharing rooms was 13.9 (see table 4.1). Two youths, a twelve-year-old girl and a sixteen-year-old boy, reported sleeping on a living room couch, despite the fact that both had older siblings occupying single rooms by themselves! Interestingly, no sex differences were documented regarding the allocation of bedrooms to single adolescents. Of the 23 adolescents having their own rooms, 10 were male and 13 were female.

In spite of the larger size of the newer housing units, many families still have trouble allocating sleeping space to all household members. A common practice is to convert a storage area into a sleeping room. Since these storage rooms are considered undesirable, generally lacking windows and ventilation, they tend to be allocated to younger children rather than to adolescents. Crowding is also partially alleviated through the practice of adoption. Parents who have a large number of children may decide to adopt out a child, often to grandparents or other relatives who have few of their own children still living at home.

Our adolescent informants universally commented that the sleeping arrangements in their households were determined not by parents, but by the kids and teenagers of the family. Older brothers and sisters were able to assert themselves to obtain their own rooms. In this respect, the desire for privacy and the need to withdraw from the rest of the family are not unlike those needs expressed by teenagers in our own culture. It may indeed be a cultural universal for adolescents to desire their own territory to which they can retreat by themselves or with visiting friends. In Holman, single bedrooms may also aid adolescent pair-bonding since they provide a place to which young couples may go to be by themselves.

The amount of living space families now have available is a dramatic change from the presettlement period when families lived in small and confined structures: snowhouses in winter and tents in summer. Even in the immediate past, government housing units tended to be so small that all family members had to share the same room for eating, sleeping, and entertaining visitors. Now that the government has started to provide larger housing units with separate bedrooms, it has become possible for kids and teenagers to sleep apart from parents. Nevertheless, the vast majority of parents still sleep with their youngest offspring until they reach three to four years of age.

TABLE 4.1

Sleeping Arrangements of Holman Adolescents and Preadolescents

AGE	NUMBER WITH OWN ROOM (n = 23)												
	10	11	12	13	14	15	16	17	18	19	20	TOTAL	AVE. AGE
Males	0	0	1	1	0	0	3	2	0	3	0	10	16.4
Females	0	0	1	3	0	1	2	2	0	3	1	13	16.1
TOTAL	0	0	2	4	0	1	5	4	0	6	1	23	16.2

AGE	NUMBER SHARING A ROOM (n = 48)												
	10	11	12	13	14	15	16	17	18	19	20	TOTAL	AVE. AGE
Males	1	3	1	3	2	3	4	2	3	1	0	23	14.7
Females	1	5	4	4	5	3	2	0	1	0	0	25	13.2
TOTAL	2	8	5	7	7	6	6	2	4	1	0	48	13.9

SHARING VERSUS OWN ROOM (n = 71)	% SHARING	% WITH OWN ROOM
Males (n = 33)	69.7%	30.3%
Females (n = 38)	65.8%	34.2%
TOTAL	67.6%	32.4%

NOTES: Based on data collected from 23 households; subjects between ten and twenty years old.

ADOPTION AND FAMILY STRUCTURE

One of the more interesting customs attesting to the notable lack of possessiveness that parents express toward children is the common practice of adoption. High rates of adoption were and continue to be characteristic of Inuit groups throughout the Arctic (Graburn 1969, 65; Guemple 1971, 67–70; Spencer 1959, 87–92; Balikci 1970, 108). Willmott (1961, 26) has stated that this relative lack of ego-involvement of Inuit in their children greatly facilitates adoption, which may occur without great suffering or trauma. As expected, family relations in Holman are significantly affected by high premarital pregnancy and adoption rates. Not all children live in their natal households with both biological parents and siblings. A large number have been adopted by grandparents, aunts, uncles or, more rarely, by unrelated households. Our 1983 household census documented 24 children between birth and twenty years of age residing in 18 adoptive households. This figure constitutes roughly 15 percent of all children and teenagers in the community. Of this number, 5 children were living with aunts or uncles, 11 were residing with maternal or paternal grandparents, and 8 were living with nonrelatives. Genealogical data suggest that high adoption rates are not a recent development in the community, but were characteristic of previous generations as well. For all Inuit residents of Holman, we were able to document 36 adoptions. In all likelihood, the adoption rate for the older generation was slightly higher since many of our household genealogies were incomplete and paternity unrecorded for many adults.

At present, adoption occuring between Inuit families is regarded as "custom" adoption and is not mediated by the Department of Social Services. Adoption is an informal practice accomplished through verbal agreements between households. As already indicated, a large number of adoptions in the community are grandparental adoptions in which a child is raised by either his maternal or paternal grandparents. The child is well aware of his adoptive status, although he may call his grandparents "mother" and "father." Grandparental adoption actually takes three distinct forms. The first involves the caretaking or adoption of an infant born to an unwed daughter still living at home. When the teenage mother gives birth, she has the choice of either caring for the baby herself or allowing her parents to adopt the infant and become its primary caretakers. If the former choice is made, the biological mother will be the child's primary caretaker and will take the child with her when she establishes an independent household. If, however, the young mother gives the infant to her parents, the child will remain with the grandparents even after the biological mother has moved out. Currently in Holman, five children between two and eleven years of age have been adopted by their grandparents in such a manner.

Another, radically different form of grandparental adoption occurs when a married couple decides to give a later-born child to either the maternal or paternal grandparents. Due to the high value placed upon newborns, it is generally a sign of respect to give a child to one's parents, especially if they are no longer able to produce children of their own. A house devoid of children is considered an empty house. Consequently, even elderly parents enjoy the presence of children whom they can care for and raise. Such grandparental adoption may be initiated by either the parents or grandparents. In fact, one woman reported that when she returned to Holman after giving birth to a boy in Yellowknife, she was met at the plane by her mother, who took the infant away and never returned it. As a sign of deference, however, the child's mother did not object even though she had not intended to part with the child. In another, quite different case, a young married couple who already had two children, and were faced with an unplanned pregnancy, arranged to have their unborn child adopted by its paternal grandparents. This was done because they felt that their two-year-old daughter was still "too young" to give up nursing.

A third, less common type of grandparental adoption involves sending an older child, usually a young girl between nine and sixteen years of age, to live with and care for an elderly grandparent. These arrangements tend to be much less formal and do not entail a permanent adoption of the young child. In one case, a nine-year-old girl was encouraged by her parents to visit her grandmother's house periodically to help with household chores. As the young girl began to spend more and more time with her grandmother, her parents decided that she should move there permanently. This arrangement was convenient for all parties involved since it alleviated crowding in the child's natal household, provided care and company for an elderly grandparent, and gave the young girl an even greater degree of autonomy than she would have if still living with her parents.

Other types of adoption include adoption between siblings, in which a child is given to an aunt or uncle, and adoption between unrelated or distantly related households. Often it is difficult to tell which children have been adopted and which children are just alternating households. Due to the large number of relatives most children have in the community, it is quite common for a child to eat and sleep for extended periods in another household.

What is particularly interesting is that the introduction of bottle-feeding now makes it possible for children to be adopted out at an early age, when in the past they could be adopted out only after they had been weaned. This may account for the common occurrence of infanticide in the past, when it was necessary to abandon unwanted children, especially in cases when a mother was still caring for and breast-feeding another child.

The fact that, today, infants and children are easily adopted out suggests that infanticide was a necessary ecological adjustment to a harsh environment rather than a cultural or expressive predisposition for small families. With the increased security of contemporary settlement existence and the availability of bottle-feeding, an unwed mother rarely has any problem finding a suitable home for an unwanted child. This accounts, in part, for why premarital, teenage pregnancy is not the catastrophic event in Holman as it often is in the South, where a young mother may have to quit school or change future career plans to accommodate her new role as a mother. In Holman the teenage mother has to make few, if any, adjustments in her activities or aspirations. If she chooses to keep her child, she can rely upon a large support network of sisters, aunts, and cousins to provide assistance with childcare. Alternately, if she decides that caring for her infant is too much of a burden, she can easily find several families who are more than willing to adopt the child.

Adopted children as well as children born to unwed mothers are rarely stigmatized to any significant degree. This is partially due to the sheer numbers who occupy such positions in the community and the markedly tolerant attitude that community members have toward premarital sex. In some respects the position of many adopted children is better in their adopted homes than if they remained with their biological parents and siblings. Often they are adopted into households which are less crowded and where there are fewer children to compete for family resources. This is especially true of children who are adopted by their grandparents. In these cases an adopted child may have a room to him or herself, be able to use the family snowmobile, and receive gifts of money from grandparents, which might not be forthcoming if he or she were living with a large number of older siblings.

In one interesting case, a young girl was adopted out to an aunt at an early age. Since the mother had given birth to three children within a three-year period, it was decided to give the middle child to an aunt for upbringing. Although the child has spent the past fourteen years living with her aunt, the mother continues to maintain intense interest in the upbringing of her daughter. In addition to providing clothing for this daughter, the mother consults with schoolteachers on her academic progress. In fact, she told one of the teachers, in no uncertain terms, that this daughter's report card was to be given to her and not to the aunt with whom she was living.

RELATIONS WITH PARENTS

I usually just wander around wherever I want without telling my parents. I started doing this at about thirteen or fourteen, when I first became a "teenager." Before that, my parents wanted to know where I was going. I also stay up as late as I want, even during school nights. I usually go to bed on my own around 1:00 A.M. My parents don't tell me when to go to bed. Sometimes they get mad if I miss school, but they don't give me a curfew.

Jack Uliktuaq, fifteen years old

Autonomy is the order of the day for most Holman teenagers and one of the most pervading "themes" of parent-child relations. Interviews conducted with our adolescent informants revealed that Holman teenagers, and many older kids as well, have great freedom to go where they want and do as they please. Activities such as visiting, eating, sleeping, going to late-night dances, and even attending school appear to be largely determined by individual kids and teenagers rather than by parents. The high degree of autonomy is not solely an index of the comparative freedom afforded Holman youngsters, but reflects the nature of parental modes of socialization and the manner in which parents relate, in almost an egalitarian fashion, to the younger generation.

Teenagers rarely indicated that there were any places their parents declared off-limits. According to Johnny Apiuk:

I usually don't tell my parents where I am going or what I am doing, and they seldom ask. Sometimes on weekends, they ask because they don't want me to go anywhere where I might drink. Generally, I can go where I want and there are no places in town that are off-limits for me.

A similar degree of autonomy was reported by teenage girls in Holman:

> I never tell my parents where I am going unless I am going fishing or swimming or something like that out of town. I listen if they tell me not to go. But in town there is no place I can't go.
>
> Emily Apsimik, sixteen years old

These were fairly typical statements for most of the teenage boys and girls interviewed. Almost none were expected to report their whereabouts when doing something or going someplace in town. Most parents consider Holman to be a safe enough community that it is unnecessary for teenage sons and daughters to report their destinations, much less ask for formal permission to go out. Only when they plan to leave town to fish, hunt, or pick berries do parents expect them to state their whereabouts.

Within the community, girls and boys are allowed similar degrees of autonomy regarding when, where, and with whom they spend their time. No explicit parental pressures restrict girls more in their wanderings about the community. Nevertheless, adolescent boys often appear to have greater mobility due to their access to snowmobiles and motorcycles. The only substantial difference in the mobility of boys and girls appears around fifteen and sixteen years of age when the boys begin to spend more time traveling out of town, on snowmobiles or motorcycles, for hunting, fishing, or just "driving around." This contrast, however, reflects more the gradual development of appropriate sex-role behavior than it reflects differences in male and female autonomy. In addition, girls are generally encouraged to take on household responsibilities, all of which function to limit the amount of time that girls have to wander about.

In the case of younger children, however, parents are more concerned with knowing their whereabouts, even if older brothers and sisters are staying out at all hours of the day and night. The following quote from Johnny's twelve-year-old sister, Annie, stands in marked contrast to the statements given above:

> I always tell my parents where I am going. Sometimes they ask me when I am going out. The only time they ever say no is when we are camping on the land and they don't want me to wander away from camp.

Because of this high degree of autonomy and lack of overt parental supervision, Inuit teenagers and parents seem almost to drift past one another and engage in minimal interaction through the course of a normal day. This is especially true during the midsummer and midwinter months when teenagers and parents maintain different activity rhythms. As already mentioned, when parents go out camping in the spring and summer, teenage sons and daughters prefer to stay in town where they can visit and play various sports and games with peers at all hours of the day and night. Younger children, however, are more likely to accompany their parents on these camping expeditions.

Despite the apparent minimal contact, teenagers maintain close emotional bonds to their parents. Nevertheless, these close attachments are rarely expressed verbally by either parents or offspring:

> I often go to my parents when I am feeling sad about something, but I have never sat down and had long talks with them about anything. That's just the way it is up here in the North.
>
> David Ageok, eighteen years old

One of the characteristic features of Inuit culture is the nonverbal nature of interpersonal relations. Inuit do not openly express their feelings verbally, but rely more upon nonverbal modes of expression. During an interview on ethnic affiliation, one of our eighteen-year-old clinical informants, Peter Nilgak, commented that the major difference between whites and Inuit was that Inuit rarely expressed their feelings openly with one another the way whites did. Inuit place greater reliance upon nonverbal modes of communicating their feelings and desires. Thus, parents do not sit down and have long and intimate conversations with their offspring. Intimacy and emotional attachment are expressed in other ways, with a smile, a nod, a mother sewing a new parka for one of her children, or a father showing his son the proper way to make a sled. These are ways in which emotional attachments between the generations are established and maintained.

During interviews on parent-child relations, the vast majority of our informants cited one or both parents as the most important people in their lives. This suggests that the close emotional bonds established between parents and children in the early years continue into adolescence, even when interactions between the generations have decreased in frequency. Nor did there appear to be any significant preference for one parent over the other. Teenage boys and girls cited both parents as equally important. Nevertheless, as children get older they are more likely to spend greater time with the same-sex parent. Teenage boys will begin hunting and trapping with their fathers, while teenage girls will spend increasing amounts of time engaged in household activities with their mothers.

The relative rarity of physical punishment is a partial reflection of indulgent child-rearing practices. Many teenagers commented that they were spanked only when they were little and that such corporal punishment did not extend into later childhood or the teenage years. From my observations of such alleged "spankings," this punishment usually involves a slight pat on the child's behind when he or she is misbehaving. Teenagers reported that when their parents become angry at them, their anger usually takes the form of mild verbal rebuke or chastisement. During three years of fieldwork in the community, I heard of only one, unsubstantiated, case in which a parent physically punished an older child for a misdeed. The transgression in question involved the child's theft of an object from the Bay store. In most cases, parents chastise their children verbally for misdeeds. The most common misdeeds reported by teenagers include fighting with brothers and sisters and "not listening to parents" when told to do something. The relative rarity of physical punishment was expressed by the following eighteen-year-old boy:

> Only once did I get punished by my parents. When I was walking out of the house, I slammed the door on my mother's fingers by accident. She got really mad and hit me with a stick that she was carrying. This was the only time that one of my parents ever really got mad at me. They usually don't yell and scream when they are mad, but just tell me what I should and shouldn't do.
>
> David Ageok

Parents' interpretations of misbehavior are particularly revealing. A child who misbehaves is not considered to be a bad child who intentionally engages in culpable acts, but is simply referred to as a child who "really can't listen." In fact, this inability or unwillingness to listen was most frequently cited by youngsters as the primary reason for parents getting mad at them. Children do not intentionally violate the wishes of parents, but misbehave only because they have not yet learned the skills that enable them to be attentive to parents. As they get older, these children gradually learn socially acceptable behavior by listening to and observing parents and other adults, thus making parental scoldings less and less necessary.

One characteristic of teenage boys and girls was the openly expressed fear that their parents might observe them in an act of which they would not approve. This fear was expressed even by teenagers who claimed that their parents rarely punished or scolded them for misdeeds. While parents are extremely tolerant, they highly disapprove of many aspects of adolescent behavior, even though this disapproval is subtly stated. For their part, young people are aware of these parental concerns, especially those pertaining to such activities as staying up all night, establishing sexual liaisons with multiple partners, and engaging in sports activities at the expense of other more productive tasks. Despite claims that their parents let them do whatever they want, many adolescents experience anxiety when they are not fulfilling parental expectations of proper adultlike behavior. The suggestion is that teenagers fear parents not because of the threat of physical or verbal punishment, but simply because parental disapproval alone has a powerful socializing influence upon kids and teenagers. This in itself is indicative of the close emotional attachment between the generations.

During interviews with our adolescent informants, we were particularly interested in exploring whether or not youngsters recognized generational conflicts as a salient dimension of parent-child relationships. The vast majority indicated that they got along well with parents and rarely had conflicts with them. In the words of eighteen-year-old Johnny Apiuk:

> My parents have never really gotten mad at me. I cannot think of any major conflict between us. Once, when I was caught drinking at Akaitcho Hall [the dormitory in Yellowknife], my parents called me on the phone and scolded me, but they never really got mad or raised their voices at me. Once, when they found out that my older brother was playing poker at home with friends while they were out at camp, they got mad at him. They raised their voices a little, but didn't yell or scream. I have never been spanked by my parents.

While conflicts between parents and children are rarely expressed openly, either in a verbal or behavioral fashion, there is one area where children and teenagers indicated some resentment over the behavior of parents. This is the domain of parental drinking, which appeared to be a source of some anxiety for many youngsters. Approximately half of the youngsters interviewed indicated that their parents drank, while the remaining youths claimed that their parents were abstainers. Many of those with drinking parents expressed some disapproval and claimed to be uncomfortable when parents had drinking parties. Others claimed to feel sorry for kids and teenagers whose parents drank excessively. For many, the anxiety over parental drinking occurs largely because adults often become very loud and aggressive when they drink. It is not uncommon for fights, particularly domestic fights, to occur during or immediately after adult drinking parties. As a result, most kids and teenagers avoid parents and other adults who are drinking. In at least one instance, however, a seventeen-year-old boy intervened during a drinking party to break up a physical fight between his parents.

The apparent lack of parent-child conflict in Inuit society may be largely a function of the absence of pronounced physical or verbal punishment. The cultural emphasis on avoiding or denying conflict, which permeates all aspects of adult social interaction, also affects the nature of parent-child relationships. Since parents are so indulgent and accepting of their offsprings' behavior, children rarely have the opportunity to resent parents' attempts to control them. The dominant parental view is that children should be allowed to develop at their own pace without excessive interference or pressure from parents. In this respect, Inuit adults seem overly tolerant of their offspring when compared to southern parents, who encourage and sometimes even force their children to succeed in school, excel in athletics, and make early decisions about what they want to do with the rest of their lives. One might say that Inuit parents demand little of their children other than that they simply be themselves. During interviews on parent-child relations, adolescents frequently reported that their parents had little to say about aspirations or future occupational goals and that such decisions were entirely their own. Most of the parents interviewed concurred to a certain extent. The father of one fourteen-year-old girl, for example, stated that he hoped his daughter would attend high school but that he did not want to force her to make a decision that was hers alone. Another father, when commenting upon the future marriage plans of his twenty-year-old son, said that he had no idea what decision his son would make. Lack of parental interference may also be a consequence of the limited number of choices available to adolescents regarding future careers.

Despite an apparent laissez-faire method of child rearing, parents can actually be extremely, but subtly, calculating in socializing children. Adults seek not to force appropriate behavior upon their offspring, but to encourage them to distinguish appropriate from inappropriate behavior and to gradually acquire, at their own pace, the behavioral and attitudinal repertoire befitting Inuit adults. Some children and teenagers simply take longer than others to do this, and parents adjust their expectations accordingly.

Parental socialization often takes on a very subtle tone. A typical example I observed was a mild rebuke made by a mother to her nine-year-old daughter who had been running around the community hall playing with the other children. When the daughter returned to sit with her parents, her mother said, very quietly: "You're running around just like a little kid. You should sit down." In this case, the daughter in question was the first born of the family, upon whom the parents were beginning to place more responsibilities in baby-sitting and helping around the house. The mother's criticism was phrased more as a suggestive comment than as an ultimatum. Nevertheless, it had the desired effect and the daughter ceased running around the hall.

Other parental attempts to change or modify the behavior of children take on a similar "suggestive" tone, although they may not always be successful, especially with older and more independent offspring. Children are told what they should or should not do, but rarely in an absolutist sense, with the threat of punishment if the child does not respond appropriately. Another example demonstrates the non-ultimatumlike tone of parental control. While I was visiting Albert, a hunter and trapper, the community dog officer came in and told him that one of his dogs was loose and should be tied up right away or the dog would be shot. Albert turned to his twenty-year-old son, Mark, and told him that he should get the dog and bring it back before it was shot. Mark, who was having a cup of tea and enjoying our conversation, said that he would get him later. After ten minutes went by, Albert again said that Mark should get the dog, and Mark responded by saying he would get it later. Fifteen minutes later a similar exchange occurred. Soon afterward, a neighbor came in with the dog, which had fortunately escaped the dog officer's clutches. Neither father nor son said anything that might indicate they had had a difference of opinion.

In another instance, however, Albert was more successful in modifying his son's behavior. According to Albert, when he learned that his son was beginning to drink heavily, he had a brief talk with him.

Albert, who does not drink at all, told Mark that he was a young and healthy man and that if he kept on drinking he might "harm his body" and be confined to his house for the rest of his life. According to Albert, as a result of this conversation, Mark stopped drinking right away. The important consideration in this episode is that the father did not yell at his son or forbid him to consume alcohol, but merely suggested to him a wiser alternative.

Albert may be unique in his attempts to modify his children's behavior, especially when they are older offspring in their twenties. Albert expressed the opinion that parents rarely talk to their older off-spring about such matters, but just let them do as they please. Because Albert and Mark are now trapping partners, they spend a lot of time together out on the land and have attained a degree of intimacy that was lacking when Mark spent more time with his peers.

Parent-child relations in Inuit society have undergone significant modifications with the introduction of schooling, the concentration of the population within the settlement, the building of larger housing units, and the rise of the adolescent peer group. All of these phenomena have served to limit the amount of daily contact and interaction with parents. Many parents complained that their children were getting much harder to handle since they spend so much time outside of the household. In fact, Albert commented that he preferred being out of town at his outpost camp because he felt that he had more contact with and control over his children than when his family was in town. Many parents also complained that their children's school attendance was poor because they are unable to get the children up in the morning. During a 1981 community meeting convened by the N.W.T. Special Committee on Education, the topic of poor attendance was discussed at length. At first a number of parents said that attendance was poor because the teachers were mean or because the school was not teaching relevant topics. Finally, a woman got up and told everyone that the only reason school attendence was poor was because the parents themselves were not strict enough to force their children to attend on a daily basis. After her commentary the entire hall was silent, suggesting that her critique went straight to the core in diagnosing the problem.

In general, the tone of parent-child interaction is marked by tolerance and mutual respect. While there is undoubtedly a subtle "generation gap" developing between parents and children as a result of the introduction of schooling, the linguistic transition from Inuktitut to

English, exposure to television, school trips to the South, and changing career expectations of youngsters, these have not led to any pronounced generational conflict. Just as parents do not openly condemn the new attitudes, life-styles, and aspirations of their children, the younger generation retains a healthy respect for their parents and their occupational pursuits. Since the Holman economy is still largely oriented toward fishing, hunting, and trapping, children can readily see that their parents are masters of the arts of arctic hunting, travel, and survival. If the adult residents of Holman were ever to abandon these time-honored activities and become completely dependent upon wage employment or welfare, this healthy respect between the generations might be significantly altered.

As in any society, parent-child relations are also a function of the sex and sibling order of offspring. Despite parental indulgence, female children are invariably encouraged to take on greater responsibilities at an earlier age than their brothers. Many girls reported that they did more chores than their siblings simply because they were the oldest children in the household. While all adolescent girls are expected to perform various household chores, first-born daughters are generally encouraged to carry out these duties at an earlier age. This is especially true if the mother is a wage earner and spends most of the day out of the house. Later-born daughters receive less active encouragement to perform household chores since many of these tasks are already being performed by an older sister.

These responsibilities include a wide range of household tasks such as baby-sitting, doing dishes and laundry, cleaning house, skinning and scraping seals, filleting fish, and so forth. Within the community there is wide variation in the amount of parental pressure placed upon daughters to assist with household chores. Some parents exert more pressure than others upon their daughters, so while some girls spend much of their free time helping around the house, others barely lift a hand. Girls appear to exercise some free choice regarding the amount of household chores they performed. Again, the pattern of parental flexibility and tolerance emerges. Daughters are not forced to perform these chores, but are encouraged to help around the house as much as possible.

Adolescent boys are another matter. Informants, both adult and teenager, uniformly commented that boys are more "spoiled" than girls and are assigned fewer responsibilities. This indulgence is most vivid for first-born males, who are not only exempted from many household chores, but have greater access to parental resources than other siblings. It is common for first-born sons to have their own snowmobiles, generally hand-me-downs from their fathers. Even when the first born son does not have his own snowmobile, he will usually have preferential access to the family machine. Boys also have a knack for running snowmobiles into the ground. One parent commented to me that he would have liked to buy a three-wheeled all-terrain vehicle, but knew that he would not be able to prevent his teenage son from abusing it.

This "manhandling" of snowmobiles (and other vehicles) is most vividly seen in the high speeds that teenage boys and many young adults like to attain when out hunting or just driving around. There seems to be great pleasure, and a certain amount of subtle competition, derived from seeing who can maintain high speeds for the longest period of time. During the "Fish Lake" season, for example, conversations often center around who made it to and from Fish Lake in record time. A young man may comment with great satisfaction that he made it back from Fish Lake in two hours with his skis never touching the ground![1]

Boys are also a more significant drain on parental cash resources than are girls and continue to be so for a longer period of time. Boys require snowmobiles, rifles, hockey skates, hockey sticks, while girls seem to have less extravagant tastes or needs. While both sexes ask parents for money to buy soda, candy and other nonessentials, many older girls obtain employment at the co-op craft shop and earn their own spending money, part of which may be spent on groceries for the household. Girls who are still too young to work at the craft shop may sew items at home to be sold to the craft shop. Boys are less likely to have access to year-round wage-generating activities. Many boys, especially between sixteen and twenty years of age, complained that there is no work around town for them to earn money. When part-time or temporary jobs are available, such as during the unloading of the barge, there are generally more applicants than positions to be filled, so not all boys have the opportunity to generate their own incomes.

While boys often pose a drain on family resources, they assist parents in such things as snowmobile repair, fishing, and hunting and trapping. This is especially true of older teenagers who have matured enough to recognize the contribution they can make to their families by assisting in subsistence activities. Those teenage boys who do obtain some kind of employment, whether temporary or part time, will occasionally give part of their paychecks to parents to help buy food. Many reported that they did so voluntarily, without any coercion from parents. When these adolescents get older and establish their own households, they tend to be much more responsible in helping out parents, especially if their parents are no longer active in hunting and trapping pursuits. For sons this generally involves gifts of fresh meat and fish, while older married daughters will visit their parents to help around the house. Thus even after they have married and moved out of the house, the close spatial proximity of settlement life allows parents and children to maintain close social and emotional contact with one another.

With regard to sex and marriage, few children interviewed said that their parents had any say in whom they were going out with or whom they should marry. As recently as ten to fifteen years ago, the majority of marriages were arranged by parents. Although the potential partners had the power to veto such arrangements, the general tendency was to abide by parental wishes. In addition, given the extremely narrow field of selection for potential partners, sons and daughters rarely had many alternatives available to them. Today, however, with the increased size and importance of the peer group, young people are able to make their own decisions. Parents continue to encourage their children to marry certain individuals, but ultimately the son or daughter makes the final decision. In discussing the spouse selection of one of his daughters, one father commented that he really did not approve of the young man with whom his daughter was living, but felt that he could do nothing to change her mind.

Parental pressures for achievement and success are largely lacking in Holman. While parents are undoubtedly pleased when their children show the potential for being good hunters or good seamstresses, they do not brag about these abilities to other parents, and they do not push children beyond their potential. Not one kid or teenager interviewed indicated that he felt his parents were putting excessive pressure upon him to succeed. Parents allow their children to be themselves and make their own life decisions. Also, there does not exist in Holman the notion that if children turn out "bad," it is the fault of the parents for failing to raise their children properly. Children develop according to their natures, and an entire household is not shamed if a child fails to live up to parental expectations.

In sum, parent-child relations in Holman are characterized by minimal conflict and a high degree of mutual affection and respect. The rapid rate of social change has led to a decrease in parent-child interactions, which is most pronounced during the teenage years when children begin spending more time with peers and less time with parents. Social change has also resulted in a gap between the knowledge, language skills, and aspirations of parents and children, but this gap has not resulted in any overt generational conflicts so often cited as endemic in southern society. Parents maintain a tolerant and flexible outlook on the behavior of their children, which undoubtedly contributes to this healthy relationship between the generations, even as children enter the presumably turbulent and stressful period of adolescence.

SIBLING RELATIONS

After parents, siblings occupy the next most important social category for adolescents. Throughout an individual's life, siblings are a primary source of social, emotional, and financial support. Due to the small size of the community and the low degree of out-migration, close sibling bonds established in childhood continue even after siblings have married and set up separate households.

Relationships between siblings are as much a function of disposition as they are of age and sex. Throughout the research period, we documented a high degree of interaction and comradery among same-sex siblings who were approximately the same age. Siblings of the same sex and age category can be seen playing or working with one another as frequently as with nonsibling friends and relatives. They are also much more likely to share rooms with one another, another factor contributing to intimacy and mutual support. Most of our informants commented that friends and siblings were pretty much the same in terms of shared activities and interests, but all agreed that siblings were much more important because they were family members. The only noticeable difference was that one did not have to worry about fighting with siblings as much as fighting with friends. As one fourteen-year-old girl in our survey sample commented:

> You can have arguments with them [siblings] and you can ask them to do things without being scared. If you argue with your friends, you may never get back together. It's different with brothers and sisters.

Most adolescents told us they felt closer and had more respect for older than for younger siblings, who tended to be more bossy and difficult to get along with. Older siblings could be entrusted with secrets, could give advice, and could be approached for money. Adolescents almost universally expressed a preference for older sisters who help around the house and perform baby-sitting chores. In this respect, older sisters often occupy the same close nurturant position as mothers and fathers. Nevertheless, younger siblings can often be a source of "cheap" labor for their older brothers and sisters. In response to the question "Which was better, younger siblings or older siblings?" Johnny Apiuk responded as follows:

> I don't really know. I'm right in the middle. I like them both. You can ask for money from older siblings, while you can get younger siblings to do stuff for you—like make you tea or coffee. Older siblings can teach you stuff. I'd also like to have a baby brother and wish my parents would adopt one. I really like babies, even though they can be so bossy at times.

Older siblings of all ages and both sexes expressed close emotional attachments to and a high degree of nurturance for siblings much younger than themselves. Johnny Apiuk is typical in expressing a fondness for young infants and toddlers. Such fondness is reflected in the frequency with which older teenagers, both male and female, care for their younger brothers and sisters. While older sisters are more likely to be put in charge of baby brothers and sisters, older brothers as well can often be seen engaged in such caretaking activities. Such frequent caretaking is undoubtedly excellent preparation for having and caring for their own children when they reach adulthood.

The typical teenager in Holman has a large sibling cohort, often with a ten-to-fifteen-year difference between oldest and youngest siblings. Thus, he or she will have older married siblings living in other households as well as younger siblings still living at home. While relations between siblings living together in the same household are understandably close, individuals are often extremely attached to these older married siblings, especially if they have had a nurturant relationship with one another. Frequent visits will be made to these households, where younger siblings provide household and baby-sitting services. In exchange they may be given gifts of money or simply a place to hang out when there is nothing else to do. It is common for a young sister to spend almost as much time in the household of an older married brother or sister as in her own home. The households of older siblings are sometimes ideal places to have drinking parties or meet members of the opposite sex.

In Holman an individual who marries and moves out of his or her parents' household does not curtail familial obligations to parents and siblings. While married sons and daughters are expected to help their parents with gifts of meat, fish, and occasionally money, similar support is often provided to younger siblings, especially if it is apparent that the parents are having trouble supporting their remaining offspring. In Holman it is quite common for a married man to give his secondhand snowmobile, sled, or rifle to his younger brother, which will enable the latter to assist in providing food for the family. One middle-aged hunter commented that he was always giving things to his twenty-one-year-old brother who was still living at home, primarily because his parents did not have the resources to provide the brother with hunting equipment and supplies.

Sibling cohorts are even larger when one considers half siblings and adopted siblings as well. Relations among these half siblings and adopted siblings are also very close, even when they are living in different households. Siblings who have been adopted out to another household spend large amounts of time playing, working, and visiting with their biological brothers and sisters. Siblings generally recognize these complicated interrelationships and claim close sibling ties to a large number of half siblings, full siblings, and adopted brothers and sisters. One young man serves as an example in point. Having been born to a young unwed mother, he was adopted and raised by his maternal grandparents. In time, his mother married and set up a separate household. To this day, this young man has close emotional ties to his five maternal half siblings, his seven paternal half siblings, and two adopted brothers.

The closeness of sibling bonds is especially evident when families are out camping. In these circumstances, brothers and sisters spend a great deal of time with one another and with parents. One presumes that sibling bonds must have been more intense in the presettlement era, when families spent most of their time out on the land in isolated units. The same close contact that was established between parents and children was also maintained among siblings. With the concentration of the population in the community, however, siblings have started to have less and less contact with one another, especially if age gaps are large.

Johnny Apiuk, for example, commented that he spends much more time with his younger siblings when out at the family's camp, but rarely sees them in town because they are always out with their friends.

In sum, family relations remain a significant aspect of the interpersonal relations of Holman youngsters. Nevertheless, the evidence points to the conclusion that the peer group has taken on greater importance in the modern era. It is to this level of adolescent interpersonal relations that we turn in the next chapter.

■ 5
Friends and Peers

In American society, adolescence is often cited as a period in the human life cycle when individuals change the nature of their relationships with age-mates (Douvan and Adelson 1966; Dunphey 1963; Bowerman and Kinch 1959; Sullivan 1953; Piaget 1965; Youniss 1980; Hartup 1983). In general, friends and peers play a more important role in the social and emotional lives of adolescents than of children. The same may be said of Holman teenagers, who not only spend greater amounts of time with their peers but begin developing close emotional attachments to a smaller group of intimate friends. For kids, peer groups are often play-oriented groups that are fluid in composition. In the small community, personal likes and dislikes are often overshadowed by proximity, and a kid is likely to play with whomever is available at the moment. For teenagers, however, relations with friends are more a function of shared emotions and intimacy than of social circumstance or spatial proximity. Through parents, these young people learn culturally appropriate values and behaviors, while through friends and peers they begin to learn the finer points of social interaction (and negotiation) which will help them in their gradual acquisition of adult roles and responsibilities.

For Holman teenagers, the valuations of peers have assumed greater significance than the valuations of adults, not only because more time is spent with peers than with parents but because the stresses and strains experienced by young people today are very different from those of their parents at a similar age (see also DeVos 1978). New social and economic circumstances require radically different coping strategies for young Inuit maturing into adulthood. Based upon his research on young Inuit men in Sanctuary Bay, O'Neil (1983, 254–255) has suggested that the peer reference groups of young Inuit provide a kind of refuge from the often critical expectations of parents and other adults. Those apects of teenage behavior viewed in negative terms by adults are "reconsidered" in positive terms within the mutually reinforcing context of friends and peers.

Who are the friends of Holman teenagers? They are neighbors, siblings, cousins, aunts, uncles, and more distant relatives. Friends constitute a subset of the larger group of age-mates (or peers). Interaction with friends is frequent, and emotional ties are intense. Patterns of friendship and peer interaction in Holman are invariably overlaid upon a complex system of kin networks. In this respect, interactions with friends and peers provide continuity with kin relations, which is often lacking in larger communities. All age-mates, as well as their parents and siblings, are known; rarely does a teenager have to contend with the trauma of moving to a new community where he or she has to establish new friendships.

PEER RELATIONS AND THE LIFE CYCLE

In Holman a child's first play partners are parents, siblings and other close kin. These older family members take the child on visits to other households, where the child meets and plays with other youngsters. More often than not, these young playmates are close kin since related households are frequently visited on a daily basis. Thus, a child's first contacts inside and outside the household occur within the tight network of kin relations.

As the child becomes older and more mobile, he or she begins exploring the immediate neighborhood, either with or without supervision. The child begins playing with other children and developing a peer group. Neighborhood play groups tend to be mixed-sex groups that encompass a broad age range (four to thirteen years) of individuals. Social functions at the community hall provide another opportunity for kids to see and play with other children. These functions are generally marked by much running around, screaming, and rough-housing by kids. For younger kids, community functions provide an opportunity to interact with children not seen on a daily basis. Thus, the peer group is expanded.

School, however, provides the major vehicle for expanding the peer group. With the beginning of school at age five, a kid is exposed to other children with whom he or she may not have had any previous regular contact. While the beginners (or kindergarten) class meets only three hours a day and rarely exceeds six or seven students, the next class (grades 1, 2 and 3 combined) regularly exposes students to larger numbers of peers as well as a greater age range. Although initial contact with peers is often facilitated by school, peer interactions extend beyond school hours. Most kids walk to school and join up with classmates along the way. Similarly, at the end of the school day, many kids remain together to play.

During middle childhood (roughly from first attendance at school to the attainment of puberty), mixed-sex play groups remain very common. Kids in this age group seem to place less emphasis upon male-female distinctions than do teenagers. Neighborhood play groups that include siblings, cousins, other relatives, and neighbors are a common focus of social interaction. The fact that middle childhood play groups are composed of a greater age range than the groups of teenagers suggests that availability and willingness to play are more important determinants of playmate selection than either age or sex. Given the small size of the community and the limited number of potential playmates available, Holman children do not have the luxury of restricting their social interactions exclusively to a narrowly defined age and sex group. Also, play activities at this stage are often noncompetitive, spontaneous, and relatively unorganized pursuits that may be undertaken by both sexes. As children become older and meet age-mates residing in other parts of the community, peer networks gradually expand beyond the immediate vicinity of the household.

In those years immediately preceding the onset of puberty (approximately ten to thirteen), the interests of boys and girls begin to diverge and there is a tendency for young people gradually to spend more time in same-sex groups. This transition to same-sex groups as the primary focus of social interaction occurs somewhat earlier for females, presumably due to an earlier onset of physical maturation. While mixed-sex play groups are still fairly common, smaller and more intimate same-sex cliques begin to form, providing the context for the formation of close friendships. Thus, when a ten-to-thirteen-year-old preadolescent goes out visiting, he or she usually visits the household of a same-sex friend. While the preadolescent will continue to play and be seen in mixed-sex neighborhood play groups, the companions who are actively sought out for prolonged and intimate social interaction are invariably individuals of the same age and sex.

At puberty, segregation between the sexes becomes much more pronounced and same-sex groups predominate. This is not due to any active avoidance or hostility toward the opposite sex, but is largely a function of the increasing divergence of the recreational interests and work responsibilities of males and females. Both in and out of school, teenagers spend the vast majority of their time with members of the same sex and contacts with the opposite sex appear tenative and strained. Segregation between the sexes may be partially the result of the difficulties inherent in adjusting to a changing self-image and coping with changing external demands and expectations. Such difficulties may be partially resolved in the context of friendship and peer interaction. Thus, social relations become naturally concentrated upon those same-age and same-sex comrades with whom there is a basis of shared emotions and experience.

Since the emotional needs and expectations of teenagers are very different from those of children, friendships and peer relations become much more selective. Casual and spontaneous neighborhood play groups can no longer provide the adolescent with the kinds of intimacy and emotional support that are required. As a result, the teenager's peer group develops into a network of significant others spread throughout the community.

Just as puberty contributes to physical and behavioral differences between adolescent males and females, it also alters the nature of each sex's friendships and peer relations. Female groups become smaller and more cliquish while male groups tend to become larger and less intimate. The social and recreational activities of teenage boys begin to revolve around competitive sports that involve the participation of large "aggregations" of youths who share a common sporting interest. While boys are engaged in such athletic ventures, which invariably entail a lot of showing off, small groups of girls will either watch as spectators or play along the sidelines less organized and less competitive games such as tag, hide-and-seek, and dodgeball.

Perhaps the most noticeable difference between the sexes during adolescence is that girls spend significantly less time in public settings than do adolescent boys, who, when not playing competitive sports, may be seen hanging out or casually socializing at the Bay store, coffee shop, hardware store, and numerous outdoor settings. During the period of our fieldwork, we were surprised at the infrequency of our observations of adolescent females, especially those in late adolescence. The tendency for females to spend more time in private settings and less time hanging out in public is the result of their being assigned a greater number of baby-sitting and household chores at an early age (beginning usually at ages nine to thirteen). Adolescent boys, on the other hand, have few, if any, assigned chores and consequently more time to spend interacting and playing with friends and peers in public. In general, girls spend more time indoors in small groups playing cards, sewing, cleaning house, baby-sitting, and watching television.

One of the consequences of female task assigment is that girls are more likely to come under the direct supervision of parents. Within this context, adolescent girls learn a higher degree of nurturance and responsibility, both of which are essential to the female's acquisition of adult roles. Perhaps for this reason adolescent girls perceive themselves as more mature and adultlike in comparison to boys, for whom the transition to adult roles and responsibilities takes a much longer period of time. (This theme is explored in greater detail in the following chapter.)

The activities of adolescent boys and girls define, in part, the nature of their respective groups. Since boys invest so much time and energy in competitive sports, their groups are necessarily larger and more task oriented. Girls' groups, on the other hand, tend to be slightly smaller and more person oriented. While a teenage girl may have trouble breaking into a clique of same-age peers, any teenage boy who displays an interest in a certain sport may become a part of these group activities. His acceptance is even further ensured if he displays a high degree of athletic talent.

Despite an increased orientation to same-sex peers, Holman teenagers do not spend all their time playing, working, and interacting in such groups. Informal mixed-sex groups occasionally form and tend to be more common as teenagers become older and develop a sexual interest in the opposite sex. These mixed-sex groups, however, are much more spontaneous and shorter lived than same-sex groups and cliques. A group of teenage girls and boys, for example, may form at the coffee shop for a brief period of interaction. More often than not, such meetings represent a coming together of two same-sex groups, almost as though boys and girls prefer the emotional support of gender mates when approaching the novelty, and perhaps uncertainty, of cross-sex interaction. Such meetings often take place when there is nothing else to do and disperse as soon as other activities are available.

The mixed groups of teenagers take on a very different character from the mixed groups of children. While the latter are often spontaneous play groups that barely recognize sex differences, the former are more goal directed (not to mention strained), with the ultimate aim of establishing dating relationships. As expected, cross-sex dyads become increasingly common in the late teenage years, a phenomenon rarely seen with younger children.

By the time young people establish a permanent pair-bond, set up a neolocal residence, and begin rearing children, peer group interaction becomes much less frequent. While the friends and peers of the young adult's teenage years continue to be an important source of social, emotional, and even economic support, the amount of time spent with these individuals becomes noticeably curtailed. At this point of the Inuit life cycle, social interaction and visitation expands to include a much greater age range of individuals and families, including parents, grandparents, and other more distant relatives. (See Appendix B for a detailed analysis and discussion of our formal behavioral observation data.)

TEENAGE ATTITUDES TOWARD FRIENDSHIP

In the early teenage years, friendships begin to take on greater importance than during childhood, when friends were simply those people a child happened to be playing with or hanging out with at a particular time. For teenagers, however, intimacy with one or more close friends becomes more important than proximity. Not only are these friends actively sought out for their company, but much of the day is spent hanging out and playing with them.

When kids and teenagers were asked to define friendship, a number of consistent themes arose. Friends were described as nice, kind, easygoing, fun, and caring. Almost all respondents emphasized the importance of friends having a good sense of humor. Older teenagers were more likely to emphasize the intimate and emotional aspects of friendship rather than the simple "instrumental" aspects of friendship. Older teenagers described friends as people one could talk to about problems or go to for advice. Older teenagers were also more likely to report that their friendships had changed as they got older. However, it was only with much difficulty that they could articulate what these changes were. Johnny Apiuk explained it in the following way:

> I don't fight as much now with my friends and I'm not as bossy as I used to be. I always used to fight with my friends when I was younger. Now, I can talk with them before I fight. I have the same group of friends now as before, but I can talk with them better.

As previously mentioned, kids tend to be extremely "bossy" or demanding of other people. Conflicts between kids often occur because of this unwillingness to compromise or negotiate. For this reason, kids make and break relationships at a faster rate than teenagers. Since kids have not yet learned the importance of talking and listening to others, long-lasting friendships are harder to establish. Teenagers, because they are beginning to act more like adults, negotiate with both friends and antagonists. Therefore, difficulties that arise between teenage friends rarely escalate to the point of enmity or termination. In addition, teenagers are much less likely than kids to make backbiting comments about others.

When members of our survey sample were asked to name their friends, 82 percent of those responding ($n = 31$) listed only same-sex friends. Only seven teenagers, all of whom were older (ages sixteen to nineteen), listed one or more opposite-sex friends. Even these older teenagers, however, listed same-sex individuals first and in greater numbers than cross-sex friends, suggesting that the primary focus of friendship during the teenage years is with members of the same gender.

One notable finding from our friendship interviews was that females of all ages listed more friends than did males (see table 5.1). Surprisingly, within each sex there was no difference between age-groups in the number of friends listed. This finding is contrary to what might be expected as young people develop more mature and intimate relationships. The most significant difference was between boys (who listed a mean of 5.8 friends) and girls (who listed a mean of 7.4). Several explanations for this sexual disparity are possible. One is that girls are better able to get along with one another than boys, who are more

TABLE 5.1
Mean Number of Friends by Age and Sex of Respondents

	AGE OF RESPONDENTS		
SEX OF RESPONDENTS	11–13	14–19	TOTAL
Males	M = 5.7	M = 5.8	M = 5.8
	SD = 1.6	SD = 2.4	SD = 2.1
	(n = 7)	(n = 13)	(n = 20)
Females	M = 7.3	M = 7.4	M = 7.4
	SD = 2.9	SD = 5.2	SD = 3.9
	(n = 12)	(n = 9)	(n = 21)
Both sexes	M = 6.7	M = 6.5	M = 6.6
	SD = 2.6	SD = 3.8	SD = 3.2
	(n = 19)	(n = 22)	(n = 41)

actively engaged in competitive sports play. In this respect, females may more closely embody the Inuit values of nondemandingness and agreeability. Males, on the other hand, are less likely to be as compatible in their peer interactions, even though they are seen more often in larger groups. Another possibility is that boys, because they interact in large groups, find it necessary to establish close relationships with a select group of peers (i.e., friends). Girls, because they do not spend as much time in large task-oriented groups, have fewer opportunities, or perhaps need, to develop such a limited number of close friendships; they simply "get along" with the peers with whom they interact on a daily basis.

Kids generally commented that there was little difference between cross-sex and same-sex friends. As would be predicted, however, teenagers noticed significant differences between their same-sex and opposite-sex friends. Teenagers were especially aware of the divergence of activities and interests of males and females. One fifteen-year-old girl commented that her boyfriends and girlfriends were basically the same type of friend, but that she talked about different things with each group. Peter Nilgak (age eighteen) put it more bluntly:

> Girls, I can fool around with. Boys, I can talk around with about the girls. I think that I can talk to the boys better than I can talk with the girls. I ask boys for favors that I don't ask of girls. I can talk about my problems better with boys. I guess I don't have any deep conversations with girls.

Johnny Apiuk, on the other hand, had more complimentary things to say about girls:

I can talk more freely with boys about things than I can with girls. Talking with female friends, however, can be more interesting since they know things that your male friends don't know.

It is not terribly surprising that teenage boys and girls have different conversational interests and that this difference is recognized by both sexes. Boys spend a great deal of time talking about sports, whether their own or those they have viewed on television. Like adult men, teenage boys also converse about hunting, fishing, and snowmobile or motorcycle repair. All are frequent activities of boys. Conversations about these activities are much akin to the "car talk" of boys in the United States and southern Canada. The conversations of teenage girls, however, concentrate more upon female activities such as sewing and baby-sitting and, more commonly, upon other girls. Nevertheless, the common thread between boys and girls is that both like to talk about the opposite sex.

Most of our teenage informants claimed that it was fairly easy to establish good friendships. According to thirteen-year-old Sarah Kitigak:

It's easy. You just start visiting one another and doing things together, and you start being friends. I knew that Mary A. was my friend when she came to visit me in my tent and fell asleep on my blanket.

Older teenagers, however, recognize that, while it is easy to establish casual friendships with other teenagers, close friendships are completely different and require a lot of work to learn about one another's feelings and needs.

Our teenage informants were loathe to admit that there were any persons whom they regarded as enemies or with whom they did not get along. Since conflict avoidance remains a strongly held value in Holman, it is difficult to tell whether there is a true absence of enmity between individuals or just an avoidance of admitting such relationships. Both are probably true. Only eleven-year-old Ricky Kitigak admitted to having an enemy:

Yes, Stanley, my uncle [also 11 years old]. That kid always bothers me at school. He likes to make trouble at school and then blame it on me.

COOPERATION AND COMPETITION: PEER RELATIONS AND SOCIAL VALUES

By the time children reach adolescence, they begin to exhibit more accurately the dominant social values of society. For this reason, adolescents tend to view themselves as more like adults, behaviorally and socially, than like children. For teenagers the domain of friendship and peer interaction provides the "playing field" in which social behaviors can be fine-tuned. For Holman youngsters, appropriate social behaviors include emotional inhibition, sharing, a good sense of humor, and conflict avoidance. The emphasis upon "getting along" is especially important in a community where everyone will remain together for the rest of their lives. While a few may move to other settlements and towns, the vast majority will remain in the community where they were born and raised. Thus, the persons who form the focal point of a teenager's peer group continue to occupy an important status throughout his or her adult life.

While Holman teenagers struggle to acquire the dominant social behaviors and values of Inuit society, they are also inundated with the values, social expectations, and behavioral norms of southern society, to which they are exposed through television, radio, movies, schooling, and school trips to the south. In many respects, teenagers are the group hardest hit and most greatly influenced by these contrasts. Since many of the recently introduced values and behavioral norms are incongruent with those of Inuit society, teenagers are often precariously balanced between two distinct ways of behaving and viewing the world around them. In the remainder of this chapter, I discuss the impact of these changes as they affect the values of cooperation and competition within the adolescent peer group. Since adolescent boys have been much more affected by these rapid changes than adolescent girls, I make separate observations for each sex. Of particular interest are the behavioral and attitudinal changes that have taken place since 1978, when I first conducted fieldwork in the community. Even over a short time span of five years, the changes have been dramatic.

Traditional Inuit society maintained a delicate balance between self-reliance and cooperation between individuals, families, and groups. Self-reliance, individuality, and achievement were all aspects of behavior essential for successful exploitation of a harsh arctic habitat. The nuclear family, however, was unable to survive without the assistance of other households. This assistance took the form of cooperative hunting, meat sharing, and information exchange. Since mutual assistance was so necessary, the individual's qualities of assertion, self-reliance, and individuality were secondary to behaviors that emphasized the welfare and continuity of the cooperative unit.

In the modern settlement, the need for intensive cooperation has become minimal. Wage employment, government assistance, subsidized housing, and health care have dramatically improved the economic condition of Holman residents. These recent innovations have significantly reduced the need for cooperation between households. Food once obtained through cooperative hunting may now be bought at the store using cash or harvested by a single hunter using a snowmobile and high-powered rifle. The increase in economic autonomy is not the only significant change that has occurred. More recently, the introduction of television has contributed to the social autonomy of households, with families spending more time at home watching television than visiting friends, neighbors and relatives.

It is within this new, secure economic order that Holman teenagers have been raised. While their parents still remember a rugged and precarious way of life in which mutual economic and social cooperation was necessary to ensure survival, such a life-style is foreign to today's kids and teenagers. For many teenagers it is simply a past way of life occasionally recounted by parents and grandparents. One elderly informant stated dispairingly that the younger people rarely asked him to tell stories about "the old days," but were much more interested in learning about life in the South.

Exposure to the southern world has come about through schooling, television, radio, and school trips to the South. Through the school, with its typically southern teaching styles and curriculum, youngsters are taught the importance of individual achievement. They are taught to work by themselves and expect evaluation of individual performance. Through television, these same youngsters are exposed to programs and personalities depicting values and behaviors often antithetical to those of Inuit society. The impact of programs like "Dallas," "Three's Company," and "Edge of Night" has been extensive. Unfortunately, many Holman residents believe that television, with all its aggressiveness, materialism, and sexual obsessiveness, provides an accurate picture of life in the South.

Holman teenagers watch television with a passion unmatched by their participation in many other social or expressive activities (with the possible exception of hockey for boys). The television is a window to the "southern" way of life, a way of life with which these youngsters are only now becoming familiar. The strange values, behaviors and norms which are beamed into Holman via satellite are often viewed with greater reverence than those of their parents and grandparents. As expected, teenagers respond by modeling many of those presumably desirable behaviors.

The impact of television upon the behavior and values of teenagers is demonstrated by two isolated events. Both events involved the sports play of teenage boys. The first occurred during the winter of 1979, prior to the introduction of television. The second occurred eight months after the introduction of television.

Twice a week, during 1979, the students in the older grades (5 through 9) were taken to the community hall for physical education. This usually consisted of playing team sports such as basketball, volleyball and kickball. The students went to the community hall one by one as they finished their school work and were joined later by the teacher. When volleyball was the sport of the day, the first arrivals to the hall would set up the net and then start to hit the ball back and forth. Youngsters who arrived subsequently would evaluate the relative strength of either side and then join the team they felt needed an additional member. This process continued until everyone had decided upon a team. During the warm-up period, the youngsters would look around at their own teammates as well as the members of the opposing team and then switch sides if any imbalance were evident. By and large, the youngsters were adept at dividing up into two evenly matched groups. Remarkably, however, they did not divide consistently into the same teams. On one occasion the teacher decided to select teams in a southern fashion by appointing captains to choose their own teammates. In this situation, the students appeared very uncomfortable and were hesitant to comply with the southern selection procedure. The teacher had to apply some pressure for the process to be completed. The anxiety and hesitation were most evident among those who had been chosen as team captains.

Due to the resistance the teacher encountered in these situations, he quickly abandoned the process in favor of the youngsters' own "natural" selection process, which proved less time-consuming and more efficient. The fact is that these youngsters were capable of an implicit evaluation of one another's skills, while at the same time avoiding an explicit ranking that would prove embarrassing to one or more youngsters. The "southern" selection procedure proved inappropriate for a number of reasons. First, appointing a team captain not only called attention to a particular individual, but momentarily placed that youngster over and above the others in terms of social status. Second, the appointed team captain was put into the uncomfortable position of making vital decisions in team selection that would ultimately affect the outcome of the game. His responsibility was thus heightened in comparison to his teammates. Third, the youngsters were visibly uncomfortable in any situation involving the explicit evaluation and ranking of one another's capabilities. The normal cultural process, on the other hand, emphasized a consensual mode whereby every person was allowed to make his or her own decision based upon the implicit recognition of his own and each others' capabilities.

This incident stands in dramatic contrast to a situation that occurred three years later in 1982. Curious about the effect that television and other recently introduced southern phenomena were having upon Holman teenagers, I requested that the same teacher attempt to replicate this event. When the youngsters were brought into the hall, the teacher casually asked if any of them would like to be appointed team captains. Almost immediately the teacher was inundated with raised hands and impassioned requests to be appointed one of the team captains. When two captains were selected, they had no difficulty deciding which individuals they desired on their teams. In fact the entire selection process was accompanied by numerous comments on the relative playing abilities of certain individuals. Those youngsters with a high degree of athletic skill were selected first, while less able youngsters were selected last amidst the uncomplimentary groans of teammates. When the game finally got underway, it became clear that winning assumed primacy over the pleasure of playing the game. Similar findings by O'Neil (1983, 208) suggest that the increased emphasis upon competition in teenage sports is not unique to Holman but indicative of social and attitudinal changes occurring throughout the Arctic.

Such competitiveness and overt ranking of skill have extended outside of the school setting as well. During the Easter games of 1982, the teenage boys and young men of the community organized a series of hockey matches. Unlike the situation with the first school volleyball game, captains were easily chosen and teams were easily picked. Not only was there some competition between the better players over who would be selected as team captains, but the team selection was accompanied by explicit remarks concerning each participant's playing ability. Many boys and young men were quick to point out in which round they had been chosen to play. The hockey matches were organized in a very southern fashion, with semifinal and final matches. The team that won the last round was quick to claim its superior talent over all the other teams.

In the first incident, the youngsters displayed the behavioral norms expected of Inuit adults. That those behavioral norms are no longer firmly entrenched is vividly expressed by the willingness of the teenagers in the more recent incidents to openly rank one another. Similar observations made during the second fieldwork period suggest that overt competition has become more common than in the immediate past. Competition is most pronounced among teenage boys who spend a great deal of their time engaged in team sports. In this context it is important to determine whether there has been an increase in competitiveness among these youngsters or if increasing exposure to southern values and behavioral styles has made the overt expression of competitiveness more acceptable. The latter explanation may, in fact, be the most feasible. Competition, both friendly and hostile, has always been a major feature of traditional Inuit society. While individuals were socialized to inhibit aggressive tendencies and hostile feelings, it was acceptable for these feelings to be indirectly expressed through controlled competitions. Competitions included wrestling matches, song duels, and other contests that matched the strength, physical dexterity, and wit of two opponents. The competitions were always conducted under the guise of joking and good humor, often belying more intense personal rivalries. While the good-natured aspect of such duels persists to the present day, especially among adults, the open expression of hostility and competitiveness appears commonplace among the younger generation.

Sports have become an integral part of adolescent life in Holman. With the increased security and leisure of settlement life, young males have begun to spend greater amounts of time engaged in such expressive activities. However, sports events are also a recent development in the community. During my first field trip to Holman, teenage sports events were a relatively rare event. Baseball and volleyball were occasionally played, usually under the auspices of the school, but hockey games were few. The introduction of television in the fall of 1980 contributed a great deal to the increase in teenage sports activities. Baseball, football, and especially hockey can all be viewed on television, and most teenage boys, as well as many adults, are dedicated sports enthusiasts. When hockey games are televised, the entire community appears deserted as people position themselves in front of their television sets for the duration. Often as soon as these events are over, the teenage boys take to the ice with a vengeance.

The viewing of television sports events has lead to a substantial increase in competition and conflict. Of all the professional sports televised in Holman, hockey is undoubtedly the most violent. Rarely does a professional hockey game occur without a fight. Teenage boys take great pleasure in watching such fights, believing that it adds excitement to the game, and often mimic such behavior in their own sports play. Verbal confrontations and even some physical fights occasionally occur during hockey and baseball games. One of these was described to me by nineteen-year-old Jason Ikpakoaq:

> A group of us were playing street hockey in front of Oliktoak's house. My team was winning. Albert Kagyut [my nephew] got mad at me because he thought that we didn't deserve one of the goals. At one point I slipped and fell on the ground, and Albert came up to me and kicked me several times in the face. Some of the other boys pulled him back. I had blood streaming down my face and had to go to the nursing station for bandages. When my father found out, he went to have a talk with Albert's father [my older brother] and told him what had happened and that it wasn't right for Albert to fight, especially with his relatives. I don't know if Albert's father ever talked to him though.

Such incidents of physical assault are, however, relatively rare. Teenage boys are more likely to engage in brief shouting matches when they feel there has been an irregularity in the progress of a sporting match. While open expression of hostility has become more common in recent years, the majority of verbal and physical confrontations are quickly forgotten, if not right away, at least by the following day. Consequently, although the expression of aggression has become much more frequent, adolescent management of conflict has remained very traditional in style. Like their parents, teenage boys rarely hold grudges for a long time. This, in fact, is one of the primary characteristics of Inuit interpersonal relations: an emphasis upon avoiding conflict and a pronounced ability to forgive transgressions. In the words of Robert Nilgak:

Some kind of quarrel, fight, or jealousy [can make friends break up]. Girls seem to break up more often than guys over jealousy—over girl stuff I guess. They talk more about one another than guys do. Guys don't break up as easily. . . . I had a fight with Roger once up at the hall. The next day, we were friends again. We don't stay mad long. . . . I also fight sometimes when I play hockey, but I never stay mad for long. We get back together. It just comes naturally. You start laughing, they start laughing, and you just forget what you were mad about.

Other informants expressed a similar attitude by asserting that people in Holman really got along with one another and that fights were quickly forgotten.

The significance of competitive sports goes far beyond their importance as a recreational forum for teenagers. In a community with limited prospects for employment or occupational advancement, sports provide the opportunity for young males to strive for excellence in athletic ability. Many of these teenage boys are excellent athletes and display a high degree of skill in hockey, basketball, volleyball, and more traditional "northern games."[1] Young Inuit realize that, due to a lack of jobs and education, they occupy a status subordinate to whites, who are seen as having positions of power and authority. The resulting insecurity is partially alleviated through the satisfaction young people derive in mastering these games (O'Neil 1983, 213–214). Teenagers most certainly realize that they are better at these activities than any other age and sex group within the community. Any anxiety felt by these sports enthusiasts as a result of parents' opinions that game playing is a waste of time is partially diffused through their attempts to excel. This athletic ability is recognized by many adults, who often observe the springtime hockey tournaments of teenage boys from the sidelines.

As expected, teenage girls conform to a very different pattern of peer group interaction. While hostilities are known to exist between teenage girls, these are rarely expressed openly. By the very fact that female groups tend to be smaller than male groups, less opportunity exists for aggressive encounters. Girls are more selective in peer group interactions and focus their social activities upon small groups of friends and relatives. Boys, on the other hand, congregate and play in much larger groups, where a greater possibility exists for conflicts. All other factors being controlled, teenage boys, whether they be in same-

sex or mixed-sex groups, are more adept at boasting, fighting, and calling attention to themselves.

Another factor that may account for male-female differences in
peer group interaction relates to the greater emphasis placed upon responsibility training for girls. Girls, especially those who have completed school, are encouraged to assist their mothers with household
chores. Most important among these chores is the caretaking of younger
siblings, nieces, and nephews. Through these activities, girls learn the
values of nurturance and responsibility. Boys rarely have the opportunity to practice nurturing behavior.

Peer interaction among teenage girls is vividly portrayed by the
manner in which they play games. The play groups of girls are smaller,
more spontaneous, and less highly organized than the sporting ventures of boys. While boys place greater emphasis upon keeping score,
thereby determining winners from losers, girls' games are more oriented toward the enjoyment that comes from playing the game and interacting with others. While minor disagreements may break out, they
tend not to be subject to the prolonged litigation that often characterizes disagreements among boys. In general, male games and sporting
activities are subject to more planning and organization, while female
games are invariably more spontaneous and shorter in duration.

One of the characteristics that permeates all aspects of teenage
peer interaction is heavy reliance upon humor, joking, and laughter.
Playfulness, when expressed in the interactional setting, is a double-
edged phenomenon. On the one hand, Inuit joking and laughter represent true expressions of pleasure and joy. On the other hand, these
playful behaviors are often used by both adults and teenagers to diffuse
sensitive or potentially embarrassing social situations. Interactions between teenagers are often accompanied by subtle insults or critical
comments tactfully qualified with the expression "I fool." In this manner, hostilities can be expressed in an open and playful manner without escalating to more disruptive verbal or physical conflicts. An individual who has been insulted in such a playful manner is expected to
respond in a similar joking manner, otherwise he or she is considered
socially immature and childlike. Like the ready forgiveness of transgressions, humor and joking provide a powerful mechanism for both
the avoidance and resolution of conflict in all social situations.

This ability to respond to stressful social situations with playfulness and good humor is a primary characteristic of teenage and adult
behavior. The social and psychological functions of Inuit humor have

been noted by numerous researchers working in the North. According to Briggs (1968, 50), laughter and joking can be used "to express, and simultaneously deny, hostility and fear." In fact, through the child-rearing process, children are encouraged to channel anger into amusement and fear into laughter. This is accomplished most effectively through parental modeling. A child who has become angered or frightened will become the object of adult laughter. While the child may become even more angered to see adults laughing at his or her misfortune, the child will eventually learn that this is the appropriate response to such disconcerting social situations. Since the open expression of such emotions is a natural response on the part of a young child, it is usually not until the teenage years that he or she is able to master this essential form of socially adapted playfulness. Mastery not only indicates that the young Inuk is approaching social maturity but also ensures smooth interpersonal relations in the peer interactional setting.

Holman teenagers live in a social world dominated, in part, by a large adolescent peer group. This expanded peer group is a recent development in Inuit society. Social and demographic changes that have occured in Holman over the past thirty years have created a larger cohort of young people than existed before the population increase and concentration of the 1960s. In addition, the introduction of schooling and southern television programming have provided these young people with a distinctive view of themselves as an age set, more similar to the teenagers of the South than to their parents and grandparents at a similar age. Holman adolescents now spend the greater part of their day playing, working, and hanging out with friends and peers. All of these companions are in close spatial proximity, thus increasing both ease of access and amount of time spent with these persons. Because of noninterventive child-rearing practices, parents grant their children a degree of autonomy not experienced by young people in many other cultures. This autonomy simply serves to reinforce the primacy of the adolescent peer group as it dominates the daily activities and interactions of Holman teenagers.

■ 6
Gender Preference Sexuality, and Mate Selection

If any aspect of adolescent development approaches universality in the human species, it is undoubtedly the awakening of sexual interest and desire. The very physiological basis of puberty entails significant increases in sex hormones, which have an undeniable and often dramatic influence upon behavior. The simplicity of childhood gives way to the hormonal, emotional, and social complexities of the adolescent stage of human development. But to state the universality of this life stage serves only to mask naïvely the social and cultural embellishments that determine the manner in which the physiological changes find expression.

In discussing the sexual aspects of teenage life in Holman, primary concern is directed to three interrelated topics: gender-role preference, dating and sexual activity, and pair-bonding. To examine these topics, we gathered data from behavioral observations, informal discussions, and formal clinical interviews. The clinical interviews were specifically designed to examine gender-role preference, gender ambivalence, and sexual activity. While I have already mentioned the difficulty of collecting data from verbally restrained informants, our data collection proved most challenging in the area of adolescent sexuality. The reticence and restraint normally encountered in the interview situation were magnified in those interviews dealing with sexual activity and pair-bonding. While we were able to obtain candid responses to our highly personal inquiries from a small number of informants, most displayed some discomfort in responding to these questions. Not surprisingly, the most open interviews were conducted with boys, while our female informants were rarely as forthcoming with the kind of information we were seeking to record.

Gender-Role Preference

The concept of gender-role preference is admittedly ambiguous, but it is precisely this ambiguity that makes it a useful cross-cultural tool since it forces researchers to examine culturally specific modes of gender assignment and preference. As used here, the term simply refers to the individual's preference for either the male or female role as expressed in overt behavior, values, and emotions.

Gender-role preference was examined using three interview techniques: the draw-a-person interview, the magic man interview, and a clinical interview designed to elicit information on gender conflict and ambivalence.

The draw-a-person interview was administered to our survey sample of forty-one youngsters. The procedure was very simple and involved minimal verbal instruction. Each respondent was given a pencil and a piece of paper and asked to draw a person. Informants inquiring about the kind of drawing we expected were told that they could draw whatever they wanted as long as it was a person. When the first drawing was completed to the subject's satisfaction, the interviewer asked a series of "projective" questions regarding the content of the drawing. These included the sex of the person drawn, the approximate age, whether the person depicted was real or imagined, and in what activity the person was engaged. The children were then asked to make another drawing of the opposite sex, followed by the same projective questions.

Our primary concern in collecting the drawings was to note which sex was drawn first, the degree of sexual differentiation between male and female drawings, the age of the individuals drawn, and the type of activities depicted in the drawings. The most interesting finding was that the vast majority of informants (90 percent) drew members of their own sex first. Only four of the forty-one informants (two males and two females) made cross-sex drawings for their first picture. While one must be careful in interpreting the significance of such a phenomenon, the data suggest a well formulated sense of gender self-ascription for both males and females. The same results might not be true in a culture where there is significant sexual differentiation in terms of social status, economic self-reliance, and political power.[1]

Other interpretations of the draw-a-persons were more difficult to make. We had assumed that draw-a-person would be an ideal vehicle for the examination of sexual differentiation, and in the other research settings this proved to be the case. In Holman, however, both male and female informants tended to draw figures wearing heavy, and unrevealing, parkas. This made it difficult to assess our informants' recognition of physical differences between the sexes. In many cases, the only difference depicted between males and females was that the latter were more often portrayed packing babies on their backs or wearing calf-length parkas with wide fur trim. A small number of boys, however, made drawings showing extreme sexual differentiation. All of these exaggerated drawings were done by older adolescent males (ages fifteen through nineteen). One sixteen-year-old drew a nude female figure in a spread-eagle position. Another boy, age eighteen, drew a buxom female figure wearing tight blue jeans and high-heeled boots. One had no doubt as to these boys' adolescent preoccupations! In contrast, none of our female informants drew such revealing figures. Thus, the modesty displayed by females in the interview situation is also evident in their drawings.

The magic man interview explored both sex and age preferences of informants. Informants were asked to pretend that they were participating in a school play requiring five different players: a mother, father, girl, boy, and infant. The sex of the infant was not specified. Informants were then given a choice between two of these "roles" and asked to choose which they would prefer to play. A total of ten paired choices were given, allowing each informant to choose between various ages and sexes.

The results of the magic man interview were exceptionally revealing of the differences between male and female informants. When generation was held constant (mother versus father and girl versus boy), almost all informants chose a same-sex role (see table 6.1). Despite this overwhelming tendency to choose the same-sex player, this preference was more pronounced for male informants than for female

TABLE 6.1
Role Selection for Magic Man Interview

	FATHER	MOTHER			BABY	MOTHER
Boys	18	2		Boys	14	3
Girls	1	21		Girls	8	11
(chi-square = 27.6; $p < .001$)				(chi-square = 4.53; $p < .05$)		

	BOY	GIRL			BOY	FATHER
Boys	19	1		Boys	14	6
Girls	4	18		Girls	17	5
(chi-square = 21.9; $p < .001$)				(chi-square = 0.033; NS)		

	BABY	FATHER			GIRL	BABY
Boys	9	8		Boys	2	18
Girls	15	4		Girls	19	3
(chi-square = 1.69; NS)				(chi-square = 21.48; $p < .001$)		

	BOY	MOTHER			BOY	BABY
Boys	13	3		Boys	19	1
Girls	6	13		Girls	6	16
(chi-square = 6.74; $p < .01$)				(chi-square = 17.26; $p < .001$)		

	GIRL	FATHER			MOTHER	GIRL
Boys	3	14		Boys	7	13
Girls	12	7		Girls	11	11
(chi-square = 5.88; $p < .05$)				(chi-square = 0.45; NS)		

NOTE: Chi-squares calculated using Yates' Correction for Continuity.

informants. The females in the sample, while prefering same-sex play-ers, made significantly more crossovers than did the males interviewed. This difference was most visible in the number of times the same-age opposite sex player was selected. Females selected the boy player 33 times as opposed to only 19 girl choices for males. The male informants seemed especially uncomfortable selecting the girl player and gener-ally did so only in circumstances when the choice given was between playing the mother or playing the girl. When confronted with this par-ticular choice, male informants seemed uneasy and often responded with nervous giggles. The same response was true of the females when asked to choose between the father and the boy. In addition, both males and females preferred to play the part of the genderless baby rather than select a cross-sex player.

When sex was held constant (boy versus father), male respon-dents preferred their own generational role to that of the parental gen-eration (14 versus 6). The same tendency was not true for the females in our sample, who were evenly split in choosing between the role of the mother and the role of the girl (11 versus 11). Since adolescent boys in Holman generally have fewer responsibilities compared to females, it is understandable that male informants would prefer the same-generation player to the parental-generation player. Due to cultural expectations that females attain social maturity at an earlier age than males, it is reasonable to assume that girls recognize little difference between their own social roles and those of their mothers. Thus, girls perceive themselves to be more to be like adult women than boys perceive themselves like adult men. This conclusion is supported by clinical interviews in which both male and female informants report that adolescent boys have a great deal more freedom to do as they please and are subject to significantly fewer assigned chores.

The clinical interviews on gender identity and gender ambivalence provided the most revealing data collected for the examination of sex differences. This interview was conducted with 10 different youngsters, 5 males between eleven and eighteen years of age and 5 females between the ages of eleven and sixteen. (All but one of these informants were members of our clinical interview sample.) This particular interview was given after several previous interview sessions and at a point when the informant was comfortable with the interviewer and the interview situation. The interview with eighteen-year-old Johnny Apiuk transpired in the following manner:

▪ R.C.: *I am going to ask you a few questions about the differences between boys and girls and what you think about these differences. First, let's talk about girls. Do you like or dislike them?*
JOHNNY: *I like girls. I like their bodies, their looks, and their breasts.*
R.C.: *Any other things besides physical appearance?*
JOHNNY: *I like them because you can talk to them about different things than with boys. Some have a good sense of humor.*
R.C.: *How important is it to you for girls to get dressed up so they look nice?*
JOHNNY: *Dressing up is okay, but it's not that important. I've never seen girls get really dressed up here in Holman.*
R.C.: *What makes girls different from boys?*
JOHNNY: *Their sex. They don't do heavy kinds of work the way boys do. Some of them are really sexy and wiggle their bums a lot.*
R.C.: *Should girls be different from boys?*
JOHNNY: *Yes, they should!*

R.C.: *Do you like girls who show off a lot?*

JOHNNY: *No, not really. If you stick around with girls like that, it might be embarrasing. I don't like girls who are too straightforward or aggressive. I prefer girls who let the guy be the boss.*

R.C.: *Do you like girls who are real shy?*

JOHNNY: *Not really. They may be kind of cute, but they're really boring after a while if they don't talk back.*

R.C.: *Do you like girls who act like boys?*

JOHNNY: *I don't really like girls who act like boys. I've seen some in Yellowknife, but they don't look too good. But there are no girls here in Holman who are like that.*

R.C.: *What do you think of boys who act like girls?*

JOHNNY: (LOOK OF DISGUST)

R.C.: *What do you call boys who like to have sex with other boys?*

JOHNNY: *Homos, gays, fags.*

R.C.: *Have you ever met anyone who was a homosexual?*

JOHNNY: *No, I've never met any boys who were gays.*

R.C.: *Have you ever heard of anything like that here in Holman?*

JOHNNY: *Never!*

R.C.: *Have you ever wondered what it would be like if you were a girl rather than a boy?*

JOHNNY: *Not really.*

R.C.: *Are you glad that you're a boy?*

JOHNNY: *Yes. It's more fun to be a boy, because boys have more freedom, can travel, and play games. Girls have more work to do around the house. My sister, works around the house, baby-sits, and does sewing for the co-op.*

R.C.: *Do you think that boys are smarter than girls?*

JOHNNY: *I don't know. In school, some of the girls were pretty smart, smarter than some boys.*

The responses of Johnny were fairly typical of all the males interviewed. All stated unhesitatingly that it was much better to be a boy than to be a girl. The reasons for this preference were also uniform: boys had much more freedom, while girls were expected to do chores around the house.

There is also intimation of some tension between the sexes. Johnny avoided answering questions regarding which sex was perceived as smarter. The response of "I don't know" was qualified by the observation that some girls were, in fact, smarter than some boys. Another informant, David Ageok (age eighteen), was more explicit in his evaluation:

Of course [boys are smarter than girls]! Girls are so dumb. Maybe it's because they don't get out as much.

Three of the six adolescent boys interviewed also displayed a distinct tendency to perceive girls as sex objects, indicating that their primary interest in girls was for sexual gratification rather than for enjoying their company as persons. Only eleven-year-old Ricky Kitigat claimed that he enjoyed both sexes as playmates and admitted that both boys and girls were equally smart.

A similar theme of tension appears in the interview responses of girls. The following interview with sixteen-year-old Emily Apsimik was fairly typical:

▪ P.S.: *Do you like or dislike boys?*
EMILY: *I dislike them.*
P.S.: *Why?*
EMILY: *Because they pick on kids that are younger than them and make them cry. They touch anybody's stuff that isn't theirs.*
P.S.: *Are there any good things about boys?*
EMILY: *Sometimes they're fun to be with, when they are giggling and running around with you, and when they're not bad.*
P.S.: *When are they bad?*
EMILY: *When they break stuff—like sticks for pulling up boats.*
P.S.: *Do you know any boys who act like girls?*
EMILY: *No.*
P.S.: *How about girls who act like boys?*
EMILY: *No.*
P.S.: *Have you ever thought about what it would be like to be a boy rather than a girl?*
EMILY: *No! (look of disgust)*
P.S.: *Surely you like to fool around with boys?*
EMILY: *No. . . . (pause), sometimes.*

In general, the girls agreed that boys were not as nice as girls, that they were bossy, dirty, and more likely to get into fights than girls. One thing the girls especially disliked about boys was that they were always seen as trying to get the girls to fool around (have sex) with them, even when the girls did not want to. While both sexes viewed girls as more "adultlike," boys were viewed as having more fun since they were not required to work as much as girls. Despite the fact that most girls claimed they preferred being girls, fourteen-year-old Emma Mikitok commented that:

> It would be better to be a boy. If I were a boy, I could follow my Dad all the time, go hunting and trapping with him, and have my own ski-doo.

Overall conclusions of the gender ambivalence interviews suggest strongly that both sexes have a well developed gender-role preference. Both sexes uniformly agreed that boys have a great deal more freedom and are not burdened down with the same responsibilities as girls, who are expected to acquire many aspects of adult roles at an earlier age. As would be expected of any group with a relatively high degree of freedom and few responsibilities, boys enjoyed being boys and expressed no desire to occupy any other age or sex catagory. Girls, while recognizing the greater freedom experienced by their male counterparts, displayed a certain degree of maturity in accepting their more demanding roles.

The underlying, and extremely subtle, tension between the sexes during adolescence may in part reflect the recent recognition of male and female differences and the fact that both groups are expected to behave in dramatically disparate ways. From the female perspective, boys may have more time to "run around" and do as they please without too much parental intervention, but they are nevertheless bossy, aggressive, and mean. From the male perspective, girls are much more likely to be boring and shy and are rarely as much fun to be with unless one is interested in "fooling around."

Further characterizations of male-female differences were obtained through intensive semantic interviews conducted with twenty-eight adolescent informants, many of whom also participated in the magic man and draw-a-person interviews. For this interview, a number of commonly used personality descriptors were elicited from several informants. These terms, thirty in all, were written on three-by-five-inch filing cards. Informants were asked to sort the cards into piles depending upon whether they more closely described the behavior of males or females or both sexes. Since there was a surprising amount of agreement between both male and female informants, the results are presented for both groups combined (see fig. 6.1). As expected, males were more likely to be described as bullyish, scary, aggressive, hard-

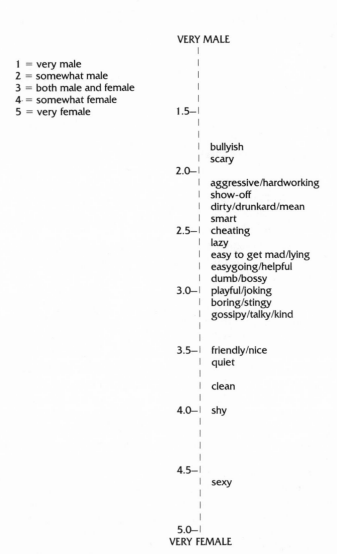

FIG. 6.1.
Male versus female traits. *Note:* 13 female and 15 male respondents.

working, show-offs, dirty, and mean. Females, on the other hand, were described by both sexes as sexy, shy, clean, quiet, friendly, and nice.

The responses to our questions on gender affiliation and sex differences must be interpreted within the context of gender roles in traditional and contemporary Inuit society. In traditional Inuit society, the social and economic duties of men and women were viewed as complementary. Due to the unusual demands of the harsh arctic environment, an individual could not survive without the assistance of a member of the opposite sex. A woman needed a man to provide food and other raw materials obtained through subsistence hunting. Although the man's contribution to the household economy might be perceived as more dramatic, the woman's contribution was every bit as essential. A man could be an excellent hunter, but without a seamstress to make warm clothing and waterproof boots, a man's subsistence activities could be seriously hindered. Which sex's contribution was more important was totally inconsequential since both male and female activities were oriented to the same outcome: survival in a harsh and unproductive habitat.

Largely as a result of this mutual dependency, relations between the sexes were highly charged emotionally and a source of great strain. There was also great competition among men for wives. In fact, competition and jealousy over women were major causes of homicide in the precontact period (Balikci 1970, 179). According to Graburn (1969, 63):

> Eskimo marriage was not only fraught with the probabilities of the loss of a spouse but was also notoriously fragile. Parties could leave each other if they did not get on well together or if they thought they would get on better with someone else. . . . All men wanted to get married and many wanted more than one wife. When bereaved or separated, a man would make every effort to get a new wife, to the point of stealing another's. Adultery was rife and sexual jealousy the norm.

One strategy for diffusing such sexual jealousy, and also for cementing ties of friendship, was the common practice of spouse exchange.

In general, husbands and wives had separate but complementary roles and duties. A woman was expected to maintain the household, care for children, attend to the soapstone lamp (*qullik*), sew boots and clothing, and distribute the meat harvested by her spouse. A man was responsible for most subsistence activities, for cutting and placing the blocks of the snowhouse, for maintaining all hunting equipment, and for deciding when and where the family should move when local food sources had been depleted. While both sexes generally attended to their separate tasks, it was not unheard of for members of either sex to engage in activities regarded as within the domain of the other.

In the political sphere, men appeared to have primary authority, and in public a woman was expected to defer to her husband. In fact, behind the scenes women made significant contributions to all decisions. In general, due to their important economic contributions, women occupied relatively important economic and political positions.

Today, Inuit women are no longer the objects of intense competition and jealousy, nor does the same tension exist between the sexes as reported for the precontact era. Much of this decline may be due to the increased security of settlement existence in which men and women are no longer so dependent upon one another for survival. The disappearance of female infanticide may also have had a significant impact by evening the sex ratio, thereby eliminating the need for males to compete for a limited number of prospective spouses. Nevertheless, the position of women has not changed dramatically in contemporary Inuit society. Women continue to make significant contributions to the household economy. In addition to attending to such traditional tasks as sewing, skin preparation, butchering, and food distribution and preparation, women are active in the modern cash economy. In Holman the vast majority of wage-earning positions are held by women. In many households the husband is responsible for hunting and trapping activities, while his wife maintains a relatively steady, if low paying, wage-labor job. As a result, the woman's contribution to the household economy remains significant, and many households would be unable to make ends meet if not for the cash generated by women. Of particular importance is that the cash generated by women is often necessary to purchase equipment and supplies used by men in subsistence hunting and trapping.

In the public arena, Inuit women continue to pay deference to their husbands. Men are still more likely to run for public office and attend political conferences in other settlements. As in the traditional period, the power of women is both subtle and behind the scenes, with household decisions continuing to be made jointly.

Returning to the domain of adolescent gender attitudes in the modern settlement, it is interesting that tension between the sexes is a dominant theme. Such tension may partially reflect the recognition of significant gender-role differences. For female informants, such strained relations may be due to resentment over the greater freedom and parental indulgence extended to boys. Such resentment is tempered by the belief that girls are better behaved and more socially mature than most boys. With maturity, and ultimately pair-bonding with a member of the opposite sex, tension gives way to the recognition of the complementarity of these divergent sex roles. The adolescent boy who feels that females are shy, silly, and perhaps a little dumb will change his tune when, after marriage, he recognizes that the activities of his spouse are indispensable to himself and his newly formed family. In addition, marriage will extract him from the influence of the adolescent male peer group where gender-chauvinistic attitudes are easily and perhaps necessarily reinforced.

SEXUAL ACTIVITY

In Holman the arousal of adolescent sexual interest and sexual play is unaccompanied by any serious parental surveillance or disapproval. While most parents disapprove of early sexual play (i.e., in the early teens), this is not due to any moral condemnation of adolescent sexual activity, but to the pragmatic concern that a young girl might become pregnant before she is mature enough to care for an infant. The response of some parents is to discourage pregnancy rather than sexual intercourse. One mother of a thirteen-year-old girl, for example, took her daughter to the nursing station to get birth control pills when she learned that the daughter was sexually active. This kind of response is admittedly rare since most parents tend not to intervene at all in the sexual exploits of their offspring. In general, the autonomy experienced by Inuit adolescents in other areas appears to extend into the domain of sexual activity as well.

Adolescent sexual activity commences with little or no knowledge of reproductive physiology. All the teenagers we interviewed stated that their parents had given them no advice whatsoever about sex or pregnancy. In most cases, mothers even avoid discussing the implications of menarche with their daughters. When one young girl had her first menses and asked her mother what was happening to her, the mother simply replied that she was "growing up." The father of three daughters stated that most parents are just too shy and embarrassed to discuss such things with their children. The lack of parent-child discourse regarding sexuality may be due also to parental ignorance regarding reproductive physiology. Because of the lack of sexual knowledge, some girls who have become pregnant may not realize it until the second or even third trimester of their pregnancy.

Sexual activity among adolescents usually starts with kissing and heavy petting, often around ages twelve to fourteen for males and one to two years later for females. By sixteen to eighteen, most adolescents have experienced sexual intercourse. O'Neil (1983, 261) reports similar findings in which 69 percent of his sample of sixteen-to-nineteen-year-old Inuit males reported having first intercourse by age eighteen or younger. Needless to say, reliable data on sexual activity were difficult to obtain. As expected, the best and most revealing data were gathered from a few of our less inhibited informants. The following interview with eighteen-year-old Peter Nilgak, a teenager with a reputation for being sexually active, was the most striking:

■ R.C.: *Did your parents ever give you any advice or training about sexual matters?*
PETER: *No. Not that I know of. My mom just tells me not to knock up any girls, but she doesn't mind if I screw around.*
R.C.: *Do people around here look down on unmarried mothers or give them a hard time?*
PETER: *I don't think so. The parents of the girl just take the kid away and adopt it themselves. People may look down on these girls a little, but I don't think they give them a hard time.*
R.C.: *Would you marry a girl who already had a kid?*
PETER: *No, I don't think so. I wouldn't want to raise another person's kid.*
R.C.: *Do you ever hear people complaining about certain boys who screw around a lot and get girls pregnant?*
PETER: *You mean guys like G.? I've never heard anyone complain about guys like G. I'm always really careful about that. I don't have any kids around town.*
R.C.: *How do you get together with girls to fool around?*
PETER: *Maybe I go out walking around, meet some girl, and invite her over to my place for tea or coffee. Sometimes I may just call up a girl and ask her to come over. After we have had tea for a while and talked a bit, I might say, "Hey, you want to fool around?" And*

*then we do it. We usually do it at my place or at the girl's place. My
mother doesn't mind if I do it at home.*

R.C.: *Are there any other places where you do it?*

PETER: *My place, the girl's place, anywhere.*

R.C.: *What time of day do you usually fool around?*

PETER: *Usually fool around late at night or early in the morning
when adults are sleeping. If I fool around during the day, the parents might find out and encourage me to see and fool around with
their daughter a lot and eventually encourage us to get married.
But I don't want to get tied down like that now. That's what a lot
of parents do.*

R.C.: *Do you think many girls around here are virgins when they
get married?*

PETER: *Virgins? No way! Maybe a long time ago when people used
to get married when they were really young.*

R.C.: *Would you marry a virgin?*

PETER: *Doesn't matter to me.*

R.C.: *In the South, there are a lot of men who only want to marry
virgins.*

PETER: *Yuk! (look of disgust)*

R.C.: *Do you ever hear boys bragging about their sexual conquests?*

PETER: *Yeh. I brag a lot. So do other guys. We brag among ourselves, not to girls.*

R.C.: *When was the first time you had sex?*

PETER: *When I was 12 or 13. I really forget. I guess I was 13.*

R.C.: *How old were you when you started necking. You know, kissing and feeling?*

PETER: *I think I was about 8 years old.*

R.C.: *Why didn't you screw then?*

PETER: *I didn't screw because I didn't know anything about it.*

Teenage dating behavior in Holman is invariably an informal process. Contact with a member of the opposite sex is usually initiated
within a group context. A group of boys may start hanging out with a
group of girls. In time, individuals will begin pairing, either to go to a
dance or to find a secluded spot for sexual intercourse. Both boys and
girls may actively seek out the attentions of a desired partner. Rather
than approaching the individual directly, contact is often accomplished
through an intermediary. Thus, a boy who wishes to go out with a girl
will start visiting that household with a male friend who is in some way

related to that household. Once the initial contact is made and both parties have expressed an interest in one another, they may start seeing one another in the absence of an intermediary.

Adolescent couples rarely go "steady" in the same way that teenagers do in the South. Most young people will have multiple partners, sometimes seeing a number of partners at the same time. Holman teenagers appear to "play the field" as long as they possibly can before establishing any permanent pair-bonds. Although there is some jealousy and competition, it is rarely expressed. One boy reported that when his girlfriend started "screwing around" with another boy, he just stopped going out with her but did not resent the girl or her new partner.

The sexual activity of teenagers, and to some degree that of adults, is affected by the change in seasons. With the constant sunlight and warmth of spring and early summer, teenagers display an increased interest in the opposite sex. Just as spring fever has a pronounced impact upon young people in the South, its impact is even more noticeable in Holman. During the winter months, teenage conversation rarely centers around sexual matters, but in spring and early summer this topic is frequently the focal point of conversation.

Boys and girls have little difficulty finding secluded places for lovemaking. Sexual intercourse may be most common in the spring and summer for the simple reason that young people can go out of town and find a comfortable bed of grass or moss. Also, at this time of year many parents leave town for summer seal hunting camps. While it is common for parents to take along their youngest children, most teenagers prefer to stay in town with their friends, peers, and lovers. Consequently, it is common for these partially empty households to become the focal points of teenage gatherings and sexual intercourse. If parents are in residence, many young couples simply retire to the room of one partner while the parents are still sleeping.

Given the apparent frequency of adolescent sexual encounters, we were interested in finding out what happened during these lovemaking sessions, especially the amount of pleasure and satisfaction afforded each partner. These data were impossible to obtain in any formal interview situation, so we relied heavily upon informal questioning during the social visits of our closest informants. Unfortunately such information could be obtained only from a few older boys and young unmarried men. Female informants were extremely reticent to discuss sexual matters of any kind in any setting, formal or informal. It is also necessary to emphasize that much of this data is of an anecdotal nature and therefore should be interpreted with great care.

Adolescent boys and young men commented that genital-genital intercourse was by far the most common form of sexual intercourse. A number admitted to engaging in limited degrees of oral sex, but almost always with "older girls" between eighteen and twenty-four years of age. Some evidence suggests that most sexual activity is performed primarily for the pleasure of the male, with the sexual needs and desires of the female taking a low priority. One young man (age twenty-one) commented:

> When I have sex with different partners, I don't care too much if I give pleasure to a woman, as long as I get a chance to "get off." Pleasing a woman can be pretty hard work so I usually save it for somebody special who I really like. A lot of girls are just people you go out with for your own pleasure. Also, most girls just giggle after a man comes, probably because they are shy or something.

This same young man admitted that he preferred to have sex with white girls because they are more talkative and aggressive than most local girls:

> I don't think that most local girls get too much out of having sex. One of the problems is that they are too shy to say anything or demand anything of their sex partners. White girls are more likely to moan and groan when having sex, while Eskimo girls just lie there. They don't talk and never tell you what they want when it comes to sex.

Similar opinions were expressed by a number of other male informants. One eighteen-year-old qualified his comments by saying that some of the older girls (eighteen to twenty-four years of age) really knew a lot about sex and that some of the younger girls were beginning to learn a lot too by talking to these older, more experienced individuals.

Despite these claims on the part of adolescent boys that young inexperienced girls are overly shy, at least one of the boys interviewed, David Ageok, claimed that he too was shy when it came to discussing sexual matters with the opposite sex:

■ DAVID: *When I get married, I'd like to ask my wife a lot of personal questions, like who she has fooled around with . . . but I don't think I can ask her because I'll be too shy.*

R.C.: *Why not? If you can't ask your wife questions like that, who can you ask?*

DAVID: *I just can't.*

R.C.: *How well would you be able to get along with her then? Where I come from, husbands and wives are more open about such things. Like a man might ask his wife where she likes to be touched or what her favorite intercourse position is.*

DAVID: *I could never do that. People around here don't ask those kinds of questions.*

R.C.: *Then how will they know what their girlfriend or wife likes?*

DAVID: *I guess they don't.*

These admittedly rare and candid interviews with a few male informants suggest that teenage sexual partners rarely communicate their desires to one another. While girls were accused of being overly shy and sometimes embarrassed when engaging in intercourse, many boys may also experience a degree of inhibition during sex. The absence of effective communication between adolescent lovers suggests a lack of sexual fulfillment for females. In all probability, the establishment of a permanent dating relationship or pair-bond creates a situation where both partners are more responsive to the needs of the other, whether or not these needs are expressed verbally.

While it is certainly tempting to extrapolate further upon these anecdotal observations, to do so would be pure speculation. Without a more substantial and uniform data base gathered in interviews with both girls and young women, it is impossible to determine the nature of female sexual fulfillment. Much more work needs to be done in this area before a thorough and reliable discussion of adolescent and adult sexual relations can be provided.

Despite the high degree of parental tolerance for adolescent sexual activity, many young people try to hide their sexual exploits from parents. Several boys commented that they were afraid their parents or the girl's parents would tease them or encourage them to marry the partner they were seeing. None, however, expressed the fear that their parents would disapprove or scold them for engaging in such activity. These interesting comments reveal that parents may have more input into the pair-bonding decisions of offspring than many young people like to admit. Even though parents no longer arrange marriages for their children, they do exert some subtle influence through encouragement, teasing, and offhand remarks about how nice it would be if their son or daughter settled down with a desired partner.

The recent introduction of southern media, primarily television, has had some fascinating effects upon the dating behavior of adolescents. During my first period of fieldwork before the introduction of television (1978–1980), adolescent dating and sexual behavior was much more clandestine than it is today. Prior to television, boys and girls were rarely seen together in public, even if they were known to be going out with one another on a regular basis. Even at community dances, couples arriving together would usually split up upon entering and sit with their respective age and sex groups, sometimes at opposite ends of the hall. Meetings with regular partners generally occurred late at night in the home of one of the individuals, where they would have a degree of privacy away from family and peers.

This tendency for covert dating was recorded in the following 1979 interview with a nineteen-year-old boy:

> During the course of our converstion, A.B. mentioned that he had to go off and visit his girlfriend. I commented that I didn't know that he had a girlfriend in the settlement, whereupon he responded that he had been going out with her for the past four years. This surprised me since I had known A.B. for over a year and had never seen him with a girl. When I inquired who she was, he insisted that I had to know the girl in question. Even though I claimed total ignorance, he refused to name her outright. I proceeded to name several girls whom I thought might be his girlfriend, but with no success. Since he still refused to name her outright, I pulled out my population survey of the settlement and began to name all the girls in the community who fell into the appropriate age group. After several minutes, the correct name came up, and my visitor confirmed my "guess."

After some dicussion, A.B. admitted that most dating in Holman was done in a covert fashion and that couples going out with one another avoided being seen in public together. He also observed that this was not necessarily the way it was done in other communities: when he was going to high school in Yellowknife, he would often go out in public with the girlfriend he had down there. His observations were summed up with the comment, "I guess it's just the way we do things here in Holman." Another factor not mentioned by A.B., which may account for the difference in dating behavior, is that neither he nor his girlfriend had parents in Yellowknife to encourage, however subtly, the young couple to establish a more permanent relationship.

During my second field visit (1982–1983), however, I observed significant changes in the dating behavior of teenagers. Boys and girls were frequently spotted together in public, sometimes holding hands or hugging. Young couples arriving at the community hall no longer split up to sit apart in same-sex groups, but often sat together by themselves or with other couples. When inquiring about these recent changes in courting practices, I was told by several informants that these changes had, in fact, occurred and were probably due to the recent introduction of southern television programming. Many of the most popular television programs among Holman adolescents are those dealing with teenagers and teenage problems. Of these, the most frequently viewed is a program about teenagers growing up in the 1950s called "Happy Days." In all probability, these new forms of dating and emotional expressiveness were acquired by watching and modeling these new forms of entertainment.

Another factor contributing to the change in adolescent courting behavior is the recent introduction of school trips to southern Canada. For a two-week period each year, Holman youngsters have the opportunity to live with a southern family and establish friendships with southern teenagers. As Holman teenagers receive increased exposure to southern styles of courtship, emotional expression, and friendship formation through both television and firsthand contact, they are more likely to conform to the southern model of adolescent behavior.

Another interesting observation is that these changes have not been without some, albeit minimal, impact upon the parental generation. Even many married couples are beginning to more openly express affection for their spouses. Not infrequently, middle-aged couples may be seen holding hands in public or kissing one another good-bye when one spouse goes off to work. None of these forms of emotional expression were observed among either adolescents or adults during the previous fieldwork period.

As would be expected in a community where adolescents have a great deal of sexual autonomy, premarital pregnancies are fairly common. While parents of young unwed mothers may mildly disapprove of early pregnancies, they tend to be extremely tolerant and accepting. Part of this tolerance is due to the adults' great pleasure in having infants around the house. The infants resulting from premarital pregancies are managed in a number of ways. The first is that the young mother may decided to take on the primary responsibility for child care, while obtaining occasional assistance from parents and siblings. Generally, only the more socially mature young mothers opt for this arrangement since having and caring for an infant places significant constraints upon the mother's social life. If, however, the young mother is unable or unwilling to take on the burden of child care, she may offer the child for adoption to her parents or to another household.

Theoretically, another response to premarital pregnancy is abortion. While available, albeit with some difficulty, abortion is not an option chosen by either pregnant teenagers or adults. Lack of information concerning the availability of this procedure may be one reason why there are no documented cases of abortion in the settlement. For adolescent girls, abortion is especially problematic since many do not seek medical attention or advice until the second or third trimester of their pregancies. Even so, it is unlikely that many young girls would choose to have an abortion since there are so many families within the community willing to adopt infants.

While there is no moral condemnation of premarital pregnancy, slight evidence suggests that if an unwed mother chooses to raise the child herself, her marriage prospects may be somewhat limited. For an older teenager girl, however, pregnancy often helps cement a relationship with a boy she has been seeing on a regular basis. Many teenage boys commented that they thought it was unwise for fifteen- and sixteen-year-old girls to have babies and keep them. A large number of these boys also pointed out that they would not want to marry a girl if it meant raising "someone else's kid." However, if the child is adopted by the grandparents or other relatives, the girl's marriage prospects remain unchanged.

The biological fathers of these premarital infants are not required to supply social, emotional, or economic support to either the mother or the infant. In many cases, the exact paternity of the child is unknown. Teenage boys and young unmarried men will sometimes speculate about the paternity of a particular child, but never in a way that is overtly condemning. Parents may disapprove if a young man who is known to be the genitor of a certain child refuses to acknowledge his parental responsibilities. Rarely, however, is any pressure applied on the individual boy to establish a permanent relationship with the girl and provide support for her and the newborn. Only in cases where a young man has fathered a number of children with different partners will adults make explicit and condemning comments about the young man's irresponsibility. In these cases, parents may tell their daughters to avoid going out with this particular boy.

As mentioned in the beginning of this chapter, interviews on sexual attitudes and behavior were frequently accompanied by nervous laughter and giggles, especially when the interviews were conducted in a formal manner. Contrary to popular beliefs concerning the lack of sexual inhibition among Inuit, adolescent boys and girls displayed a high degree of anxiety when discussing sexual matters. Whether this anxiety was unique to adolescents is difficult to say since no adults were interviewed in a formal fashion. There appears to be an inherent paradox in local sex patterns. While many adolescents are extremely shy and modest when questioned about sexual matters, there is nevertheless a high frequency of premarital sexual activity. A logical conclusion may be that adolescents are inhibited when questioned about all personal matters, whether sexual or nonsexual. The difficuties we encountered in gathering other kinds of personal data appear to substantiate such an assumption. In short, since Holman is a noninterventive and noninterrogative community, our young informants had rarely been exposed to such prying questions. Nervous giggles and laughter were one strategy for dealing with uncomfortable interview situations.

Despite these apparent inhibitions, sexual joking is a common phenomenon among both adolescents and adults. Just as other forms of joking and laughter are used to diffuse sensitive and potentially embarrassing social situations, so sexual joking may be a means of eleviating the anxiety associated with this mode of behavior. During interviews, we discovered that it was very easy to get people to talk about sex in a joking manner, but quite difficult to get them to talk seriously and personally about such matters. Even adults, who are normally inhibited when discussing any personal matters, make joking references to the sexual exploits of themselves and others.

On the surface the sexual activity of contemporary Holman adolescents appears very similar to that of the traditional period. Both the popular and scientific literature on the Inuit abounds with references to spouse exchange and general sexual promiscuity. The traditional Inuit practice of spouse exchange, for example, was functional since it provided a means for establishing alliances with members of unrelated families or groups. Nevertheless, reports of traditional sexual freedom can be misleading if not interpreted in an appropriate context. It is important to emphasize that extramarital arrangements were often in the form of socially legitimate exchanges, in which all parties involved gave their consent to such arrangements. Despite the disppearance of these ritualized exchanges, largely due to the influence of missionaries, extramarital sex continues to be fairly common, although it is now more likely to occur behind the backs of spouses. As one adult informant explained to me, sexual promiscuity was introduced from the South! Such an assertion may, in fact, be valid given the suppression of traditional and socially legitimate mechanisms of spouse exchange.

As for adolescent sexuality, concentration of the population into settlements with the consequent creation of large peer groups has lead to an increase in premarital sexual activity among teenagers. In the traditional period, adolescent sexual activity would have been significantly limited due to population dispersal and lack of nonrelated sexual partners. Another important factor in this increase has been the disappearance of arranged marriage at an early age, thereby prolonging the period of time during which sexually mature but as yet unmarried youths can experiment with different partners.

Although contraceptives are available at the nursing station, their use by adolescents is limited and seems to be confined primarily to older teenagers. This is partly due to the absence of any organized public health program to provide teenagers with birth control counseling or sex education, either at school or during nursing station clinics. As a result, many teenagers are ignorant of both birth control methods and reproductive physiology. Other obstacles to birth control lie in the methods available. Condoms are the only barrier method available in the settlement. Intrauterine devices and birth control pills are used more frequently, however, with limited success. During 1982, for example, at least six adult women and older teenage girls became pregnant with IUDs in place. Also, the irregular sleep-activity cycles that many people, especially teenagers, maintain in midsummer and midwinter make successful use of the pill difficult.

A small number of older adolescent boys and young men we interviewed claimed to use condoms when engaging in sexual intercourse. All obtained their condoms from the nursing station, which distributes these items at no charge. Not all sexually active males, however, take advantage of this service. Many simply cannot be bothered with birth control, while others are just too shy to request condoms from the nurse. Those who do go to the nursing station are extremely embarrassed and arrive with some imagined complaint, only to request "some of those things" when leaving.

Adolescent girls are less likely to request contraceptives or birth control counseling from the nurse. In fact, most adolescent girls and young women do not start using contraceptives at all until after their first pregnancy. The only adolescent girls using contraceptives during 1982–1983 were those who had been encouraged by their mothers to receive birth control counseling at the nursing station. Due to the modesty of our female adolescent informants, it was difficult to obtain any accurate information concerning the use of contraception. Data collected from medical files indicate that only five girls (ages fifteen to eighteen) had received counseling and contraceptives from the nursing station.

PAIR-BONDING AND MARRIAGE

Permanent pair-bonds are established in a casual and noneventful manner. In this respect, pair-bonding is an informal outgrowth of adolescent sexual "play." A young couple, having determined their mutual compatibility and affection, will start seeing one another on a frequent basis, thereby giving notice to family and friends that they will cease seeing other partners and will eventually set up a household with one another. Compatibility, more than romantic love, appears to be the most important variable in determining potential partners.

Young couples often go through a series of stages before submitting to a formal marriage ceremony, suggesting that there is no single ritual signifying the creation of a long-term commitment. The first stage is marked by either the boy or girl moving into the same bedroom as his or her partner. Household size and space availability often determine which partner will move. While these young couples have not yet submitted to a formal marriage ceremony, parents are usually delighted since such arrangements mean that their son or daughter is on the way to establishing a permanent pair-bond. Another factor accounting for such "bedroom pair-bonding" is that housing in Holman is scarce, requiring young couples to wait some time before a housing unit becomes available. One father of a fifteen-year-old girl was delighted when her boyfriend moved into her bedroom. The girl's younger sister, however, did not share her father's enthusiasm since she was required to move out of the bedroom and onto the living room couch. A few months later the father's enthusiasm turned to elation when he learned that his daughter had become pregnant.

While "bedroom pair-bonding" is clearly the first step to a lifelong commitment, the individuals involved recognize that these relationships are qualitatively different from marriage relationships. When one young man in such a relationship was asked if his bedroom mate was his "girlfriend" or "wife," he just shrugged his shoulders and said:

"I don't know what I would call her—I just call her Jamie." Perhaps such hesitation is a reflection of the transitional nature of these relationships. Nevertheless, all of these "bedroom romances" result in a permanent pair-bond and the creation of an independent household.

Not all pair-bonding in Holman entails the sharing of a bedroom during the initial stages. In some cases a couple will simply begin seeing one another on a regular basis, both in public and in their respective natal households. This will also entail one partner occasionally sleeping over in the other's bedroom with the parents' recognition and acceptance of the arrangement. At this point the young couple no longer attempts to hide their intimate relationship from parents and other adults; thus they make it known that they intend to establish a more permanent relationship.

In time, and when suitable housing becomes available, a young couple will set up an independent household. Often this may not occur until a child has resulted from the union. Of the fifteen new households created since my first census in 1978, almost half of the couples had children before moving into their new homes. For the first year or two, these new households take on a "satellite" quality, with the husband and wife spending large amounts of time visiting, working, and eating in their natal households. Gradually, as they purchase or are given more material household items, increasing amounts of time are spent in the new household. As in the pair-bonding process, the creation of independent households is a gradual process.

As previously mentioned, parents have much less control over their children's spouse selection than was true in the past. While some parents may try to encourage their children to choose certain partners, the ultimate decision rests with the child. Occasionally parents may express some distress over their offspring's selection of partner. More often than not, parents are simply pleased to see evidence of their children's settling down to a permanent relationship. Parents may also be uninformed about the intentions of a young couple going through the initial stages of pair-bonding. One father of a twenty-two-year-old son whose girlfriend had been living with the young man for over a year commented, "I don't know what they plan to do. . . . George doesn't discuss these things with me." As this statement suggests, the increase in adolescent autonomy, as well as the greater availability of prospective spouses due to population growth, has made it less essential for parents to be the primary arbiters of spouse selection. For this reason, pair-bonding in the contemporary period tends to be delayed until young

people themselves are willing and able to make such a lifelong commitment to another person. More than any other event, pair-bonding and
the creation of an independent household signal the individual's entry
into the adult world. At this crucial point in the life cycle, the young
couple is expected to dispense with the carefree behavior of youth and
take on the roles and responsibilities of their newly acquired adult
status.

■ 7
School, Work, and Aspirations

Prior to the introduction of formal schooling in Holman, children acquired all knowledge and skills through the observation of and interaction with parents and other adults. Not only did this method provide continuity in parent-child relationships, but it allowed children an opportunity to learn the skills necessary for survival in the arctic ecosystem. These skills were neither academic nor abstract, but ones that had visible importance and applicability. Learning always took place within the context of the immediate household unit, with parents serving as the primary instructional agents.

Perhaps one of the greatest changes to occur in Inuit communities throughout the Arctic has been the transfer of education from the household to federal and, ultimately, to territorial schools. Children who previously spent their days helping parents with hunting, trapping, fishing, skin preparation, and general household chores now spend much of the day in an institutional setting learning skills unrelated, and sometimes antithetical, to those emphasized at home. As a result, schools have become the primary acculturative agents in most modern Inuit settlements. Not surprisingly, the teenagers of Holman are the first age-group to be noticeably affected by the introduction of southern-style schooling, resulting in changes in behaviors, language, and aspirations.

SCHOOLING AND EDUCATION

Roman Catholic and Anglican missionaries introduced the first formal schooling to Inuit children in the 1930s and 1940s. The missionaries not only nurtured the Inuit's conversion to Christianity but also contributed to their secular education by operating day schools in community mission buildings as well as regional boarding schools. In Holman the Roman Catholic mission established a grade school in the mid-1950s, which operated up until 1962 when the federal day school was built. Parents of older children were also encouraged to send their children to a mission-operated secondary school located five hundred miles away in Aklavik. During the late 1940s and the 1950s, a small number of Holman schoolchildren were sent to these boarding schools. The emotional toll of residential schooling was often dramatic since many Inuit youngsters would be separated from their families for several years at a time (Hobart 1970). These schoolchildren were transported out of their small, kinship-based communities and placed in large, understaffed, and impersonal residential schools where all instruction was provided in English. After completing their schooling, many of these youngsters had difficulty readjusting to life in their home communities. In addition to being ill prepared for the kinds of physical privations awaiting them at home, a number of these residential students had trouble communicating with parents after spending several years in an environment that discouraged speaking Inuktitut (Hobart and Brandt 1966).

In 1962 the federal government, through the Department of Northern Affairs and National Resources, constructed the first classroom building in Holman. As was true of all northern federal schools at that time, the Holman school was staffed with white teachers from the South who by and large were provided with no special training to assist them in adapting to and providing instruction in isolated northern communities. The vast majority of the southern teachers were enticed into northern service with the promise of high salaries and partially subsidized living expenses. Teachers were provided with housing that was luxurious compared to the housing available to native residents. All this, the government reasoned, was necessary to attract the most qualified teachers to bring Eurocanadian education to the North. Despite highly lucrative salaries, many teachers, unable or unwilling to contend with the difficulties of living in an isolated community, returned south after one to three years of service. One of the unfortunate consequences of such high turnover was a notable lack of continuity within the educational structure.

The federal government handled northern education in Holman and other Inuit communities until 1970, when the territorial government took control of northern schools and educational services. The newly formed Territorial Department of Education instituted various programs to help train native teachers and classroom assistants, with the goal of producing sufficient numbers of highly trained native teachers to staff the schools in predominantly native communities. Most arctic schools, however, continue to be staffed predominantly by white teachers.

The Holman (or Uluhaktok) school is an unassuming complex of four separate buildings. The main building is the original double classroom shipped to Holman by barge in 1962. This unit houses a small library, the principal's office, and two classrooms. The second building is a combination workshop and kitchen, while the two remaining buildings are used as classrooms. Instruction at the Holman school is provided through grade 9. Because of limited space as well as the small size of the student body, teachers instruct two to three grade levels in each class. Students who have successfully completed grade 9 may continue their education at Sir John Franklin High School in Yellowknife. Students at Sir John Franklin live in a dormitory and return to Holman for summer and Christmas holidays.

The curriculum of the Holman school is based upon that of the province of Alberta. Much of the curriculum, however, is unsuited to the special needs and learning styles of Inuit children. Language arts concentrates almost exclusively upon the reading and writing of English, which is the primary language of instruction. School instruction in Inuktitut is provided by Inuit classroom assistants for a half hour each day for kindergarten through grade 3 and for an hour each day for grades 4 through 9.

The school staff consists of four white teachers from the South and two Inuit women who act as classroom assistants.[1] The classroom assistants work closely with the teachers, providing a wide range of essential services. They are especially useful in providing a degree of continuity and familiarity in a realm that is still considered somewhat foreign to most young children.

Unfortunately there are no special training programs for white teachers prior to their arrival in the settlement. Teachers receive no detailed orientation concerning the special problems they might encounter in remote arctic communities. Nor is there any opportunity for teachers to obtain facility in the native language. The net result, an unfortunate one, is that many new teachers arrive in the Arctic with limited training and encounter a host of adjustment problems that may take several years to sort out. While the teacher turnover rate is no longer as high as it was when schools were first introduced to the Arctic, many teachers leave their posts after only two to three years of service, just when they have learned enough about northern life to be effective instructors. For this reason, the services provided by the classroom assistants are even more crucial in ensuring the smooth operation of northern schools.

Community involvement in the Holman school has been encouraged through the creation of a local school committee. The Holman Education Committee is made up of elected members from the community, who meet periodically with the school principal. The committee acts primarily as an advisory body and has no power to implement changes in the structure or content of local education. The education committee receives a yearly budget from the territorial government, which it uses to hire local residents to teach subjects not a part of the school's standard curriculum.[2] Subjects in this category include Inuktitut language instruction, sewing, soapstone carving, and survival and hunting skills. Despite good intentions, few of these programs are effectively implemented. In 1979, for example, a local man was hired to teach Inuktitut to schoolchildren. His language program involved visiting the school two to three times a week and reading directly from an Inuktitut Bible. His visits occasioned great displeasure from the students, who were supposed to benefit from this cultural inclusion. As a result of the ineffectiveness of many cultural inclusion instructors, Holman residents are gradually losing their enthusiasm for these courses. A number of parents have even requested that their children be withdrawn from all cultural inclusion programs (Peter Murray, principal, personal communication).

One of the most prevalent problems in the Holman school is extremely poor or irregular attendance. As table 7.1 illustrates for the 1981–1982 school year, attendance for all grades was only 56.6 percent, with the lowest attendance rates characteristic of the upper grade levels (7 to 9). As children get older, they are much less likely to attend regularly. Some of the children in grades 6 through 9 may not attend at all but remain on the school register until they reach age six-

TABLE 7.1
Holman School Attendance, 1981–1982

CLASS LEVEL	% ATTENDANCE		
	MALE	FEMALE	TOTAL
7–9	33.3	50.6	42.8
	($n = 16$)	($n = 20$)	($n = 36$)
4–6	71.4	60.6	64.5
	($n = 11$)	($n = 19$)	($n = 30$)
1–3	55.6	64.6	61.2
	($n = 16$)	($n = 8$)	($n = 24$)
K	92.2	93.9	93.2
	($n = 2$)	($n = 2$)	($n = 4$)
All grades	53.1	58.4	56.6
	($n = 45$)	($n = 49$)	($n = 94$)
No. of students with 0% attendance	5	3	8

teen, the age at which schooling is no longer required (or, in the case of girls, until they become pregnant).

Females appear to be slightly better school attenders overall than males. This trend is more pronounced for the upper grades. As already mentioned, male dropouts spend much of their time "hanging out" around town, while female dropouts spend more time at home helping parents with baby-sitting and other household chores. The sex of the teacher also seems to affect the school attendance of postpubescent youngsters. During 1978–1980, when the teacher of grades 7 through 9 was male, the school attendance of teenage girls was quite low in comparison to teenage boys. When a female teacher took over these grades in 1981, however, the attendance of teenage girls increased dramatically while that of teenage boys went down.

Several factors account for the high dropout rate. As kids become teenagers, they are more likely to find other activities to occupy their time, including sports and hunting and trapping for boys, household chores for girls, wage employment, and just hanging out with peers. As students begin to fall further behind in school due to poor attendance or inadequate motivation, they are unable to successfully perform the work required of their grade level. It is not uncommon for students to be working two to four grade levels behind their assigned grades. For many, this frustration is ultimately manifested in their total abandonment of schooling.

Irregular attendance places an extra burden upon teachers, who are already teaching two or three grade levels in the same classroom. When an irregular attender who has fallen significantly behind decides to come to school on a particular day, the teacher must dedicate extra classroom time to assist the student in reorienting. Occasionally this is done grudgingly if the teacher knows that the student will not come to school again for several weeks or even months.

Discontinuity between the home and school environments also presents an obstacle to effective education. The school represents a foreign, "white," environment replete with books, audiovisual materials, and other items that are uncommon in most Inuit homes. Since the school is neither spatially nor cognitively integrated into the community, it is viewed as an outside, instrusive agent rather than as a vehicle for locally controlled or relevant education. Few parents adequately understand the educational process or the ultimate goals of the school. This may be partially attributed to the fact that most parents themselves received little or no schooling and therefore have no experience with this recently introduced acculturative agent. However, the gap between the home and the school is gradually being bridged as Holman households receive increased exposure to southern values, life-styles, and material objects through television, radio, newspapers, and magazines.

Because the school's role and function within the community are ambiguous, many parents are divided in their opinions of the school. Some perceive it as an intrusion that teaches their children more about the southern way of life than about traditional Inuit values and skills. Others have a more favorable opinion of schooling; they recognize the importance of their children learning fundamental skills that will allow them to succeed in the North's changing economy and culture.

Although some of the more acculturated parents actively encourage their children to attend school, few parents place a high value upon academic achievement in the school setting. Many adults do not see the positive impact of schooling upon their children's lives. They do recognize that school removes children from parental supervision for most of the day. In one respect, parents view this as advantageous since the school provides a useful day care service for children. Nevertheless, many parents are afraid that if their children leave Holman to attend high school in Yellowknife, they may find employment in some other community and never return home. These concerns seem more pronounced for daughters than sons, perhaps explaining why it is only very recently that adolescent females have been allowed to attend high school in Yellowknife.

Most of the youngsters interviewed, both formally and informally, asserted that they enjoyed school. This claim was made even by those who rarely attended school. Only a handful said they did not like school and found the work too hard or tedious. The assertion regarding the difficulty of school was understandably most pronounced for students in the higher grades, largely because they have had a longer period of time to fall behind in academic achievement. Most appeared to enjoy school because it provided relief from the boredom that so many Holman youngsters claimed to suffer. Enjoyment may also stem from the lack of anxiety over academic achievement. One of our informants, Emily Apsimik, claimed that she quit going to school when she was fifteen, but eventually returned on her own accord because there was nothing to do during the day. Despite this young girl's assertion, a large number of older nonattenders, especially boys, are able to occupy themselves with a variety of expressive activities, even though they also complain of boredom.

The problems inherent in the local school system were brought to public attention during the 1981 community meeting with the Northwest Territories Special Committee on Education.[3] During this meeting, which was attended by residents, teachers, and the regional superintendent of education, a number of grievances were registered against the school. Many parents complained that their children were doing much of the same work that they had done in previous years, despite having been promoted to higher grade levels. These parents believed that this was the reason children were not attending on a regular basis. A few of the teachers commented that such "repeat" work was necessary for many students since they had not yet mastered the work required of them in these earlier grades. Such complaints actually pinpoint one of the major problems of the education system. In the past, schoolchildren were automatically advanced to the next grade level even if they failed to complete successfully their present work requirements. This policy was followed because it was believed that many children would be discouraged from attending school if they were not promoted with their classmates. Thus, even though these children would not advance in the overall quality or difficulty of their schoolwork, they might at least continue to attend and perhaps improve, however slowly. The overall result of this policy was, and continues to be, that many students work at academic levels significantly below their present grade.

Until recently, automatic advancement has not posed too many problems except that the quality of education has been significantly diluted, at least by southern standards. However, with the recent increase in students wishing to attend high school in Yellowknife, the problems inherent in the automatic advancement system have become much more noticeable.[4] Few of the students who have completed grade 9 at the Holman school are functioning at an academic level commensurate with the demands they will meet in the more competitive high school environment. One ninth grade student in Holman, desiring to attend school in Yellowknife, took the high school entrance exam only to discover that he scored at a grade 4 competency level.

In an attempt to combat the negative effects of automatic advancement, the Department of Education has initiated a new policy in which grade promotion is contingent solely upon academic performance. This policy represents a departure from the Department of Education's previous open admissions policy in which students were accepted to attend high school regardless of academic credentials. This policy was followed for over a decade in order to make advanced schooling accessible to as many native students as possible. It is not surprising that so many of these students did poorly in high school and quit after just a few weeks or months. At present, however, with the increase in the number of young people wishing to attend high school, students are no longer accepted at Sir John Franklin without the written approval of the local school principal. In addition, prospective high school students must pass a set of entrance exams and demonstrate at least a grade 7 working level in English and mathematics. One of the consequences of this new policy is that large numbers of students are kept back a grade until they demonstrate a mastery of the skills required for successful advancement. While this new policy has met with some disgruntlement from students and parents, the principal in Holman believes it is more constructive to set standards for academic advancement that will ultimately have a positive impact upon the quality of local education. The only alternative is that students continue to work at substandard academic levels while assuming that they are successfully advancing within the school system. The principal hopes that this new policy will provide potential high school students with the skills necessary for successfully finishing their high school careers (Peter Murray, personal communication).

Despite the territorial government's attempts to improve academic performance on the local level and make high schooling more accessible to Inuit students, few successfully complete the three-year program of study. By the winter of 1982, only one Holman youth had persisted through the entire three-year period to receive a high school certificate.[5] The stress of being in a strange environment, separated from family and friends, has been a primary factor in the failure of other students to complete high school.[6]

The experience of David Ageok (age eighteen) is fairly typical of these high school students. While attending school in Holman, David was an excellent student whose attendance was exemplary in comparison to his classmates. After successfully completing grade 9 in 1980, David went off to Sir John Franklin in the fall. Despite his recognized academic abilities, he quit after the first month and returned home. He returned to Yellowknife in January of 1981 but quit again in March. After spending the next spring and summer in Holman, David once again returned to Yellowknife in August and finished the entire school year.

David reports that he enjoys going to high school, but does not like being separated from his family and friends for long periods of time. He especially dislikes living at Akaitcho Hall (the school dormitory) since he reports the food is awful and life made unpleasant by an abundance of rules and regulations. The latter complaint is not surprising, given the relatively high degree of autonomy afforded young people back in the settlement. Social adjustment to a highly regimented lifestyle in high school is further exacerbated by being thrust into a foreign social environment bereft of the social and emotional support of family and friends.

Now that David has successfully completed his first year in high school (the interview with him was conducted during the summer after his first full year), he is committed to completing the two years remaining in his high school education. While David's parents provide him with both emotional and financial support, he claims that he is going to school because *he* wants to and not because he is being forced by his parents.

David and the three other Holman students attending high school in the fall of 1981 reflect a changing attitude toward the benefits of education. Since fewer and fewer of them aspire to be hunters and trappers, these young people believe that advanced schooling will provide access to highly skilled and better paying jobs than would otherwise be available to them. Due to the limited number of such skilled jobs in the community, however, few of these young people will actually obtain such sought-after positions. Unless they are willing to relocate to larger northern communities, many of these educated youngsters may eventually find themselves either unemployed or employed at low-paying and unskilled occupations.

In response to the hypothetical question "What would happen if there was no school in Holman?" David responded in the following manner:

> It's gonna be a drag. Kids won't be able to get an education to get jobs. White people are gonna come up and start running the town. We're gonna be bumming around. Gonna be a hard life. Gonna be dumb. Not going to be supporting our parents in the future.

Clearly David had not succumbed to a romantic notion that somehow life in Holman would be better if people returned to the old way of life, that is, life before the community and the local school had been established. David and many others interviewed realized that the North is changing rapidly and that the young people of Holman must be well educated in order to deal with imminent economic and political changes. This view is encouraged by the school and by many other acculturative agents both within and outside of the community.

Students attending high school in Yellowknife must contend with other temptations that affect their academic performance. Paramount among these are drug and alcohol abuse. Almost all of the high school students interviewed commented that they drink more alcohol when they are attending school in Yellowknife than when they are in Holman. One twenty-year-old not included in the adolescent sample stated that he first started drinking when attending Sir John Franklin because other students were doing it.

Alcohol and drug abuse among high school students is due partly to the relative ease of purchasing alcohol in Yellowknife. This stands in contrast to Holman, where there are no retail liquor outlets and all alcoholic beverages must be ordered by air freight from Yellowknife. In the substantially larger territorial capital of Yellowknife (population 10,000) it is a simple matter for underage drinkers to find an adult or older student willing to purchase beer or liquor on their behalf. In addition, Holman students occasionally come under undesirable peer pressure to drink more than they normally would. While all alcoholic beverages are prohibited at Akaitcho Hall, students are able to smuggle drugs and liquor into their rooms. At other times they are simply invited to drinking parties that take place off school grounds.

This kind of undesirable influence is precisely what parents fear when their children leave home to attend high school. One Holman student caught drinking by his dormitory supervisors was forced to call his parents to explain his behavior. While his parents were upset with him, they did not scold or punish him. Rather, they simply told him to return home.

Parental concerns over what happens to their children while away in Yellowknife are also reflected in the reticence of many parents to send their daughters to high school. Until 1984 only one girl from Holman was allowed to enroll in Sir John Franklin. While there, however, this girl apparently "fell" under the wrong influences, quit school, and never returned home. Because of this girl's experience, parents have expressed fears that the same might happen to their daughters.

In the fall of 1984, however, the trend of sending only male students to high school was dramatically reversed. Largely due to the encouragement of the female teacher of the upper grades at the Holman school, eight girls left Holman to attend Sir John Franklin. This high enrollment rate for girls may be the first sign of changing parental attitudes toward advanced education for their daughters. Whether or not Holman parents continue to allow their daughters to leave Holman for high schooling will depend upon the academic performance of these students and whether or not they are able to pursue their studies without encountering the same alcohol and drug problems of their male counterparts.

In addition to the high school in Yellowknife, the Department of Education offers various vocational training courses at the Vocational Training Institute (Thebacha College) at Fort Smith. Training programs in such trades as carpentry, welding, mechanics, and heavy-duty equipment operation are offered to qualified individuals over eighteen years of age. The education requirements for prospective students vary according to the program one desires to enter. For many, successful completion of grade 6 is required, while other more demanding training programs require either grade 9 or a high school diploma. Because of the availability of vocational training, many adolescent males and females have opted to quit school after grade 8 or 9 and hang out for one to three years with the intention of eventually enrolling in a vocational training program at Fort Smith. While a number of vocational school graduates will be able to obtain jobs in Holman, the vast majority will be able to apply their skills only in larger communities. Since few Holman residents, adolescents included, expressed a desire to live anywhere other than Holman, such nonlocal employment must take the form of seasonal labor.

ADOLESCENTS AND WORK

In a community as small and isolated as Holman, one of the major problems for both adolescents and adults is the lack of wage-employment opportunities. In the recent past families could live comfortably by hunting, carving and sewing for the co-op, and selling sealskins and fox pelts. While Holman residents have attained unprecedented opulence, the dramatic escalation in prices of southern manufactured goods has made it increasingly difficult for many to obtain these highly desired objects. Items such as snowmobiles, rifles, ammunition, camping equipment, televisions, radios, and washing machines can cost 25 to 75 percent more in Holman than in the South. Perhaps more important, exposure to southern life-styles and material standards of living through television, radio, and schooling have increased local expectations of object wealth. A family that was once content with a government-subsidized home and a working snowmobile now desires as many modern conveniences and recreational diversions as possible. These expectations have been raised at a time when, due to natural population increase, the settlement labor force is vastly exceeding local employment prospects. An alternative for many older adolescents and young adults is to seek temporary employment outside the community in the industrial sector. The largest employer in the industrial sector is Canmar (Canadian Marine Drilling Ltd.), which has been exploring for oil in the Beaufort Sea since the early 1970s. Canmar has been active in hiring and training native workers for skilled and semiskilled jobs on drilling platforms and supply ships. Work cycles are arranged in such a way that native employees may return to their home communities after a work shift for a period of rest and relaxation.

Since 1976 approximately fifteen Holman residents, mostly male, have taken advantage of these high-paying employment opportunities. The majority have been older adolescents and young adults. Since the drilling season is limited to the period of open water, Canmar employees may work from late spring to late fall, allowing them to spend the rest of the year back home. Individuals who work through most or all of the drilling season make enough money to support themselves and their families through an entire year. During the 1979–1980 season, one young man grossed $6,700 in just a six week period. Despite high salaries and other benefits, few local residents are able or willing to be separated from their families for such long periods of time.

The adolescent boy or girl who has recently dropped out of or graduated from the local school has extremely limited job prospects. Available work tends to be temporary, often requiring a large number of able bodies for a short period of time. During the late summer and early fall there is an increase in temporary wage employment, which includes road repair, housing construction, and other community rennovation projects. Most of these jobs go to older teenagers and young adults with the necessary skills and previous experience. Employment for younger adolescents is limited to short-term and unskilled projects such as unloading the barge and helping with the community beach cleanup. Permanent, full-time jobs are few. The Hudson's Bay Company usually employs two older teenage boys to work as stock clerks. By far the single largest employer of young people in Holman is the co-op craft shop, which hires older girls (age seventeen and over) to help with silk-screening, sewing, and packing arts and crafts items for export.

Frequently adolescent boys may decide not to attend high school or to delay their entry for several years. During this period they may alternate their activities between hanging out, casual employment when available, and hunting and trapping with their fathers. The length of this transitional period varies significantly, depending upon the individual involved, and may last anywhere from several months to several years. Since Holman is very much a self-pacing culture, little parental pressure is placed upon these youngsters to find employment or to continue their formal education by going to high school in Yellowknife or enrolling in a vocational training program at Fort Smith. Of all the adolescents interviewed, only one boy indicated that his parents encouraged him to seek employment. Since 1981 this nineteen-year-old boy has been working as a stock clerk at the Bay; his parents are proud that he is working and not "hanging out" like many of his age-mates. In fact, most of his earnings are used to purchase food and other items for the entire family.

In many respects the work prospects of young girls are less problematic. Since girls, more than boys, have been socialized from an early age to assist with household chores, the end of formal schooling does not necessarily result in a transitional period of idleness. Many of these girls begin to take a more active role in household management and child care. Their contribution to the household economy is even more crucial if their mothers and older sisters work outside the home. These girls also have more prospects for wage earning, either working at the craft shop or sewing at home. Thus teenage girls hang out considerably less than do teenage boys, presumably because they are occupied with either wage employment or household chores.

Not surprisingly, girls who are engaged in wage employment contribute a larger proportion of their earnings to the household than do boys. Cash is used primarily for food, but may also be used for clothing, hardware, snowmobile parts, gasoline, oil, and other hunting supplies. Few, if any, families have a household budget whereby the earnings of specific household members are allocated to cover specific expenses. Generally, cash earnings are spent on whatever expenses come up at a particular time. Teenage boys, with a few exceptions, are less likely to contribute their earnings to the family coffers. Given the adolescent male obsession with snowmobiles, motorcycles, and hockey equipment, most of their earnings are expended on personal material possessions.

There is no doubt that adolescent boys represent a more significant drain on household resources than adolescent girls. According to one twenty-one-year-old female informant, the socialization of responsibility is much more effective with girls than with boys; this is the major reason grandparents prefer to adopt granddaughters over grandsons. This same young woman expressed some disapproval of her younger nineteen-year-old brother, who contributed very little to the household but who expended her own earnings to maintain his own snowmobile and motorcycle.

ASPIRATIONS

During adolescence, aspirations for future vocations, material wealth, and social position are often unfettered by the kinds of pragmatic constraints that affect adults. What adolescent in our own society has not aspired to be a brain surgeon, lawyer, senator, president, or millionaire?

Before the impact of Eurocanadian culture upon the residents of Holman, young people were not faced with the kinds of choices contemporary teenagers must face. A young man would aspire to be a good hunter with a hardworking wife and healthy children. He would seek to be respected as a wise and knowledgeable member of the community. Nevertheless, the number of alternatives available to him would be limited. He was expected to be a hunter and a provider for his family. Beyond this, however, no other opportunities were possible.

This scenario stands in marked contrast to the myriad choices now available to Inuit adolescents. Political, economic, and educational developments have opened up a plethora of alternatives that were nonexistent when the parental generation came of age. Such choices include attending high school, receiving occupational training, working in local and regional politics, deciding where to live, and so on. In this respect, Holman teenagers are gradually becoming more like adolescents in the South for whom making future life plans assumes critical importance even before the completion of high school.

When Holman adolescents were interviewed regarding their aspirations, they were questioned about a host of future alternatives, including future occupations, marriage plans, residence preferences, and possible involvement in local and regional political organizations. The following interview was conducted with eighteen-year-old David Ageok:

■ R.C.: *What are your future plans?*
DAVID: *After finishing school, I would like to be a mechanic working on trucks and diesel engines. I'll probably get the training at Fort Smith.*
R.C.: *Where would you like to live?*
DAVID: *Right here in Holman. I'd like to try to get a good job here and not have too many whites in town. It would be good if we could work for ourselves.*
R.C.: *Would you ever like to live someplace else?*
DAVID: *I've never thought about living anyplace else. I want to live where I know all the people.*
R.C.: *Have you thought about when you would like to marry?*
DAVID: *I don't know. I guess I'd like to marry in my early twenties.*
R.C.: *Is there anybody who you are interested in marrying?*

DAVID: *There's nobody in town that I'm interested in. I'll probably marry an outsider. I had a girl-friend from Coppermine when I was in Yellowknife, but I'm not seeing her anymore.*
R.C.: *How many kids would you like to have?*
DAVID: *I want just one, but I'll probably have more. Maybe about three. I can make them work around the house.*
R.C.: *What kinds of qualities would you want your wife to have?*
DAVID: *I don't know. I've never thought about it. I'm not going to make her work—just make her work around the house. That's all.*
R.C.: *What about personality?*
DAVID: *Nice, kind, soft-hearted, not lazy.*
R.C.: *When you get married, would you like to live with your parents a while or get your own house?*
DAVID: *Like to get my own house right away—for privacy.*
R.C.: *Is there anything else you would like to do in town, like be on the settlement council or the hunters and trappers association?*
DAVID: *I'd like to be on the education committee—to be caring about how students are taught.*
R.C.: *Do you think your chances are good for attaining all these things?*
DAVID: *If I graduate? I don't know. Hard to say.*
R.C.: *Would this be the best of all possible worlds?*
DAVID: *Yes.*

The almost dizzying pace of social change in the community is partially reflected in teenagers' choices of future occupations. Youngsters are well aware that the world they will occupy as adults is significantly different from that of their parents and that it is no longer feasible to earn a livelihood exclusively as a hunter, trapper, or carver. Table 7.2 lists the occupational preferences of twenty teenage boys and twenty-one teenage girls, some of whom listed two or three possible alternatives.

As the table shows, teenage boys were much more likely to be attracted by highly skilled occupations requiring either high school or vocational training. Youngsters choosing jobs such as welder, electrician, and mechanic indicated that they would go off to the vocational school at Fort Smith to get the required training. One fairly sophisticated youngster stated that he wanted to work as a resource development officer advising various corporations engaged in mineral and hydrocarbon development in the North. While this may appear to be somewhat unusual occupational preference, this boy's uncle is engaged in such work in the neighboring community of Inuvik.

TABLE 7.2
Occupational Aspirations of Holman Adolescents

OCCUPATION	BOYS (n = 20)	GIRLS (n = 21)
Carpenter	3	0
Mechanic	4	0
Heavy-equipment operator	1	0
Electrician	1	0
Dental therapist	1	0
Teacher	1	0
Welder	3	0
Hockey player	1	0
Nurse	0	3
Bay clerk/cashier	0	4
Co-op worker	1	5
Stewardess	0	1
Hairdresser	0	1
Resource development	1	0
Songwriter	1	0
Hunter/trapper	3	0
"Some job"	1	1
"Don't know"	3	8

NOTE: List includes second and third choices when given.

Turning to the teenage girls, significantly fewer had any definite occupational aspirations. Eight of the twenty-one girls stated that they had no idea what they wanted to do in the future. The majority who did have a preference selected realistic occupations such as co-op worker or Bay clerk/cashier. Unlike most of the boys, who chose occupations requiring some kind of advanced training, only five girls chose similarly highly skilled vocations: three chose nurse, one hairdresser, and one stewardess.

The sexual disparity in occupational choice may be a function of a number of factors. For one, females have access to more employment opportunities within the community that do not require any advanced schooling or vocational training. In this respect the co-op provides a valuable source of employment for a large number of women and older adolescent girls. For males, on the other hand, there is a marked dearth of jobs, so these youngsters understandably direct their occupational aspirations to skilled jobs such as welding, carpentry, mechanics, and electrical work. Another determining factor may be that it has only recently become acceptable for teenage girls to leave Holman for high school or vocational training. As more and more girls leave Holman to attend high school in Yellowknife, one may expect a gradual change in the occupational preferences of girls.

TABLE 7.3
Future Living Preferences of Holman Adolescents

LOCATION	BOYS	GIRLS
Holman	18	11
Coppermine	0	1
Yellowknife	0	2
Edmonton	1	0
"The South"	0	1
"Don't know"	0	1

When these same youngsters were asked where they would like to live when older, the overwhelming majority stated that they preferred to continue living in Holman. As table 7.3 indicates, only one boy and four girls declared that they would want to move elsewhere when older. The remaining twenty-nine youngsters asserted a clear preference for remaining in the community where they were born and raised.

This uniform preference for remaining in Holman may appear surprising given the adolescent tendency to complain about the boredom and restrictiveness of social life in an isolated community when compared to the larger urban centers of Yellowknife and Edmonton. Nevertheless, the fact that Holman is a comfortable, secure, and kin-oriented community is not lost on these adolescent boys and girls, who realize that life on the outside, while exciting, can be very stressful and lonely. In the words of Johnny Apiuk:

> I would eventually like to go to vocational school at Fort Smith and learn to become a carpenter, then find a good job and live in Holman the rest of my life because it's a nice place to live, it's small, and there's plenty of room to travel in.

While there are now numerous opportunities for advanced education and vocational training, the lack of employment opportunities within the community will severely hamper the realization of the occupational aspirations for many youngsters. While a few may be fortunate to secure good-paying and highly skilled positions in Holman, many will be forced to take up full- or part-time residence in other communities in order to utilize the skills they have acquired. It is also conceivable that many will prefer to take low paying jobs or accept social assistance in order to remain in the community where they were born and raised and within which their entire social world revolves.

■ 8
Rebellion and Deviance in Adolescence

When I was going to school in Yellowknife, [I used to drink] about
once or twice a week. I don't drink all that much here in town.
When I do drink, it's just enough so I feel good. I don't want to get
drunk since I might get caught by my parents.

(Johnny, eighteen years old)

A discussion of adolescence in any culture would be incomplete
without an examination of the rebellion and deviance that often accompany this critical life stage. As the adolescent exerts more control
over his or her own thoughts and actions, he or she starts experiment-
ing with a wide range of behaviors, attitudes, and life-styles. Driven
by new physical and emotional needs, the adolescent may test the
boundaries of social expectation as defined by the adult world. In
American society, experimentation may take the form of distinctive
clothing styles, staying out late at night, involvement in drugs and alcohol, loud and raucous behavior in public, occasional acts of juvenile de-
liquency, and other activities by which young people deny parental authority. A peculiar ambivalence often permeates adolescence: teenagers
may alternate between the denial of adult authority and the imitation
of adult behavior. Even when imitating adult behavior, adolescents frequently reject the social responsibility that is a requirement of the
adult stage of life.

In some respects, adolescence is the ideal time for the expression of inappropriate impulses. Since adolescence is viewed in many cultures as a transitional phase of life, the repercussions of nonconformity are significantly fewer for adolescents than for adults. In many societies a troublesome teenager is tolerated much more than a troublesome adult becaue the former is viewed as potentially outgrowing his or her errant ways.

Just as each society defines socially acceptable behavior among adults, so also a culture specifies what types of deviance or rebellion, if any, are a normal and perhaps necessary phase of social development. Such behaviors are viewed as activities that all young people must experience before resigning themselves to the conformity of the adult world. In Holman, adolescent experimentation with the domain of social convention may range from relatively minor forms of rebellion (including alcohol and drug use, staying up late at night, noisy and raucous behavior in public, distinctive clothing and hair styles, and truancy from school) to more extreme forms of deviance and criminality that are condemned by parents and adolescents alike (including alcohol and drug addiction, juvenile delinquency, and other socially disruptive or self-destructive behaviors).

Minor acts of rebellion are a logical consequence of the high degree of autonomy that accompanies adolescence and later childhood. Since Holman parents place few demands and restrictions upon their offspring, young people are free to behave in ways distinct from parents (e.g., staying up all night, driving around in snowmobiles, hanging out at the Bay or coffee shop, and engaging in other nonproductive activities). While parents may mildly disapprove, these activities are tolerated as a normal part of teenage existence. In their wisdom and patience, parents realize that their teenage children will eventually outgrow such behaviors on their own accord without parental interference. It is perhaps due to this understanding and tolerance that teenagers rarely strike back at parental restrictions through rebellious or asocial behavior. None of our teenage informants suggested that they engaged in any activities with the specific intent of defying parental wishes. Rather, these activities naturally develop within the context of peer group interaction and play. Nevertheless, there are instances in which adolescents engage in activities that are condemned or highly disapproved of by parents. Alcohol use, petty theft, vandalism, and breaking and entering are all activities occasionally perpetrated by adolescents that require some kind of response from parents or law enforcement agents. In the vast majority of cases, these are minor infractions initiated by youngsters bored with the normal routine of settlement existence. In other instances, such as suicide and substance abuse, the potentially self- and other-destructive behavior of the adolescent is condemned by young and old alike.

ALCOHOL AND DRUG USE

Alcohol abuse is rapidly becoming one of the major social problems in Holman and other communities in the Northwest Territories. Not only do violations of the Territorial Liquor Ordinance account for an unusually large proportion of law violations in most northern communities, but alcohol abuse is frequently implicated in other categories of crime, including homicide, assaults, sex offenses, willful damage, theft, and breaking and entering.[1]

The negative impact of increased alcohol use has not been lost on the residents of Holman. There is uniform consensus among adolescents and adults that drinking has increased substantially since the late 1970s. While there has been an overall increase in alcohol-related violence and law violations, there have been no alcohol-related homicides or accidental deaths. By and large, however, the resulting alcohol abuse has been more of a problem among the adults in the community rather than the adolescents. This is largely due to the difficulty young people have in obtaining alcoholic beverages.

Alcohol consumption among teenagers is best understood in the context of similar behavior in the parental generation. Alcohol use among Holman adults follows a distinct pattern that is similar to drinking behavior in other isolated Inuit communities. Since alcohol is a relatively scarce commodity, it is, more often than not, consumed immediately upon receipt. The predominant characteristic of drinking behavior is the conspicuous absence of any form of moderation. Regardless of the amount of alcohol purchased by any individual or group of individuals, it is usually consumed the day it is received. The pattern is not to drink socially until "high" or drunk and then stop, but to drink until the alcohol is completely gone or, alternately, until most people have passed out. The term *passed out* is frequently used to describe the physical state of many people who are drinking on any one night. This lack of moderation in alcohol consumption is similar to that described for meat consumption in the traditional period when people would gorge themselves in times of plenty. The feast or famine outlook that pervaded traditional subsistence efforts has been transferred to contemporary drinking patterns. One of our adult informants, for example, commented that he always drank in moderation while living in Inuvik, where there is easy and inexpensive access to alcohol, but he often drinks in excess in Holman when liquor is available.

Holman teenagers rarely consume alcohol to the extent of many adults, and probably teenagers consume significantly less than they would if alcohol were more readily available. As already mentioned, teenage boys are much more likely to drink when they are attending high school in Yellowknife, as a result of peer pressure, the greater availability of alcoholic beverages, and the absence of parental surveillance. Nevertheless, adolescents occasionally obtain and consume liquor in the community. Liquor is usually obtained from an older sibling or relative who is willing to purchase alcohol on the behalf of minors. Older teenagers may also attend the drinking parties given by young adults, who display little concern about providing liquor to minors. One older boy confided that he was in the habit of taking bottles of liquor from his parents when they themselves were drinking and in no condition to keep track of their liquor supply.

Like the parental generation, which is made up of both total abstainers and heavy drinkers, teenagers exhibit a wide range of attitudes regarding the use and abuse of alcohol. Younger teenagers, especially females, tend to condemn alcohol use more than older teenagers, who will often imbibe whenever the opportunity arises. Our female informants of all ages reported less interest or involvement in drinking than our male informants, although a small number of older girls are known to be frequent users. A similar sex distinction is found in the parental generation, where males are more frequent users and abusers of alcohol. As with the sexuality interviews, girls were less open about their involvement with alcohol. Our interviews with boys between the ages of sixteen and twenty provided the most revealing self-reports regarding drinking attitudes and behaviors. The following interview with eighteen-year-old David Ageok was fairly typical of the kinds of attitudes expressed by older teenage boys regarding drinking behavior:

▪ R.C.: *Have you ever consumed alcohol?*
DAVID: *Yes. The first time was in 1981 when I was seventeen years old. When I was down in Yellowknife going to school. We were*

walking around drinking from a 12-ounce mickey bottle. I got a little high.

R.C.: *When was the last time you drank?*

DAVID: *About two weeks ago at Peter's place. [Peter is a close friend and another Holman youngster attending high school in Yellowknife.] He brought back a bottle with him from Yellowknife. Allen, George, James, Rosie, and I were all there drinking. Peter's sister was there too, but not drinking. She hardly ever drinks.*

R.C.: *About how often do you drink?*

DAVID: *I hardly drink at all. About twenty times a year.*

R.C.: *What do you think of people who drink a lot?*

DAVID: *Alcoholics.*

R.C.: *Are there any people who you don't like to drink with?*

DAVID: *I only drink with my friends.*

R.C.: *What does a drunk person act like?*

DAVID: *They act stupid. They try to fight for no reason, they beat up on people, try to kill themselves. I haven't done any of that stuff.*

▪ R.C.: *Are you afraid of those kinds of people?*

DAVID: *Just a little bit. I've never had any problems with drunks.*

R.C.: *Have you ever gotten into trouble for drinking?*

DAVID: *No. I was caught once in Yellowknife for drinking. They grounded me for a week. It went by really fast.*

R.C.: *Did they tell your parents?*

DAVID: *I had to call home and tell my parents. They got a little mad and told me not to do it again.*

R.C.: *Do your parents know or approve of your drinking?*

DAVID: *They don't know about my drinking. It's all up to me. They would probably get mad at my getting drunk, but not just at my drinking.*

R.C.: *Have you ever gotten so drunk that you passed out or couldn't remember what you had done?*

DAVID: *Never.*

R.C.: *Do your parents drink?*

DAVID: *Yes, but not much.*

R.C.: *Does their drinking bother you?*

DAVID: *No. It only worries me a little bit.*

R.C.: *Would it bother you if your parents drank all the time?*

DAVID: *Yes it would bother me.*

R.C.: *Have you ever gotten drunk just by yourself?*

DAVID: *No.*

R.C.: *Would you like to drink more or less than you do now?*
DAVID: *Would like to drink less.*
R.C.: *Why do you drink at all?*
DAVID: *Just to have a little fun.*
R.C.: *Do you like the taste of alcohol?*
DAVID: *Not really.*
R.C.: *What kind of sensation do you get when drinking?*
DAVID: *I have a good feeling, get more talkative, talk about the past, about what we used to do.*
R.C.: *Are you more likely to chase girls when you are drunk?*
DAVID: *No, not me. A lot of boys do that though.*
R.C.: *Where do you usually drink when you are here in town?*
DAVID: *I usually drink at a friend's place. Next week I might have a party at my place since my parents are going out camping. I don't know. I haven't decided yet.*
R.C.: *Do you ever drink with any of your brothers?*
DAVID: *I've drunk a little with Walter. The first weekend I was back from Yellowknife, I had a little party with him at his place. When I was still in Yellowknife, I had Peter buy me a bottle to give to him.*
R.C.: *Why did you take your first drink?*
DAVID: *Everybody was doing it.*
R.C.: *What effect has drinking had on your life?*
DAVID: *None at all.*

During the course of this interview, David commented that he "didn't know why white people brought alcohol up to the Arctic." He was of the opinion that it was having a bad influence upon the community and that some people were simply drinking too much.

Nevertheless, David and other informants believed that drinking is acceptable as long as it does not result in drunkenness. Drunks were invariably described as foolish, stupid, childlike, and belligerent. Despite this assessment of drunken behavior, young people become extremely intoxicated when the opportunity arises, thus conforming to the same pattern of "binge" drinking as many adults.

Transient whites, especially, exercise a negative influence upon the community in general and the adolescents in particular. These include Bay clerks and construction workers who often ply residents with alcohol in an attempt to make friends by "showing them a good time." During 1982 a group of white construction workers spent several months in Holman working on the new nursing station. Many of them brought large supplies of alcohol and marijuana which were sold to local residents. Community ire was eventually raised when it was discovered that some of these workers were giving alcohol and marijuana to kids and teenagers. These individuals were eventually removed from the work crew and returned south.

Most parents express disapproval of teenage drinking. This is true for both drinking and nondrinking parents. As would be expected, parents are more likely to tolerate drinking by older sons and daughters than by younger offspring. Adolescents, regardless of age, are cognizant of this disapproval and try to hide their drinking from their parents.

The majority of younger teenagers who were interviewed expressed greater disapproval of drinking than did the older teenagers. A few admitted they had tasted alcohol but had not liked it. Disapproval of alcohol consumption appeared most pronounced for those young people whose parents were heavy users of alcohol. One thirteen-year-old girl commented that she wished her parents would not drink so much since she is afraid of them, especially her father, when they are intoxicated. This young girl's concerns are readily understandable since her father periodically beats her mother when he is drunk.

Holman teenagers have also used other substances to get high or dizzy. During the summer of 1978, gasoline sniffing spread among the younger teenagers of the community. When informed of these activities, the nurse and teachers embarked upon an educational campaign to inform youngsters of the potential health hazards of such activities; several months later gasoline sniffing gradually subsided and disappeared. Nevertheless, a few teenage informants commented that some individuals still occasionally sniff gasoline or drink perfume.

Among a few older teenagers and young adults, marijuana use is on the increase. Until very recently, however, marijuana was unavailable in Holman. Users of this drug now report buying it from transients who come through the community or from high school students returning from Yellowknife. As with alcohol, many older boys and young adults reported that they received their first exposure to drugs while attending high school in Yellowknife. Others, who have not attended high school outside the community, received their initiation from these returning students. Many of our informants stated that they liked "smoking dope" because it was easier to hide from their parents than alcohol and that they would probably smoke more if the drug were more readily available.

While a few young people drink to excess, none could be labeled chronic alcohol abusers. Whether moderation will continue as adolescents mature into adults is another matter. As adults, these youngsters will find it easier to purchase alcohol and may become more heavily involved in its use. In addition, the alcohol abuse of some members of the parental generation may simply provide a model encouraging increased use and abuse of alcohol on the part of these maturing individuals.

CRIME AND JUVENILE DELINQUENCY

Because of its small size and isolation, Holman has a reputation for being a relatively peaceful and law-abiding community. Part of this reputation is due to the absence of a permanent Royal Canadian Mounted Police (RCMP) detachment in the settlement, thus encouraging local resolution of civil disputes and criminal violations. At present Holman is policed by the Holman/Coppermine Detachment based in Coppermine. Since there is no resident RCMP officer on permanent duty in Holman, officers from Coppermine make periodic trips to Holman. These visits are ideally spaced two to three weeks apart, but are actually less frequent due to the more demanding work load in Coppermine.[2]

Court proceedings for all civil and criminal law violations are normally held at the community hall. The judiciary of the Northwest Territories is composed of three different levels: justice of the peace court, magistrate's court, and the supreme court of the N.W.T. Justice of the peace court, which handles minor law violations, is presided over by a local Inuk who has been formally trained and certified as a justice of the peace. This court is convened whenever there is a sufficient number of cases to be heard. More severe criminal and civil cases are handled by either magistrate's court or the supreme court of the N.W.T. All cases involving juveniles are generally handled by magistrate's court. As an indication of the overall peacefulness of the community in comparison to other northern settlements, no court sessions were held in Holman during all of 1982.

RCMP and court records involving the law violations of minors (age sixteen and under) are not available for public scruntiny. In addition, court proceedings involving cases of juvenile delinquency are closed to everyone except parents, close relatives, and witnesses. As a result, accurate data concerning such violations must be limited to the self-reports of the juveniles, the reports of others, or the observation of law violations.

Most law violations involving minors include breaking and entering, theft under two hundred dollars, vandalism, and possession of alcohol. Alcohol-induced assaults, a fairly common violation for young adults, are very rare for juveniles. Given the isolation of the community, the lack of recreational facilities, and the minimal amount of parental supervision of young people, it is not terribly surprising that a few teenagers get into varying degrees of mischief. In the vast majority of cases, either the mischief goes unreported or the perpetrators are not caught. By and large, there is an attempt to resolve cases of juvenile delinquency on a local level without the intervention of external law enforcement agents.

During our 1982–1983 fieldwork period, only one juvenile case appeared before magistrate's court. The case involved a fifteen-year-old boy from Holman (Tommy) and two friends who were visiting from Coppermine. One evening in July 1982, Tommy and his two friends broke into several buildings owned by the Holman Eskimo Cooperative and stole an undisclosed sum of money. These buildings included the post office, the hotel office, and the print shop. Later testimony indicated that one of the Coppermine youths was the instigator of this incident. While in one of the buildings, the youngsters took photographs of themselves with a stolen polaroid camera. The following day the three boys went on a buying spree at the Bay store, making themselves prime suspects for the break-ins. They also left their photographs lying around where others could see them. As a result of this carelessness, they were immediately apprehended. The two Coppermine boys were sent home while Tommy appeared in juvenile court and was sentenced to attend school everyday until the end of the school year. He was also made to work for the co-op after school to work off the money he had stolen. It was later discovered that Tommy's two friends had stolen money in Coppermine in order to pay for their airfare to Holman.

While Tommy was required to appear before the magistrate in juvenile court, a decision was made to enact "punishment" on the local level by having Tommy work for the co-op until he paid back the stolen money. In other cases, juvenile court may be circumvented altogether, with wayward youngsters being required to provide voluntary work services for the settlement council or the recreation committee. Since most illegal acts performed by adolescents are relatively minor, Holman residents and RCMP officers consider it unnecessary in most cases to institute formal court proceedings.

Stealing is by far the most common delinquent act in Holman and often goes unreported and unpunished. Most thefts perpetrated by teenagers occur at the Bay store, where it is easy to shoplift candy and soda pop. While there is no way to accurately assess the degree of such thievery, a large number of teenagers interviewed admitted to occasional shoplifting. This type of theft may be accounted for in two ways. First, there is the general sentiment among both adults and adolescents that the Hudson's Bay store is both a foreign and exploitative agent. Most items sold at the Bay are very expensive due to the high markup. Many people who have shopped at other stores in larger communities, such as Yellowknife or Inuvik, are surprised to see how much more they must pay for similar items in Holman. Second, shoplifting is viewed by many youngsters as a recreational activity—something exciting to break the monotony of life in a settlement that offers little recreation or entertainment.

Despite this apparent increase in theft at the Bay, many youngsters asserted that they would never dream of stealing from any other people or from institutions such as the co-op. The rationale is that the co-op is owned by the people while the Hudson's Bay Company is not. Nevertheless, many adults interviewed expressed some dismay that theft from individuals was generally on the rise in Holman. Hunters who have cached supplies of gasoline out on the land find that their supplies have been taken by unknown individuals. In the past, such a thing was unheard of. Now, however, the increased size of the settlement has resulted in greater anonymity and less social cohesion, two factors that have undoubtedly contributed to thefts.

SUICIDE

Suicide is one of the most extreme forms of deviance in any society. In the Northwest Territories as a whole, there has been an alarming increase in the suicide rate among teenagers and young adults. In 1983, for example, there were 21 reported suicides, for a rate of 43.1 per 100,000, which is significantly above the national average. Although they constitute only 35 percent of the territorial population, Inuit account for slightly over half of the suicides (11 male and 2 female). Examination of the age distribution of these suicides reveals that young people account for the vast majority, with 8 in the fifteen-to-twenty-four age range and 4 in the twenty-five-to-thirty-four age range (*Report on Health Conditions in the N.W.T.* 1983, 35).

As with deaths from accidents, injuries, and violence, alcohol abuse appears to be implicated in the vast majority of Inuit suicides. Alcohol, however, is only part of the problem, which is further aggravated by acculturation stress, unemployment, and low self-esteem. The recent increase of suicide among young Inuit has been a cause for much concern among health care workers. However, it has been difficult for medical administrators to implement preventative programs since suicide is viewed as a sociological rather than as an individual psychiatric problem (*Report on Health Conditions in the N.W.T.* 1978, 44).

Some researchers have suggested that the high suicide rate among the Inuit is partially due to the acceptance of altruistic self-destruction during the traditional period. Anthropological accounts abound with examples of the old and infirm who are no longer productive members of a household taking their own lives (Rasmussen 1927; Hoebel 1954; Holm 1914; Weyer 1932; Balikci 1961).

While contemporary suicide tends to be more common in larger and less integrated communities, cases of successful and attempted suicides have been documented for Holman. All of these, however, have involved young adults rather than adolescents. While not directly involved in these incidents, adolescents are nevertheless affected by this destructive form of behavior, both because suicide victims may be members of the immediate family and because adolescents are just a few years away from the most susceptible age group. Patterns of alienation and disaffection acquired during adolescence may eventually be expressed in self-destructive behavior in early adulthood.

Over the past twenty years, five Holman residents (all male) have committed suicide. The most recent suicide in the community occurred in 1980 when a young man (age twenty) shot himself in the head with a high-powered rifle. Community reaction to this event was one of shock. Almost everyone recognized that the victim was a bright, hardworking, and motivated young man with a promising future. (Just a few months before, this young man had returned from a vocational training program and had secured a good, high-paying job in the community.) No one could have possibly predicted that such an individual would take his own life. In fact, prior to the suicide there were no overt signs of depression to suggest that something was terribly wrong with this individual. In addition to this successful suicide, two suicide attempts were documented, one in 1979 and another in 1982. Both of these incidents involved young men in their early twenties.

All three of these cases are typical of the manner of attempted and successful suicide—two with a firearm and the third through the ingestion of methyl hydrate. They share a common theme in that they represent a reaction to a sense of social withdrawal and isolation. Few other options are available to such individuals in a society that condemns the open expression of anger or depression. As Foulks (1974, 23) suggests, the only alternative open to such persons is permanent withdrawal through suicide.

A thoughtful discussion of the etiology and community reaction to suicide requires a more detailed account than can be provided in this work. Also, since the two young men who attempted suicide are still alive, discretion prevents a thorough discussion of their personal lives and motivations. Suffice it to say that, while suicide has not yet been attempted by any younger members of the Holman community, there is no doubt that youngsters are profoundly affected by successful and attempted suicides. While suicide has been a relative rarity in Holman compared to larger communities, there is no reason to expect that this statistic will remain unchanged in the coming decades. As Holman continues to grow and becomes more inextricably linked with the outside world, the insulation that now characterizes the social environment of Holman will give way to increasing anonymity and social upheaval. Also, as today's adolescents enter adulthood, with its increased social pressures and responsibilities, suicide may very well increase in frequency. In addition, as young adults they will have greater access to alcohol, which may aggravate any sense of frustration and psychological withdrawal, thus facilitating the decision for self-destruction. Nevertheless, there is always the possibility that changing patterns of emotional expression among the younger generation will preclude suicide as an avenue for dealing with stress and anxiety.

■ 9
Conclusion

Theories concerning adolescent development are both abundant and varied, ranging from the developmental theories of Jean Piaget (1965), Lawrence Kohlberg (1969, 1976), and Erik Erikson (1963, 1968) to the conflict theories of Sigmund Freud (1949) and G. Stanley Hall (1904). From their varying theoretical perspectives, these researchers have sought to understand the universality of the adolescent experience as the child matures sexually, intellectually, and emotionally into an adult member of society.

Despite the abundance of theoretical perspectives, our knowledge of adolescence is deficient because it is limited primarily to the observation of adolescents in Western societies. At best we have developed an understanding of this life stage within a restricted cultural environment. At worst, we have constructed a large number of theoretical paradigms that are inapplicable outside this narrowly circumscribed population. ·

The present work in no way attempts to offer a definitive theoretical perspective upon this fascinating stage of the human life cycle. In fact, it does no more than offer a detailed ethnographic description of adolescence in another society. Despite what the reader may interpret as a marked dearth of theory, the research relies heavily upon two distinct assumptions: (1) that all human beings experience significant physical, social, and psychological changes during puberty which may be studied in an objective fashion, and (2) that comparative studies of this life stage are both useful and necessary. The descriptive ethnographic data contained within this book should offer new ideas and suggest alternate avenues of research that will eventually lead to the construction of cross-culturally valid theories.

HOLMAN ADOLESCENCE IN RETROSPECT

Three years of intensive research in the community of Holman have generated more data than can be presented in this brief work. Nevertheless, it has provided a data base for future research as the children and adolescents from the present project are followed through adulthood. This is precisely what makes the examination of human development in any society so exciting. It is ever changing and requires constant reformulation of concepts, methods, and theories.

Traditional Copper Inuit society precluded the existence of a prolonged transitional period between childhood and adulthood. Children had to acquire quickly the knowledge and skills to help them and their families survive. Girls were married at or just before puberty and boys soon after they acquired the physical skills necessary to support a wife and children. This type of reproduction-management strategy was necessary in a harsh ecosystem where people, like food resources, were scattered and scarce.

The past thirty to forty years have seen dramatic changes in the social, material, and economic bases of Inuit society. Population concentration, schooling, wage labor, and the introduction of television programming have changed not only the manner in which Inuit youngsters perceive the world around them, but also their expectations of the future. They have been subjected to acculturative pressures that did not exist when their parents were coming of age. These pressures have given rise to a generation of young people not only in transition between childhood and adulthood but also in transition between two distinct ways of life. As such, the youngsters who have been the subject of this study represent an ideal population for the examination of the effects of rapid social and cultural change upon the organization of the human life cycle. They are truly an "in-between" generation like none before in this isolated and marginal part of the world.

ADOLESCENT AUTONOMY: BEING WHERE YOU WANT TO BE

One of the most salient characteristics of Holman adolescence is the high degree of autonomy that youngsters have to go where and do as they please. Adult regulation of adolescent activities is minimal, and young people are, by and large, free to schedule their own lives. While parents exert some control over the activities of kids and younger teenagers, older teenagers, especially boys, are allowed to conduct their lives unfettered by constraints established by parents and other adults. The adolescent peer group, a social entity virtually nonexistent in the presettlement era, has become fully entrenched as the primary sphere of adolescent social activities and interactions.

The one area where parents exert a certain amount of control over adolescents is in the allocation of cash, a scarce resource in a community with limited wage-employment opportunities. Pocket money obtained from parents is used to attend dances; buy coffee and pie at the coffee shop; purchase records, makeup, hockey sticks and skates at the Bay; or order a new part for a snowmobile through the mail. A number of our informants admitted to ordering items C.O.D. and then asking parents for the money upon their arrival. As already discussed, teenage boys are more demanding materially than teenage girls and thus more dependent upon parents' good graces if they are unable to earn money themselves. The amount of money given to young people varies considerably from household to household and depends ultimately upon the parents' level of prosperity. As expected, more affluent households provide their sons and daughters with a large number of nonessential luxury items. One fifteen-year-old girl, for example, had her own television, stereo, and snowmobile, all gifts from her parents. This case is exceptional, however, since most households are more likely to indulge male offspring. Since teenage boys are much more likely to be provided with snowmobiles, usually hand-me-downs from parents, they require a fairly continuous supply of cash to buy gasoline, oil, and parts. It is not unusual, for example, to hear a teenage boy complain that his snowmobile is temporarily inoperable because his parents are unable or unwilling to provide the money needed for repairs. While such dependency does not seem to affect the mobility or activities of adolescents, it must certainly impress them with the fact that they are not totally independent of the resources and, hence, the wishes of their parents.

The assertion of autonomy among Holman adolescents is not unlike that of adolescents in many other societies. As alluded to in the introduction to this work, the quest for autonomy is one of the main themes of adolescence. Young people strive to assert more and more control over their activities, whether they are related to peer group activities, friendship formation, dating and sexual behavior, clothing styles, financial independence, and so on. Autonomy, of course, does not stand on its own, but is closely related to the "individuation" process, a concept introduced by Peter Blos (1962) to describe the adolescent's attempt to sharpen the boundaries between him- or herself and others, most notably parents. The heightened awareness of self-boundaries represents the adolescent's need to assert a distinctiveness from parents and to overcome the bonds of dependency that characterized infancy and childhood. Individuation is thus more than a simple movement away from parents, but also entails taking increased responsibility for one's thoughts and actions (Blos 1967).

It is in the area of adolescent autonomy that we see a significant departure from traditional Inuit society and culture. Before creation of the settlement and the construction of the federal day school, youngsters maintained regular and close interactions with parents and other adults. Presettlement camp life was more demanding and harsh, requiring close cooperation and contact among household members. While young people had a certain degree of freedom and autonomy, the need to learn from and work closely with parents, combined with the lack of alternate behavior settings and peers, ensured the rapid maturation of Inuit youngsters. If population concentration has done anything, it has provided Inuit youngsters with a substantially increased number of behavior settings and peers outside of the immediate household unit.

High degrees of adolescent autonomy can have both advantages and disadvantages for the social and emotional development of youngsters. Where autonomy is high and parental surveillance low, youngsters may frequently get into trouble. While acts of theft, vandalism, and alcohol use are initiated by youngsters in Holman, they are generally rare and have not resulted in an alarming rate of juvenile delinquency. If the settlement were significantly larger, delinquent acts would probably reach epidemic proportions, as is the case in the neighboring community of Coppermine.

There are also advantages to high dgrees of autonomy for adolescents. Where autonomy is high, parental pressures upon youngsters are limited. Thus boys and girls are allowed to develop at their own pace, without incessant parental pressures to do well in school, excel in athletics, or be "popular" with age-mates. This is not to say that subtle parental pressures are absent in Holman, but that they are minimized to the point of avoiding overt conflict between parents and teenagers. This is one explanation for the seeming lack of generational conflict and the close emotional bonds between parents and children in the community.

In middle-class American society, the process of individuation and the adolescent's search for autonomy can create conflict insofar as parents may be unwilling to relinquish their control over children. This may be due to the parents' unwillingess to accept that their children are growing older and bound ultimately to leave home. Alternately, parents may feel that, as long as their children remain financially dependent upon them, they must succumb to the dictates of parents and save autonomy for a day when they are able to pay their own rent and buy their own food and clothes. The prolonged period during which adolescents must be educated in order to compete in a complex society means that American youngsters must maintain a dependent status even once they have realized the intellectual, emotional, and physical competence to take control of their own lives. In either instance, parents and adolescents are bound to meet head-on in a test of wills regarding how much of his or her own life the adolescent may control without permission from parents.

Neither of these potential causes for conflict appear salient in Inuit society. Parents know that their children must eventually leave home and establish their own families and households. This, however, does not entail a termination or dissolution of parent-child bonds and interactions. Because Holman is a small community with limited outmigration, a married son or daughter will always be close by and serve as a constant source of social, economic, and emotional support. The notion of holding onto youngsters for fear of an "empty nest" is unheard of in Inuit society. Not only does the youngster *not* abandon his or her family by moving into another household, but there are always plenty of younger brothers, sisters, and adopted children to fill the gap.

In Holman, parents do not presume ownership of their children and hence do not attempt to control their thoughts, actions, and aspirations. Nor do parents attempt to live vicariously through their offspring. As most of our clinical informants stated, their parents had little say in such matters as schooling, occupational aspirations, and marriage. This lack of ownership is vividly seen in the degree to which children are offered for adoption to grandparents, related families, or unrelated households.

This nonpossessiveness does not imply that Inuit parents do not take pride in the accomplishments of their offspring. While rarely expressed openly, parents are very proud of a child who has become an accomplished hunter or trapper, obtained a good job, or started to produce offspring. Parents do not brag about the popularity or competence of their children, nor do they attempt to take credit for a child who has matured admirably to adulthood any more than they take blame for a delinquent teenager who is prone to trouble-making.

In American society, responsibility and autonomy are perceived as going hand in hand. Parents may be unwilling to relinquish control of their children until they have demonstrated the necessary responsibility and "common sense" to regulate their own lives. In Holman, responsibility and autonomy are not presumed to go hand in hand. Young people are granted high degrees of autonomy even before they demonstrate the remotest degree of responsibility, something they will eventually acquire as they mature.

The autonomy of Holman teenagers is best appreciated when compared to the notable lack of autonomy experienced by teenagers in the Romanian village of Baisoara, also included in the Harvard Adolescence Project (Ratner n.d.). Of all the communities studied for the Adolescence Project, Holman and Baisoara provide the most dramatic contrast. In this peasant-worker community located in the foothills of western Romania, adult control and regimentation of adolescent life is immediately evident. The demands of schooling and chores effectively limit the amount of time teenagers have to "hang out," play sports, or engage in other nonproductive pursuits.

All Romanian children are required to attend school through the second year of high school, after which all able-bodied males must perform a period of compulsory military service. Unlike Holman, school attendance in Baisoara is near perfect. Romania has been a socialist state since 1948, and the educational system is used to instill the socialist values of obedience, loyalty, and hard work. The work values emphasized by parents in the home are reinforced in the school with the constant reminder that work is an expression of honor, duty, and necessity. The true patriot is the individual who works hard and advances in the competitive occupational hierarchy of Romanian society.

Employment prospects in Baisoara are bleak without educational training. For this reason, parents and teachers encourage children to perform to the best of their abilities in the hopes of securing a good-paying job. Life in bureaucratic Romania is severely restricted without such training, and the only alternative is a low-paying "brute labor" job.

The regimented life of Baisoaran youths and the autonomous, almost happy-go-lucky, routine of Holman youngsters present a vivid contrast. When Baisoaran teenagers are not attending school or doing homework, they are helping parents with vital economic tasks. The economic affluence, primarily in the form of government subsidies, that characterizes life in Holman does not exist in Baisoara, where families must eke out a marginal existence from family farms and low-paying jobs in the local mine. As a result of the marginal economic status of most Baisoaran households, parents cannot afford to let their children be idle. Children must work hard not only to help support the family but also to advance themelves in a society that rewards only hard work and responsibility.

The concept of family honor is another area that distinguishes the lives of adolescents in Romania from the relatively relaxed pattern of adolescent life in Holman. Parents are deemed ultimately responsible for the behavior of their children. The child who excels in school and eventually obtains a high-paying job brings honor to the family. Those who fail to measure up to the socialist ideals of hard work, duty, and cooperation bring shame to the family. Baisoaran adults believe that children are products of the family environment in which they are raised, a notion that finds expression in such sayings as The chip does not fall far from the log. If a child is errant, it is the parents' responsibility for failing to instill the proper social values. This obsession with family honor results in parents exerting as much control as possible over offspring.

Similar concepts in Holman are markedly absent. There is neither obsession with a child's academic performance nor concern that a child's misbehavior will reflect adversely upon family honor. In few areas is this difference more pronounced than in parental and community reactions to premarital pregnancy. As we have already seen, premarital pregnancy is a relative common phenomenon in Holman. Although most parents would prefer that their daughters wait until their late teens or early twenties before becoming pregnant, young girls who do become pregnant are rarely stigmatized in Holman. The girl is allowed to make the final decision whether to keep the child or put it up for adoption. The casualness that Holman parents express for premarital pregnancy is not shared by adults in Baoisoara. Moral condemnation of premarital sexual activity, and especially pregnancy, is severe in this Romanian Orthodox community (Ratner, personal communication). It is felt that "good girls don't" under any circumstances, and the dominant cultural attitude is that girls should remain virgins until marriage. Parents express great anger over the premarital sexual activity of their children and abhorrence when premarital sexual activity results in pregnancy. Premarital pregnancies not only bring shame to the family but severely limit the young woman's prospects for making a "good match" in later life. In Baisoara, parents continue to play an active role in the marriage selection of offspring and try to arrange marriages in order to form alliances or enhance the family's social status. Since it removes from them the decision about whom a child will marry, Baisoaran parents must condemn premarital pregnancy.

Parental control over adolescent sexual activity and marriage is also an important concern for the residents of Mangrove, the Australian aborigine community included in our cross-cultural sample. Mangrove shares with Holman many similarities in terms of the traditional level of social complexity and the rapid pace of recently introduced social change (Burbank, personal communication).

The traditional marriage system of Mangrove was ideally controlled by parents and grandparents. As in traditional Copper Inuit society, females were often betrothed or married before the onset of puberty. Marriages were arranged within a complex system of kin relations, which implied reciprocity between groups of kin. Conveniently, prepubertal betrothal and marriage also eliminated any problems with premarital sexual activity or pregnancy. According to precontact marriage rules, the mother of a little girl and the mother of a little boy would decide that their children should enter a special relationship with one another whereby all of the young girl's offspring would eventually go to her partner as wives (Burbank n.d.). The arrangement not only implied a sense of obligation to one's partner, but ensured that all marriages would entail some age disparity between the male partner and his future wives. If and when the male partner died, all of his surviving wives went to his brothers. Thus, marriages were contracts between kin groups as well as between partners.

A number of interesting similarities and differences exist between Holman and Mangrove. Both societies practiced premenarcheal marriage in the precontact era, although perhaps for very different reasons. In Mangrove the traditional pattern of child marriage not only provided a period of time for a girl to "settle" into her new relationship, but the marriage occurred at an early enough age so that she, presumably, did not have enough sense to refuse her parents' wishes. Since parents were concerned that all marriages conform to the ideal system of marriage, early betrothal and marriage eliminated any possibility of a girl taking it upon herself to arrange a match, possibly with a partner who was not appropriate in the eyes of parents. Thus, parental control of marriage through early betrothal ideally ensured the integrity of the aboriginal marriage system and effectively avoided any opportunity for premarital sexual activity to result in "illegitimate" children (Burbank n.d.).

For the Copper Inuit, early betrothal had many of the same effects but appears to be motivated more out a concern that offspring obtain any reasonable partner rather than a concern with conformity to the rules of partner selection and reciprocity between groups of kin. This strategy made sense given the sparse distribution of the population and the high hunting mortality rate of adult males. While kinship and alliance formation undoubtedly played some role in Copper Inuit marriages, the inherent flexibility of the system implied less of a concern with these factors than was the case for Mangrove aborigines. Also, marriage arrangements made between Copper Inuit parents were less binding since such contracts could be broken at any time.

As in Holman, marriage forms in Mangrove have changed dramatically over the past few decades. Many of these changes can be attributed to the presence of missionaries who established Mangrove as a mission in 1952. Since the missionaries, predictably, disapproved of the traditional marriage system, they developed specific strategies to eradicate the practices of infant betrothal, polygyny, and child marriage. One effective strategy practiced in the area was that missionaries purchased from mothers the right of consent to marry. This arrangement freed large numbers of young girls from any parental dictates concerning marriage and allowed them to choose their own husbands when they reached an appropriate age, as judged by the missionaries (Burbank n.d., 95; Hart and Pilling 1960, 101–102). In addition to this interventive strategy, the missions also provided, through school and church, the social settings where young people could come together in mixed-sex groups. This allowed opportunities for young men and women to establish romances away from the watchful eyes of parents (Burbank n.d.). However, in the missionaries' attempt to eradicate "un-Christian" marriage practices, they have actually helped increase the frequency of premarital sexual activity and premarital pregnancy.

The overall result of these changes is that young men and women now have greater opportunities to arrange their own marriages, doing so with little or no consultation with parents. Parents, on the other hand, continue to expect to have a hand in marriage arrangements, often with little success. Parents in Mangrove have become upset not only because they have lost control of their daughters' marriage arrangements but also because many of these self-arranged marriages are with inappropriate partners, implying an undermining of traditional kin relations and marriage reciprocity that once formed an essential component of aboriginal social organization and social identity. Girls now have significantly altered expectations of marriage: they intend to marry only males they love or not marry at all. Also, since the missionaries have encouraged a later age of marriage, girls have the will power to confront their parents with greater conviction. In a few cases, girls may use pregnancy as a way out of prearranged marriage.

Another factor contributing to the disruption in traditional marriage practices has been the recent creation of an adolescent peer group. In this regard the similarity with Holman is most pronounced. With the concentration of the aboriginal population into the settlement of Mangrove, greater opportunities exist for peer interaction than was true in the past, when large social gatherings were limited to just a few months of the year. The creation of an adolescent peer group provides the context for the development of adolescent values and expectations that are in nonconformity with parents' values. As young people reinforce one another within this new value system, parents exert less and less control over the premarital sexual behavior and marriage arrangements of their offspring.

The Harvard Adolescence Project did not have the resources to include a field site in the United States, which would have allowed for a more thorough cross-cultural comparison of the adolescent experience. However, recent work by Csikszentmihaly and Larson (1984) provides useful data on the behavioral and emotional dimensions of adolescent life in a middle-class Chicago suburb. These researchers used a novel approach to chart the everyday experiences of their adolescent sample. Using what they call the Experience Sampling Method (ESM), adolescent participants were asked to carry an electronic pager and a pad of self-report forms. For a one-week period, the participants were paged at forty to fifty randomly chosen moments. Upon being paged, the participants would complete one of the self-report forms. These forms contained questions concerning location, activities, mood, other people present, degree of concentration upon activity, degree of self-consciousness, and so on. The value of the EMS method lies in its attempt to determine not only where, how, and with whom adolescents spend their time, but also the underlying motivations and emotions experienced by young people within these settings.

Based upon their analysis of 4,489 self-reports a number of fascinating patterns emerged. The American teenagers appear to lead much more regimented and adult-controlled lives than their northern or Australian counterparts, although significantly less regimented than the Romanian youths. The American high school students are positioned somewhere between the restrictive, parentally dominated experience of Baisoaran adolescents and the open, peer-dominated world of Holman and Mangrove teenagers. Unlike all three settings, American teenagers experience greater heterogeneity of settings, activities, and companions (Csikszentmihalyi and Larson 1984, 82). The variety of settings available to American teenagers is undoubtedly due to the presence of an urban environment that offers more in terms of people, places, and activities than is available in an isolated Arctic settlement, an Australian aboriginal community, or a small peasant-worker village in Romania.

The self-reports of the American students revealed that they spend 32 percent of their waking time in school, 27 percent in public settings, and 41 percent at home (Csikszentmihalyi and Larson 1984, 59). There is no doubt that schooling absorbs much of the time and energy of the typical American teenager. As in Romania, schooling maintains an important position in American society, and the amount of time that American teenagers spend in school or studying at home reflects the cultural value placed upon school achievement. A similar concern for schooling and education is not as evident in either Holman or Mangrove.

When examining the amount of time American teenagers spend at home, the most interesting finding is that these youths spend the largest proportion of their waking hours (13 percent) in their own bedrooms, reading, reflecting, listening to music, or simply withdrawing from the incessant demands of the adult world. Daily routine interviews from Holman adolescents reveal that a similar tendency to withdraw to the privacy of one's own room is not as prevalent. While Holman teenagers occasionally isolate themselves in their bedrooms, most of their time at home is spent in the kitchen or living area interacting with siblings and friends or watching television with family members. Of course many Holman teenagers share their rooms with one or more siblings, thus limiting the degree to which teenagers can withdraw into rooms that are off-limits to other family members. For Holman teen-agers, solitary withdrawal is probably much less important than for American teenagers because the former have been raised in a small kin-oriented community where privacy is neither highly valued nor necessary. Perhaps Holman teenagers do not spend time by them-selves because they do not need to escape from social pressures, which weigh more heavily upon the teenagers of other cultures.

When examining the activities of American adolescents, Csik-szentmihalyi and Larson discover that, in spite of the American em-phasis upon education, leisure activities consume 40 percent of the teenager's waking hours. These diversions include thinking, listening to music, nonschool reading, watching television, attending to hobbies, playing sports and games, and socializing. The remaining time is evenly split between productive tasks (studying, classwork, jobs) and maintenance activities (napping, eating, personal care, chores and er-rands). The amount of time available to these adolescents for non-productive leisure activities partially reflects the affluence of middle-class American society, which not only permits nonproductivity, but caters to the leisure needs of teenagers through television program-ming, youth-oriented record sales, organized sporting events, game parlors, ad infinitum. While so much leisure time would shock the typical Romanian parent, the average Holman adolescent or adult would not consider it unusual. Holman teenagers do not have as many distractions available to them as American teenagers, but they clearly spend as much or even more time engaged in leisure activities such as casual socializing, visiting friends, hanging out at the Bay, and playing hockey.

This, however, is only part of the story for Holman teenagers. If a similar inventory of Holman teenage activities were performed, one would probably find significant variation between younger and older teenagers and between males and females. Younger teenagers, up to fifteen and sixteen years of age, are much more likely to attend school on at least an irregular basis. As a result, the amount of leisure time available to these youngsters is limited to weekends and weekday after-noons. Older teenage boys who have dropped out of school, but not yet obtained any regular employment, spend large amounts of time in non-productive activities. Older teenage girls, on the other hand, spend sig-nificantly less time in leisure activities as they become increasingly in-volved in household chores or wage-labor jobs. That older teenage girls rarely appeared in our spot observations strongly suggests that this group has less leisure time than their opposite-sex age-mates.

While American adolescents spend much of their time in locations that are supervised or structured by adults, such as the school, the amount of time spent in the company of adults is actually quite small (Csikszentmihalyi and Larson 1984, 70–71). Only 19 percent of the adolescents' waking hours was spent with the family, and only a fraction of this family time was spent with parents or other adults. Time spent with peers and friends, either in the classroom or out, occupied fully half of the week's waking hours. In American culture, as in Holman and Mangrove, the adolescent peer group occupies a paramount position. No wonder the adolescent experience in these societies can be understood only with reference to the positive and negative qualities of peer group influence.

As stated repeatedly throughout this work, Holman teenagers spend less time with parents than was the case thirty or forty years ago. The actual amount of time spent in the presence of parents and other adults, however, is difficult to gauge. In summer, when teenagers and kids stay up all night and sleep through most of the day, contact with parents is limited, especially if the latter are at fishing and seal hunting camps. During the midwinter dark period, when adolescent activity rhythms are similarly disoriented, interactions between parents and children may also be minimal. At other times of the year, however, when parents and teenagers maintain similar sleep-waking cycles, interactions increase in frequency. The interactions that do occur, however, are generally limited to the household and not to public settings. A teenage boy who comes home from an exhausting game of hockey may grab something to eat and sit down with his parents and siblings to watch television. A daughter who has come home from school may help her mother with laundry or assist in caring for younger siblings. A young boy struggling to repair his snowmobile may get assistance from a patient and more knowledgeable father. In all these instances, parent-child interaction is of a casual nature and there is little evidence that children and parents intentionally sit down to prolonged conversations. As many of our informants asserted, they rarely talk with their parents, apart from fleeting social interactions as their paths cross in the course of a typical day.

For the American adolescents in Csikszentmihalyi and Larson's study, activities that involve the entire family are much more common. In some cases these are activities in which teenagers have no desire to participate, but grudgingly accede to their parents' wishes. Such incidents may often be a source of intense generational conflict. A family may attend church together, go to a movie, eat dinner at a restaurant, and so forth. Similar family activities are absent in Holman. If there is a movie or dance at the community hall, family members will rarely go together. The parents may walk or snowmobile to the hall with younger children, while older children go separately with friends or other relatives. When parents go to church on Sunday morning, they may take along their youngest children, but not require their older sons and daughters to attend.

Outside of the immediate household context, adolescents spend most of their time with friends and peers and, like American adolescents, are rarely seen in the company of adults. Of our 467 spot observations of kids and teenagers in public settings, less than 6 percent involved young people in the presence of a parent or other adult (age thirty or more). A difference between age groups was also apparent. Kids between nine and thirteen were spotted 8.3 percent of the time in the presence of an adult, while teenagers were spotted with an adult only 4.8 percent of the time. What emerges is a picture of Holman teenagers maintaining close emotional bonds with parents, but spending little time interacting with those parents and most of their time engaging in leisure activities with peers.

ADOLESCENT UPS AND DOWNS

One of the more interesting findings of Csikszentmihalyi and Larson's research deals with the mood variability of their adolescent participants. Adolescence in our own society is popularly regarded as a stage of life when "runaway hormones" contribute to tremendous, and at times spontaneous, mood swings. This notion creates a biologically deterministic image of the adolescent as one who is constantly subject to internal turmoil, as "raging" hormones create new feelings and sensations, not all of which are pleasurable. This notion has become firmly entrenched in the popular as well as scientific literature as the "storm and stress" of adolescence (Hall 1904).

Based upon the analysis of the self-report forms, Csikszentmihalyi and Larson (1984, 120–126) find evidence of dramatic variability in the moods of their adolescent participants. An adolescent may go from a state of total elation to a state of extreme depression and back again in a matter of minutes. While adults also experience mood swings, these swings are less dramatic and less rapid than those of adolescents. Csikszentmihalyi and Larson believe that adolescent mood variability is partly a situational phenomenon, a function of what adolescents happen to be doing at any particular moment:

> If they are more emotional, it is partly because they are exposed to more varied environments than adults are. In fact, teenagers move from one context to the next more rapidly than adults, and thus their emotions have a greater chance of being affected by situational factors. . . . Whether it is because they have not yet chosen a pattern for their lives, or because society makes fewer demands on them to conform to a predictable set of activities, adolescents are less firmly rooted in their environments. Therefore, their emotions shift more readily with the restless pattern of their lives. (Csikszentmihalyi and Larson 1984, 123).

What can be said of mood variability among Inuit adolescents? An examination of the moods of Inuit teenagers was exceedingly difficult due to the cultural avoidance of emotional expression and the high value that Inuit place upon emotional restraint and inhibition. In this respect, Inuit teenagers more closely approximate the values and behaviors of adults than of kids and do not appear subject to sudden and dramatic changes in mood. If such mood variability does exist, it is internalized to a degree where it is not recognized by others. This emphasis upon emotional inhibition was adequately expressed by one adolescent informant who stated that "Inuit just don't talk about personal things with one another like white people do."

Throughout their daily experiences, Inuit teenagers maintain an even emotional keel. Anger, depression, and anxiety are rarely expressed openly. Moodiness and unpredictability, like anger and hostility, are not traits admired in Inuit society. As previously noted, Inuit adolescents as well as adults try to maintain a pleasant demeanor in all social situations, often relying heavily upon humor and joking to diffuse senstitive social situations or psychological stress. As many of our informants commented, having a good sense of humor is a highly desired personality trait.

Mood variability during adolescence has been explained by both biological and sociocultural determinants. The biological perspective asserts that the maturational changes associated with puberty, primarily increased adrenal hormone production, are responsible for the adolescent's variability in mood, arousal, and motivation. The sociocultural perspective, on the other hand, minimizes the importance of maturational change and stresses the importance of culturally specific demands placed upon young people. Margaret Mead, for example, in her classic work on adolescent girls in Samoa (Mead 1928), concluded that the storm and stress normally associated with adolescence is unique to American culture and is due primarily to the expectations and demands placed upon American youths. Other social scientists have offered similar sociocultural explanations; they emphasize the social stress experienced by adolescents who are expected to change dramatically many aspects of behavior and personality in a relatively short period of time (Benedict 1938; Parsons 1942; Lewin 1938).

Csikszentmihalyi and Larson (1984, 123) believe that their data offer support for the sociocultural perspective and suggest that the dramatic mood swings of American adolescents are a consequence of the adolescents being exposed to a greater number of distinct behavior settings in which very different demands are made upon them. The apparent lack of mood variability among Inuit teenagers is a result of the relative homogeneity of behavior settings within a small, isolated, and kin-oriented community. While teenagers move from one physical setting to another (e.g., from the home to the Bay store to a friend's home, etc.), these do not require any significant cognitive or behavioral adjustments. The most distinctive behavior setting in the community is the Holman school, and even this is abandoned by many adolescents as they get older.

Another factor that may account for the lack of mood variability among Holman adolescents is that they are not subject to the same parental demands and constraints as American adolescents. An American youth who is experiencing a mood "high" while talking on the phone to a girlfriend may experience a dramatic downswing when his parents tell him to get off the phone and "do his homework." Similar demands upon Holman adolescents are almost totally nonexistent. The lack of parental interference and the high degree of adolescent autonomy may minimize mood variability, or at least its overt expression, among Holman adolescents.

FRIENDS ARE NEIGHBORS: LIFE IN A SMALL KIN-ORIENTED COMMUNITY:

Holman is the smallest of the research sites included in the Harvard Adolescence Project and, as such, provides a familiar and secure environment that defines so many aspects of the adolescent experience.

The size of the community also has its disadvantages, which were clearly expressed by many of our informants when commenting on how boring Holman was in comparison to other, larger Inuit settlements.

Growing up in a small, kin-oriented community provides a dramatic contrast with the experience of most adolescents in industrialized nations, for whom urbanization and suburbanization give rise to an almost frenetic pace of life. In Holman there are no strangers. Residents live in tightly clustered housing, which enhances prospects for casual daily interaction. During the course of a day, kids and teenagers interact with friends and peers who are also their neighbors and, in many cases, relatives. When a child enters school for the first time, fears of entering a strange new environment are tempered by the fact that he or she knows many of the classmates. There is not the constant social and psychological adjustment required of American youths when they enter a new school, move to a new community, or join a little league baseball team.

In Holman the individual is born into a network of social and familial relations that follow a person from infancy through old age. In short, everyone knows everyone else, and there is security in the knowledge that these physically and emotionally close relationships will never be broken. The father of one of our clinical informants stated that living in Holman was better than living in the South because "everybody shares with one another and tries to help one another out." This man also asserted that Holman was a nice place to live since he could leave town at any time and know that his family would be well cared for by his friends and relatives. The shyness that characterizes the Inuit teenagers' response to a stranger in the community (as happened when my research associate first arrived in Holman) partially reflects their lack of outgoing social skills that are a requirement of life in the South.

The advantages of living in a small community lie not only in the predictability of social interaction, but also in the support provided by friends, neighbors, and relatives. Such a community is likely to give one a sense of belonging as well as a recognition that one will be accepted for the kind of person one is, regardless of personal shortcomings. In the South many teenagers move through a social world full of strangers and often attend large, impersonal schools. Perhaps for this reason American teenagers frequently try to call attention to themselves or "act out" as though they were on stage. The need to assert an individual identity gives rise to the fads, fancies, and totems that distinguish adolescents from adults. An adolescent may join a social clique (greasers, jocks, heads, punks, etc.) in order to assert his or her uniqueness as well as to establish a sense of belonging within a peer group. Only in this manner can many adolescents maintain a sense of belonging and a sense of personal identity in a complex, competitive, and highly impersonal society.

Such expressions of individual identity (or rebellion) are not necessary in Holman, where knowledge of each person as a unique individual is a fact of life. Throughout our clinical interviews, we were provided with numerous comments such as, "I like living in Holman because I can be myself" or "I have no desire to be anything but who I am." The ease and readiness with which Inuit adolescents accept themselves may be a consequence of being recognized as unique individuals by others in the community.

A small community also provides assurances to parents regarding the whereabouts and activities of their children when they are not immediately present. While Holman kids and teenagers may occasionally get into minor trouble, the size of the community limits the settings in which adolescents can significantly harm themselves and others. A small community also allows for greater surveillance of children and adolescents, by both adults and peers. Imagine the anxiety of the typical American parent on a Saturday night when a son or daughter has borrowed the family car and, with a group of friends, has gone off to an undisclosed location. It is unlikely that the same anxiety would be felt by Holman parents since their offspring will always be close by visiting friends or relatives. American parents also worry about their offspring falling in with the "wrong crowd" and getting into varying degrees of trouble. Holman parents do not have such concerns since the friends and peers of their offspring are the sons and daughters of close friends, relatives, and neighbors. The significantly higher rate of juvenile delinquency in neighboring communities such as Coppermine and Inuvik suggests that community size has a determining effect upon both the prosocial and antisocial activities of young people.

The disadvantages of life in a small community seem to pale in comparison to the advantages, but nevertheless they exist and are recognized by adults and adolescents alike. Adolescents, especially, are prone to complain about boredom and the lack of anything exciting to do. These complaints are more pronounced now that many Holman teenagers have had an opportunity to go south on school trips. Naturally these trips are planned to keep the teenagers busy: visits to ice cream parlors, movies, bowling alleys, amusement parks, museums, and the like. Since life in Holman is sedate in comparison, it is not surprising that Holman youths fervently believe that their southern counterparts do nothing but avail themselves of these leisure activities.

Perhaps more significant than the expressed boredom of settlement life is the dearth of employment opportunities for both adults and adolescents. Since the population of Holman is steadily growing, the number of adults and older teenagers seeking full- or part-time employment vastly exceeds the community's employment base. This situation will gradually worsen as more and more teenagers come of age. Those who receive vocational training may have to seek employment in other communities. In any event, the adolescents now growing into adulthood will have to make a choice between a small number of unskilled positions in Holman and vocational training that may require residence in another community. Neither situation is desirable and forewarns of significant unemployment and underemployment problems in the future.

GETTING ALONG: THE IMPORTANCE OF BEING INUIT

With the introduction of television, newspapers, magazines, and school trips to the South, Holman adolescents are beginning to behave more like teenagers in the United States and southern Canada. This recent exposure to the adolescent subculture of the South has made Holman adolescents fully aware of how different their lives are in comparison to southern teenagers. Many Holman adolescents recognize that they have much more autonomy. They are also cognizant that life in a small community is qualitatively different from life in the large urban and suburban centers they have visited on school trips.

In spite of changes that have occurred in the adolescent subculture, Holman teenagers maintain a distinct sense of ethnic identity. Even though Holman teenagers are more interested in the fads and fancies of the South than in the cultural traditions of Inuit society, many young people have a distinct sense that their ethnic affiliation is important. The following interview with Johnny Apiuk (age eighteen) expresses some of these feelings:

■ R.C.: *Describe the differences between whites and Inuit.*
JOHNNY: Qablunaaqs *are smarter. In school, they work harder. They must be more open-minded and more straight forward. Es-*

*kimos are more shy to talk about personal things with one an-
other. Eskimo kids do whatever they want without their parents
permission. Qablunaaq kids are not so spoiled. They aren't allowed to do whatever they want.*

R.C.: *Are there any differences in the way they think or feel?*

JOHNNY: *Qablunaaqs want the land, but Eskimos don't want to
give it away.*

R.C.: *Which Eskimo traits do you think are most desirable?*

JOHNNY: *Their language, hunting and trapping techniques, land
to travel on, all free medical expenses, free housing, going to school
for free.*

R.C.: *Which Eskimo traits do you think are the most undesirable?*

JOHNNY: *Drinking (pause). Don't know.*

R.C.: *Which do you think is better, being Eskimo or Qablunaaq?*

JOHNNY: *I think I like being Eskimo. At times, I thought of what it
would be like to be a white person, like if I were adopted by a white
family. My life would be a lot different. I wouldn't know how
to travel or speak Eskimo. I wouldn't be so spoiled. I might be
smarter though.*

R.C.: *Would it be better if Eskimos acted more like Qablunaaqs?*

JOHNNY: *They're OK the way they are.*

R.C.: *How about if Qablunaaqs acted more like Eskimos?*

JOHNNY: *Yes—some, like the Qablunaaqs who want to spoil the
land. [Here Johnny is referring to the whites who have come North
primarily for mineral and oil development.] They should act more
like Eskimos. The Qablunaaqs who want to keep the land the way
it is are alright. They're nice people.*

R.C.: *Which Qablunaaq traits do you think are desirable?*

JOHNNY: *All their sports, like hockey, baseball, football. Girls—
they produce a lot of beautiful girls. Schools and teachers, their
houses, guns, ski-doos, bikes, guitars, paper, pens, games like Mo-
nopoly, cards—something to do to make the time pass.*

R.C.: *What's the single best thing about being Eskimo?*

JOHNNY: *I can be myself.*

It is apparent that Johnny appreciates the differences between
whites and Inuit, but indicates his personal preference for being Inuit.
Interestingly, Johnny defines desirable white traits in terms of the material goods that have been introduced from the South, possibly reflecting a more materialistic outlook of Holman teenagers. Most important,
however, Johnny asserts that the best thing about being Inuit is that he
can be himself.

While the Inuit adolescents of today are obviously different from the Inuit youths of just ten to fifteen years ago, many typically Inuit values and behavioral traits have persisted. All the teenagers we interviewed pointed out the importance of being nice, having a good sense of humor, and getting along with others. Life in a small community, where people are constantly interacting with the same group of friends and relatives, requires that everyone live equitably with one another and avoid placing excessive demands upon personal relationships. Because there is a limited pool of significant personal relationships, Inuit teenagers and adults are less likely to make and break friendships the way southern adults and teenagers do. My research associate and I were constantly amazed at the speed with which teenagers made up with one another after a dispute. It was not unusual to see two boys fighting on the hockey rink one day and then "chumming it up" the next. Inuit teenagers have thus been effectively socialized by parents to express the Inuit values of avoiding conflicts and forgiving transgressions.

Teenage reliance upon humor and joking is another mechanism by which equitable social relations can be maintained. Like their parents, Inuit adolescents spend much time joking around with one another and have a remarkable ability to laugh at themselves in even the most embarrassing social situations. At times this reliance upon humor makes these young people appear to take few things seriously, when in fact these characteristics enable individuals to maintain smooth and cooperative relations with one another. A teenage boy or girl will qualify an insult to a friend or peer by claiming that he or she is only joking, meaning that the friend should not take the insult seriously. Rather, the friend should laugh at the comment and respond in a similar fashion to the "assailant's" abuse. Conflict diffused in the context of "just joking around" is conflict avoided.

THE FUTURE

Our examination of Inuit youth has taught us much not only about Inuit society and culture but about the adolescent experience in another part of the world. While I have discussed many differences between Holman adolescents and adolescents in the United States, the two groups probably have many more commonalities than differences. Adolescents everywhere must deal socially and psychologically with the profound maturational changes of puberty. They must renegotiate their roles and status positions within the family. They must start to change the nature of their relationships with same-sex and opposite-sex friends and peers. Last, they must start to consider seriously what kind of occupation or life-style they would like to pursue in adulthood.

The future inspires a certain amount of fear for young people everywhere. Will they be able to get the job they want? Will they find someone to marry? Will they be able to afford the things they would like to have? Such questions may not weigh as heavily upon Holman adolescents as upon young people in other societies. Nevertheless, they are concerned for what life will be like in the future. Many would like to obtain an education and vocational training that will enable them to get secure and high-paying jobs. But will the jobs be in Holman when they return from high school or vocational training school?

For these young people the future is, ironically, both exciting and dismal. It is exciting because these youngsters have more choice in molding their futures than their parents and grandparents had before them. It is dismal because the small community of Holman will not be able to provide its young people with the life-styles promised by advanced education and vocational training. Out-migration to larger communities may be the only alternative for many. Also, as the community increases in size, a concommitant increase in alcohol abuse and law violations may occur, which will affect adults and adolescents alike. In this volume, we have had the luxury of stopping time momentarily in the "ethnographic present," but there is no doubt that the future for these Holman adolescents will be one of rapid change and dramatic challenge.

APPENDIX A: Biographical and Household Background of Primary Clinical Informants

1. JOHNNY APIUK

Johnny was among the most articulate and committed of our clinical informants. During my first field trip, in 1978–1980, I came to know Johnny quite well as one of the more responsible teenagers in the community. He started to work with me soon after my arrival in February 1982. Initially I hired Johnny as a research assistant to help collect spot observations, household composition surveys, and other basic survey data. Several months into the research, Johnny agreed to become my first clinical informant. By the end of the research, we had completed twenty-nine formal interviews, ten daily routines, and numerous informal interviews.

At the time, Johnny was eighteen years old and lived at home with his parents, one older brother, three younger sisters, and a male cousin whom Johnny's parents had recently adopted. During the period of the research, Johnny's parents also adopted an infant girl from their eldest married son.

Johnny's family lived in one of the newer four-bedroom housing units constructed in 1979. His parents were more traditional than the parents of many other adolescents. They spoke only Inuktitut at home and did not hold wage-labor jobs. Johnny's father was an active hunter and trapper who supplemented his trapping income by carving whalebone sculptures which he sold to the co-op. Johnny's mother worked occasionally in the co-op craft shop and also did carving and sewing at home. His parents maintained a camp one hundred miles east of Holman, where they spent four to six months out of the year. While Johnny occasionally accompanied his parents and siblings to the camp, he frequently stayed at home with his older brother because there was more to do in town than out at camp. Since Johnny was an older teenager, his parents allowed him to decide where to spend his time.

Johnny completed grade 9 at the Holman school in 1980 in spite of a 12 percent attendance rate for his final year. Despite his low attendance rate for grades 8 and 9, Johnny gained a reputation as a good student, and many of his teachers spoke highly of him. His first trip to the South was in 1978 when he accompanied his teachers and several other students to Toronto. Johnny reported this experience as one of the most exciting events of his life; he was fascinated by the cars, skyscrapers, escalators and elevators, which he encountered for the first time.

Johnny entered grade 10 at Sir John Franklin in the fall of 1980. Over the next two years, Johnny quit school and returned home three times, twice voluntarily due to homesickness and once by force. On Johnny's last attempt to attend school in Yellowknife, he was caught drinking by the dormitory counselors and sent home.

During the period of the research, Johnny divided his time between hanging out, working as a clinical informant, playing hockey, hunting and trapping with his father, and taking on temporary employment in the community when available. In the course of being interviewed, Johnny mentioned that he would like to go back to school at Sir John Franklin but that they would not take him back. Johnny hoped eventually to apply and be accepted into a vocational training program at Fort Smith because he was getting bored doing nothing.

The large amount of time Johnny had available made him an excellent research assistant and clinical informant. The only time Johnny did not work on the project was during a four-month period from June to September, when he was staying up all night and sleeping all day.

2. ANNIE APIUK

Johnny's eleven-year-old sister was our youngest female clinical informant. Annie came to work for us at her older brother's suggestion. Interviews with Annie did not begin until after the arrival of my research associate, Pamela Stern, in June. Several weeks after Stern's arrival, Annie and a friend started to visit her on a regular basis. Since we wanted to conduct some clinical interviews with a number of preadolescents, Stern approached her to work for us, and she agreed. With the exception of Annie's recently adopted infant sister, Annie was the youngest member of her household. At the time, she slept in a separate bed in the same room as her parents and baby sister.

Because Annie was the youngest member of her household and had two older sisters, she had few household responsibilities. She could often be seen wandering around the community with other children her age. She did not, however, have the same degree of freedom as did her older brother. When her parents would go to their camp, Annie and her sisters would always accompany them. As a result, Annie spent more time "on the land" than many of her age-mates.

At the time of our interviews, Annie had been promoted to the fifth grade. Annie's attendance at school was relatively high when she was not out at her parent's camp. Unlike her brother Johnny, Annie had never been to Yellowknife or any other southern city.

3. ROBERT NILGAK

Johnny's roommate was Robert Nilgak, a cousin recently adopted by Johnny's parents. Robert's residential history was somewhat complicated. Although

Robert's mother, two older brothers, and three sisters lived in another house in Holman, Robert had not resided with them since the age of five. At that time he was adopted by his paternal grandfather. As the only child in his grandfather's household, Robert had a great deal of freedom. As a result, his school attendance was poor, and he spent most of his time visiting, playing hockey, and hanging out.

In 1980 Robert's grandfather died and Robert was given a choice between moving back with his mother or going to live with his aunt and uncle (Johnny and Annie's parents). His aunt had talked with Robert and asked him to come and live with them. Robert eventually decided to move in with his aunt and uncle because "Mom didn't make enough money to support a lot of kids."

At the time of Robert's interviews, he was fifteen years old and had been living with the Apiuks for a year and a half. He stated that his adopted family tried to make him feel at home, although he sometimes thought he did not fit in and would rather live with his mother. Robert confessed that he had thought about this a lot and sometimes got a little angry, but never said anything about it. If he could have made his choice again, Robert claimed that he would go live with his mother.

Robert spent a great deal of time visiting with his mother, brothers, and sisters. Robert's aunt and uncle were much more strict with him than his grandfather ever was, something that appeared to be a source of tension between Robert and his adopted family. Even though he was actively encouraged to attend school, Robert's attendance for 1981–1982 was still fairly low (41 percent for the academic year).

When he would appear to work, Robert was an excellent informant. Often, however, Robert would miss our prearranged meetings or would arrive totally exhausted after having stayed up all night.

4. PETER NILGAK

Peter, Robert's older brother, split his time between attending high school in Yellowknife and living with his mother and siblings. Peter was a tall, attractive eighteen-year-old who was extremely popular among his peers. He was especially popular with girls, which he frequently boasted about in our clinical interviews. Peter and his cousin Johnny were close friends and could frequently be seen hanging out together when Peter was home on vacation. Peter also spent a lot of time with his younger brother Robert.

When Peter was twelve years old, his father committed suicide. Peter reported that he was really happy when his father was still alive and had a lot of problems when he died. For several years afterward, Peter was constantly getting into trouble and had a reputation for being a "bad kid around town." (Peter had been to magistrate's court several times for breaking and entering and underage drinking.) At the time of our interviews, Peter reported that he was much better behaved and was no longer getting into trouble. He thought that most people liked him now: "I have more pride now. When I walk around town, I want people to respect me. I want people to think that I'm a good example, somebody to look up to."

Peter's teachers reported that he had been a very difficult student to work with for many years. In the previous three to four years, however, Peter had changed dramatically and became much more cooperative and easygoing. Like Johnny, Peter was well thought of by the teachers and principal of the Holman school.

Like many other teenagers, Peter's first visit to the South was on the school trip to Toronto in 1980. The next year Peter went on another school trip to Calgary. He listed both trips as the most exciting events of his life. Peter was also extremely athletic and won first place in the Alaskan high kick at the 1982 Northern Games held in Coppermine.

Peter first went to Sir John Franklin in 1981 and successfully passed grade 10. Our interviews were conducted during the summer of 1982 when he was looking forward to grade 11. Peter expressed a desire to be the first person from Holman to attend college. Nevertheless, he reported that he frequently cut school in order to go into town and have coffee. During his first year at Sir John Franklin, Peter got drunk one night and reportedly tried to beat up one of his supervisors. As a result he was summoned to magistrate's court for underage drinking. He was fined and put on probation, but since it was his first offense, Peter was not expelled from Sir John Franklin.

Although our interview sessions were limited to summer, Easter, and Christmas vacations, Peter was an excellent informant. Due to his outgoing nature, Peter was very talkative and was more than willing to discuss many personal and sensitive topics.

5. JACK ULIKTUAQ

Jack was a fifteen-year-old who lived at home with his father, mother, three brothers, and two sisters. Their house was one of the older houses in the community and lacked both running water and flush toilets. Jack shared a room with his younger brother, Paul. His parents were much more acculturated than Johnny's parents, and both had schooling to at least grade 4. In addition to some hunting and trapping, Jack's father maintained a number of part-time jobs. His mother held a permanent wage-labor job.

Jack was in grade 8 at the time of our interviews. His attendance was poor (58.7 percent for 1981–1982). Jack's first trip to the South was in 1981 when he went to Calgary on a school trip. The following year Jack went on another school trip to Kingsville, Ontario.

When Jack was not attending school, he could frequently be found hanging out at the Bay or the co-op coffee shop. Like other teenagers his age, he spent a great deal of time hanging out, visiting, and playing hockey, often during school hours.

Jack's teachers reported that Jack used to be very shy, but started to come out of his shell as he became a teenager. At the time of our interviews, he was a very sociable and outgoing person. Although Jack was an extremely pleasant young man, our interviews were not as successful as those with many other teenage males. Jack had a great deal of difficulty answering many questions, often failing to answer at all or giving only very brief, unrevealing responses.

6. SARAH KITIGAT

Soon after their arrival, newcomers to Holman would invariably make the acquaintance of Sarah. Due to her outgoing nature and curiosity, Sarah was quick to appear at the house or hotel room of most new arrivals with a barage of questions about who they were and what they were doing in Holman. Although thirteen years old at the time of the research, Sarah's precocious and inquisitive behavior was much more characteristic of "kids" than of teenagers.

Sarah lived with her father, mother, older sister, and three younger brothers. Her family resided in an older housing unit that did not have running water or flush toilets. She shared both a bed and a bedroom with her older sister. In addition to being an active hunter, Sarah's father was a wage earner who had been employed by the Holman Eskimo Co-operative since its inception. Her mother was primarily a housewife, but also sewed at home for the co-op.

While Sarah's father was fluent in both Inuktitut and English, her mother spoke only Inuktitut. The household linguistic situation was similar to many other Holman households, with the parents speaking to one another and their children in Inuktitut and the children responding in English. Sarah's mother had not had any formal schooling, but her father attended both the Roman Catholic mission school in Aklavik and Sir John Franklin High School in Yellowknife. Even though he never finished high school, Sarah's father was one of the better-educated adults in the community.

Because her father recognized the importance of education, Sarah and her brothers and sister were all encouraged to attend school regularly. Although a poor reader, Sarah's math skills were excellent. Sarah's school attendance was exemplary. During 1981–1982, when Sarah was in grade 7, she had a 93 percent attendance rate.

We hesitated at first to use Sarah as a clinical informant, worrying that her energetic nature (bordering on hyperactivity) would make it difficult for her to sit through long interview sessions. Sarah was most interested in working for us, due in part to her natural curiosity as well as her need for pocket money. While we put her off for a long time, we finally agreed to try her out. Much to our surprise, Sarah turned out to be a model informant. While her responses to our questions were often brief and nonrevealing, as though she wanted to get through the interviews as quickly as possible, she was highly conscientious and always punctual. When Sarah was finally paid for her services, she went to the store with her mother and bought food and some clothing for the entire family. To our knowledge, she was the only clinical informant who did not use her paycheck for "pin money."

7. RICKY KITIGAT

Sarah's younger brother Ricky was eleven-years-old during the time of our interviews and the youngest of our male clinical informants. Ricky lived in the same household with his sister and shared a room with his ten-year-old brother Fred. While Sarah and her older sister shared a bed, Ricky and Fred had their own beds.

Ricky was extremely "low key" in comparison to Sarah. During the period of the research, Ricky was attending grade 5. He was not as good a student as either his two sisters or his younger brother. While his three siblings had an excellent attendance record, ranging from ninety to ninety-three percent attendance, Ricky's attendance was much poorer (67 percent for the 1981–1982 academic year). Ricky's parents seemed to tolerate his poor attendance, in part, because he was the first-born son.

Ricky reported that he was not terribly interested in school and would rather be out hunting and trapping. In fact, Ricky's hunting abilities were outstanding for an eleven-year-old. He was a good tracker and an excellent marksman. His father recognized these abilities and took great pride in the knowledge that Ricky would mature into a fine hunter and trapper. For this reason also, Ricky's parents tolerated his poor school attendance and academic achievement.

Unfortunately, Ricky was not a terribly reliable clinical informant. He rarely came to work on time and frequently missed appointments. Often he arrived at inconvenient times and expected me to drop whatever I was doing in order to interview him. In this respect also, he was a striking contrast to his sister Sarah. While Ricky's parents encouraged his sister to come to work on a regular basis, they did not seem to emphasize the same responsibility to him. Because of his pleasant and innocent nature, it was difficult to chastise him for being late or skipping our interview sessions.

Like Annie Apiuk, also eleven-years-old, Ricky's responses to interview questions were not well thought out or revealing. Ricky would often vacillate on many questions, giving "yes," "no," "must be," and "I don't know" responses. Ricky also had trouble concentrating during our interviews, preferring to talk about fishing, trapping, and hunting. In all probability, Ricky's responses were fairly typical of children his age, who have not reached the stage of personal reflection and introspection more common among our older informants.

8. DAVID AGEOK

David was another eighteen-year-old who, at the time of our interviews, was home on summer vacation from Sir John Franklin. His parents and two younger siblings lived in one of the original three-bedroom houses that lacked running water. David also had an older married brother, an older married sister, and an older sister who lived with his grandmother. David's father had a full-time, wage-labor job, but also engaged in hunting and trapping. In addition, his father was widely recognized as one of the best carvers and artists in the community. During the fieldwork period, David's mother held several temporary, part-time jobs.

When he was home, David shared a room with his younger brother Simon. David completed grade 9 at the Holman school in 1980. An excellent student, David's attendance was much better than many of his age-mates (95 percent and 75 percent attendance for the 1979–1980 and 1978–1979 academic years respectively). In the fall of 1980, David went to Sir John Franklin in Yellowknife but quit after the first month. He returned to high school in January 1981, but quit again in March. He finally returned once again the following August and successfully completed the entire year without incident.

David reported that he liked going to school but did not like being separated from his family and friends for long periods of time. He especially disliked living at Akaitcho Hall, the school dormitory, because "the food is awful and there are too many rules and regulations."

David had been outside of Holman several times. He reported that he went to Coppermine about once a year. In 1980 David went on the school trip to Toronto. Like many of our other informants, David reported that this was one of the most memorable events of his life.

David reported that he was going to high school because he wanted to and not because he might get a better job and more pay with a high school diploma. While he received much encouragement and financial support from his parents and siblings, he asserted that it was his decision to go to high school. After finishing school, David planned to attend vocational school at Fort Smith and receive training as a diesel mechanic.

During our interview sessions, it became apparent that David had a cynical streak, which I had not seen in any of our other informants. For example, David expressed great disapproval of teenagers who did not work or go to school, but who sat around complaining about how boring it was in town. He also complained that many of the young people were not learning much about the old way of life, such as hunting and trapping.

During a number of interview sessions, I sensed a lot of latent hostility in David, who made frequent references to "beating people up." On a number of occasions David said that he would "beat me up" but would then qualify his statements by saying that he was only joking. Even though David liked to "talk tough" and was critical of others during our interview sessions, in public he was as passive and restrained as most other Inuit. While David's cynicism and hostile remarks often made our interview sessions strained, he was conscientious in answering all questions to the best of his ability. David also had a better understanding of the goals of the research than most of our other informants. More so than any of our other informants, David was truly "caught between two worlds," which may have accounted for his unique outlook.

9. EMMA MIKITOK

Emma was fourteen-years-old and lived at home with her parents in one of the larger, four-bedroom housing units equipped with running water and flush toilets. Emma's family was one of the largest in the community. She had ten brothers and sisters, five of whom were married and living in other households in the community. The remaining siblings all lived at home and included an older brother, two older sisters, and one younger sister. In addition, her parents had adopted two grandchildren.

Emma's father, Peter, was a highly respected elder in the community. Because he had five married sons and daughters, he had a large network of kinsmen, including twenty grandchildren. Peter was an active hunter, trapper, and carver, but occasionally engaged in temporary wage employment. Since Peter was in his midsixties, he had curtailed his hunting and trapping somewhat. Emma's mother spent most of her time at home, doing housework and sewing for the co-op.

During the 1981–1982 school year, Emma was in grade 7, having been kept back a year due to poor attendance. Emma frequently skipped school and could often be seen hanging around the Bay store and the co-op coffee shop. When Emma first started to work for us, she would often arrive during school hours. Since we did not want to encourage her skipping school, we decided not to interview her during school hours. There was no indication, however, that our prohibition improved her school attendance at all.

Emma was our most cooperative and talkative female informant, despite her young age and the fact that she frequently missed her interview appointments. Emma was also unusual for a teenage girl since she spent a lot of time with her father. During the period of the research, she started traveling with her father as a trapping partner.

10. EMILY APSIMIK

Our last clinical informant was Emily Apsimik, a sixteen-year-old girl. There were nine members of the Apsimik household, including Emily's parents, an older brother and his girlfriend, an older sister, two younger sisters, and an infant adopted from Emily's oldest married sister. The Apsimik family lived in one of the newest four-bedroom houses. Since Emily and her older sister both had their own bedrooms, her parents converted a large storage closet into a bedroom area for two of their youngest daughters.

Emily's parents were relatively traditional. Her father was an active hunter and trapper while her mother worked at the co-op print shop. Her father was also active in the Holman Anglican church, where he was a lay minister. Emily's sister and brother also worked at the co-op and contributed part of their earnings to the household. Emily's parents operated a camp one hundred miles north of Holman, where they spent part of their summers and winters. When they were at the camp, Emily usually accompanied them.

During the period of the research Emily was enrolled in grade 9, having repeated one grade (7) during her school career. Emily had been on two school trips, one to Kingsville, Ontario, and another to Calgary. In school Emily had a reputation for being extremely stubborn and contentious. According to her teacher, Emily often refused to do schoolwork and would grumble that she shouldn't have come to school if forced to complete her assignments. About one-third of the way through the year, however, Emily's attitude changed dramatically, and she started doing all her work without complaint. Her attendance, however, was quite low, averaging about a half day per week. Emily reported that she went to school only when she wanted to go. When not in school, Emily often did housework and baby-sitting at home.

Emily had no idea what she wanted to do in the future and had not decided whether to go to high school. She asserted that this was something she never discussed with her parents, although her mother had told her that it would be easier for her to get a job if she finished high school.

Emily's contentious nature came through during many interview sessions. Her responses were often abbreviated, and at one point she announced that she was tired of working and wanted to quit. We persisted, however, and she continued to work until we had completed all interviews.

APPENDIX B: The Behavioral Observation of Adolescents

Formal behavioral observations collected during the fieldwork period provide valuable insights regarding the sex and age composition of preadolescent and adolescent groups (defined here as approximately ages nine through thirteen and fourteen through twenty respectively). These data do not provide easy answers to the compexities associated with adolescent and preadolescent peer groups, but offer an interesting data base from which to interpret our interview data.

A total of 467 spot observations were collected during the twelve-month fieldwork period. Most were limited to public and outdoor settings frequented by preadolescents and adolescents between the ages of nine and twenty. A smaller number of observations were collected from private settings during regular social visits to individual households. While the collection of these spot observations was not totally random, we attempted to visit as many settings as possible at different times of the day and different seasons of the year in order to record a representative sample of preadolescent and adolescent behavior. In conducting a spot observation, one of the researchers or our research assistant would enter a behavior setting and record all of the individuals present between the ages of nine and twenty. Also recorded were the ages of all individuals in the group, the group activity, proximity of individuals to one another, group size, presence or absence of adults, and bodily contact. If only one individual was present at the time of the observation, the name and activity of that person were duly recorded. These data were later coded and transferred to disk for analysis. During the data-coding stage, one individual from each spot observation was randomly selected to be the target, or "ego," of that particular observation. Subsequent analysis of group size, activity, and sex and age composition were based upon the age and sex characteristics of the sample "egos." While a limited number of running spot observations were collected (i.e., recording activities over a five-to-fifteen-minute interval), all of the spot observations subjected to computer analysis represent activities at one point in time.

Table B.1 displays the number of observations of 9-to-13-year-olds and 14-to-20-year-olds seen in same-sex and mixed-sex peer groups (defined as three or more individuals). The findings show that preadolescent males and females

TABLE B.1

Adolescents and Preadolescents in Same-Sex versus Mixed-Sex Groups

NUMBER OF OBSERVATIONS	TARGET OF OBSERVATION			
	MALES 9–13	FEMALES 9–13	MALES 14–20	FEMALES 14–20
Same-sex	8 (50%)	29 (60%)	68 (71%)	18 (36%)
Mean size	4.75 ± 1.58	3.93 ± 1.03	4.11 ± 1.78	3.38 ± 0.78
Mixed-sex	8 (50%)	19 (40%)	28 (29%)	32 (64%)
Mean size	4.87 ± 1.55	4.52 ± 1.98	4.17 ± 1.70	4.25 ± 2.02
TOTAL n	16	48	96**	50*

NOTE: Difference between number of observations of same-sex versus mixed-sex groups: *p < .05; **p < .001 (chi-square, one-sample test of significance).

(9 to 13 years of age) were spotted frequently in both same-sex and mixed-sex groups. Older boys, however, contrast dramatically with their younger counterparts. While 9-to-13-year-old males (kids) were spotted with equal frequency in same-sex and mixed-sex groups, older boys were spotted 71 percent of the time in same-sex groups and only 29 percent of the time in mixed-sex groups. This pronounced change may be partially accounted for by the older boys' greater involvement in competitive sports play. Interestingly, a similar change was not documented among the older girls in our sample. In fact, these girls were spotted slightly more often in mixed-sex groups (64 percent of the observations) than in same-sex groups (36 percent of the observations). This finding is noteworthy since the data collected from interviews, daily routines, and casual observations suggest that both boys and girls begin to concentrate their social interactions with members of the same sex as they grow older. One explanation is that the social developmental sequence of females may be slightly different from that of males. While older boys appear to be more obsessed with competition within the ranks of their own age and sex group, and limit their interactions therein, the interests of females are less likely to result in exclusive same-sex interactions. Unlike older boys, adolescent girls were more frequently spotted in mixed-sex groups that included males and females of a broader age range.

Another explanation is that significantly more adolescent boys than girls were spotted in public settings. Since adolescent girls, especially those between 17 and 20 years of age, reported spending more time in private settings (i.e., individual households) and have more household responsibilities than males, few venture out in public with the same frequency as do boys. In all probability, girls are more likely to restrict their social interactions to other girls who assist with a variety of baby-sitting and household chores. The adolescent girls who do venture out to public settings on a frequent basis may, in fact, be the more outgoing girls in the community who are more likely to seek male companionship within mixed-sex groups. Thus, the finding in table B.1 that older girls were spotted more often in mixed-sex groups may be the result of a sampling error that inadvertently selected a small group of the most outgoing girls in the community as targets for our spot observations simply because they were the only ones present in these settings. (In fact, three teenage girls accounted for almost half of the observations of adolescent females in the 14-to-20 age group. All of these girls had reputations for being extremely sociable and physically mobile.)

A related finding from table B.1 is that across all age and sex categories, mixed-sex groups were observed to be slightly larger on average than same-sex groups. The difference is most pronounced between preadolescent and adolescent females and less so for males. This suggests that same-sex groups tend to be slightly smaller and hence more intimate than mixed-sex groups. Due to the gender ambivalence that exists at this age and the uncertainty associated with cross-sex interaction, it is feasible to assume that individual boys and girls find "strength in numbers" when interacting in mixed-sex groups. A similar tendency has been described by Dunphey (1963, 236) in which American adolescents were observed establishing mixed-sex groups through unisexual cliques coming together in group-to-group interaction. At this stage of peer group development, adolescents presumably approach the novelty of mixed-group interaction with the protection and support of unisexual clique members.

When examining the frequencies of mixed-sex groups for different ages and sexes, a logical consideration is the age of these opposite-sex playmates. Thus, we must ask if 9-to-13-year-old boys are spotted mostly with 9-to-13-year-old girls or perhaps dividing their time between 9-to-13-year-old girls and 14-to-20-year-old girls. Table B.2 provides a breakdown of the ages of these opposite-sex playmates by age and sex of the target of the spot observation. As expected, girls and boys of all ages tend to prefer the companionship of op-

TABLE B.2
Number of Opposite-Sex Interactants by Age and Sex of Target (mixed-sex groups only)

	TARGET OF OBSERVATION			
OPPOSITE-SEX INTERACTANTS	MALES 9–13	FEMALES 9–13	MALES 14–20	FEMALES 14–20
Age 9–13				
Abs. Freq.	9	18	3	10
Mean	1.13	0.95	0.11	0.31
Age 14–20				
Abs. Freq.	7	9	33	32
Mean	0.88	0.47	1.18	1.00
TOTAL number of observations	8	19	28[a]	32[a]

[a] Difference between number of 9 to 13-year-olds and 14 to 20-year-olds significant at $p < .001$ (chi-square, one sample test of significance).

posite-sex playmates of roughly the same age. This preference, however, is not terribly pronounced for preadolescent boys and girls. Younger boys, especially, were spotted almost as frequently with adolescent girls (14 to 20) as with pre-adolescent girls (9 to 13). When examining adolescent boys and girls, however, we see a preference for opposite-sex playmates in the same age class. For both groups the difference is statistically significant at $p < .001$ using the chi-square, one-sample test of significance. Nevertheless, 14-to-20-year-old girls were more likely than their male age-mates to be spotted with preadolescents of the opposite sex. The overall results suggest that older males are more concerned with age *and* sex as criteria for inclusion in peer group activities than are females. A seventeen-year-old boy would never want a ten-year-old sister or niece following him around with his friends. Since females are often charged with the care of younger siblings, cousins, nieces, and nephews, they are socialized for a higher degree of nurturance and tolerance than adolescent males. As a result, they are less likely to restrict their interactions to a narrow age and sex group.

Paradoxically, cross-sex dyads increase in frequency in the later teenage years. While kids and younger teenagers are likely to limit their contact with the opposite sex to play groups, older teenagers (generally around age sixteen to seventeen) begin to develop dating relationships and cross-sex friendships, which are a natural outgrowth of initial contacts established within mixed-sex groups. Table B.3 provides a breakdown of the number of spot observations involving same-sex and opposite-sex pairs. When young males and females were spotted in pairs, it was invariably with members of the same sex (90 percent for boys and 86 percent for girls). Older boys and girls, on the other hand, were much more frequently spotted with opposite-sex companions (30 percent for boys and 29 percent for girls). For boys, these opposite-sex companions were almost exclusively in the same age category as themselves.

TABLE B.3
Observations of Same-Sex and Cross-Sex Pairs

| | PRIMARY EGO (TARGET OF OBSERVATION) | | | |
SECOND EGO	MALES 9–13	FEMALES 9–13	MALES 14–20	FEMALES 14–20
Same-sex				
Age 9–13	4	19	3	7
Age 14–20	4	7	42	18
Age unknown[a]	1	4	2	2
TOTAL same-sex	9 (90%)	30 (86%)	47 (70%)	27 (71%)
Cross-sex				
Age 9–13	1	4	1	3
Age 14–20	0	1	18	5
Age unknown[a]	0	0	1	3
TOTAL cross-sex	1 (10%)	5 (14%)	20 (30%)	11 (29%)
TOTAL number of observations	10	35	67	38

[a] Age and identity of second ego unknown.

These findings are especially interesting when we note that older boys display a clear preference for interacting in large same-sex groups even as they are developing an interest in more intimate dyadic cross-sex interaction. One explanation is that while these older boys prefer the companionship of same-age and same-sex companions, they are not completely disinterested in the opposite sex. In fact, it may be that awakening sexual interest in the opposite sex leads these older boys, and older girls, to seek out more intimate contact with potential sexual partners outside of the mixed-group context. Thus while young boys and girls are likely to limit their contact with the opposite sex to mixed play groups, older teenagers begin to develop dating relationships and cross-sex friendships that are an outgrowth of initial contacts established within mixed-sex groups. Even as teenage boys spend much time in large same-sex groups, they tend to increase contact with the opposite sex in intimate cross-sex dyads. The fact that boys spend significantly less time in mixed-sex groups than in same-sex groups may not necessarily be due to any conscious segregation between the sexes, but simply because they enjoy the thrill of competitive sports play, in which teenage girls do not participate.

APPENDIX C:
Holman Draw-a-Persons

Draw-a-persons done by an eleven-year-old girl. Above: a girl going inside her house after sliding on a hill. Below: a boy driving to the Bay on a snowmobile.

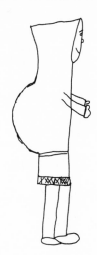

Above: *Draw-a-persons done by a thirteen-year-old girl.* Left: *a young boy going to school.* Right: *a woman packing her baby and going to the Bay store.*
Below: *Draw-a-persons done by a fifteen-year-old girl.* Left: *a young girl walking to the Bay store.* Right: *a boy seeing how big his muscles are and getting ready to go to school. (He is saying, "my muscles are not big enough.")*

Draw-a-persons done by a sixteen-year-old boy. Above: teenage boy playing hockey. Below: teenage girl playing softball.

Draw-a-persons done by a sixteen-year-old boy. Above: a man pulling up a seal from a breathing hole ("I got a seal!"). Below: a woman fishing and packing a baby.

Draw-a-persons done by a seventeen-year-old boy. Above: a man about to go seal hunting. Below: a woman butchering a seal and singing to herself.

Draw-a-persons done by an eighteen-year-old boy. Left: teenage boy just hanging around. Right: *teenage girl walking around and looking sexy.*

Draw-a-persons done by a thirteen-year-old boy. Above: boy ice fishing. Below: girl walking to a lake to play on the ice.

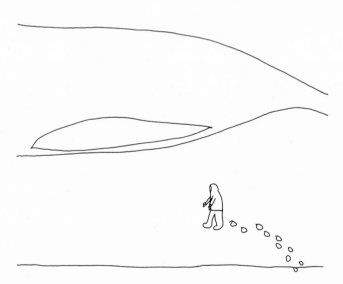

Draw-a-persons done by an eleven-year-old girl. Above: woman packing a baby and waving to a friend. Below: *man ice fishing.*

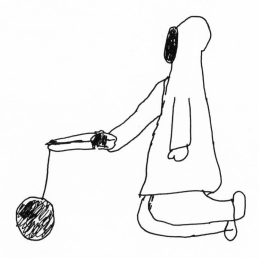

Draw-a-persons done by a thirteen-year-old girl. Above: *woman packing a baby.* Below: *an Eskimo man playing with his puppy.*

Draw-a-persons done by an eleven-year-old boy. Above: *an eleven-year-old boy walking to his desk at school.* (*He is saying, "I should go to the store at recess time."*) Below: *a thirteen-year-old girl playing outside.* (*She is saying, "I should dig a hole in the snow."*)

Draw-a-persons done by a nineteen-year-old boy. Above: a man seal hunting at a breathing hole. Below: a woman drum dancing and singing in Inuktitut.

NOTES

CHAPTER 1. THE COMMUNITY
1. In 1984 Holman was elevated by the Government of the Northwest Territories to hamlet status. As a hamlet, Holman has more control over its own affairs. Settlement employees who used to work directly under the N.W.T. Department of Local Government are now employed by the Holman Hamlet Council. All buildings and equipment previously owned and operated by the territorial government were transferred to the hamlet council, which now receives a larger operating budget to accommodate these increased responsibilities in financial management and settlement development.

CHAPTER 2. LIFE STAGES AND CYCLES
1. Our original methodology was to obtain the mean age for the 25 percent fastest growing males and females. For both samples, however, a natural break appeared between the six fastest growing boys and girls and those who scored lower on height and weight velocity.

2. In traditional Inuit society, marriage did not imply the same legal, ceremonial, or religious obligations as it does in Western society. It is used here for lack of a better term. From an emic point of view, a man and woman were considered married when they established a separate household and were recognized as husband and wife by members of the community.

3. Despite Health and Welfare Canada's program to encourage bottle-feeding in the 1950s and 1960s, later studies provided evidence that bottle-fed infants were more susceptible to various upper-respiratory and middle-ear infections (Schaefer 1971, 1973, 1976; Ling, McCoy, and Levinson 1969; Brody, Overfield, and McAlister 1965; Reed, Struve, and Maynard 1967; Maynard 1969). As a result, Northern Medical Services reversed its policy in the late 1960s and implemented programs to encourage breast-feeding.

4. On only two occasions in twenty-nine months of fieldwork did I observe a parent spank a child. In both cases, the punishment involved a very mild swat on the bottom of a misbehaving child.

CHAPTER 4. FAMILY LIFE OF ADOLESCENTS

1. Young people who are obsessed with high speeds and fast snowmobiles often complain when they have to travel with older hunters, for whom high speeds are superfluous and dangerous. O'Neil (1983, 141) suggests that this difference between young people and older, more experienced hunters is due to the former's fear of camping out. While older hunters have an intimate knowledge of the land and have mastered the skills of cold-weather camping, these skills are not as well developed in the younger generation. As a result, there is a tendency for young people to go on midwinter hunting trips that can be accomplished in one day. Also, at the first sign of bad weather, young Inuit will, more likely than not, race back to the settlement, while older hunters will set up camp and wait for better traveling conditions. Another reason adolescents prefer day trips is that they are eager to get back to the comfort and warmth of town to watch a favorite television program or engage in some late night sporting activity.

One of the unfortunate sides of the day trip mentality is that young people, having the attitude that they can always make it back to town if bad weather suddenly moves in, frequently go out hunting without sufficient camping equipment or supplies. Older hunters, most of whom have had numerous "close calls," do not travel with such self-assurance. My own experience with such an ill-equipped day trip nearly resulted in disaster when a spring blizzard blew in suddenly. My hunting companions and I traveled all night in zero visibility. We finally made it back to town, but only after having to abandon two broken-down snowmobiles. We later discovered that we had spent most of the night traveling in the wrong direction!

CHAPTER 5. FRIENDS AND PEERS

1. The term *northern games* refers to a category of traditional Inuit games that continue to be played in Holman and other northern communities. The entire repertoire includes several dozen games that have either been modified or elaborated as a result of Eurocanadian influence. In addition, there has been a great deal of exchange with other areas of the Arctic, so Holman youths will often play northern games introduced from other areas such as Alaska and Greenland. Examples include the musk-ox push, in which two contestants will lock heads and shoulders on all fours and push; the one-foot high kick, in which a single contestant will jump up and kick a small sack suspended from a pole with one foot; the toe jump, in which a contestant will hold his toes with his hands and jump as far as possible without losing his balance; and the kneel jump, in which a contestant will jump as far as possible from a kneeling position. In general, northern games emphasize a range of skills and abilities, including balance, strength, manual dexterity, and endurance.

Northern games are not played with the same frequency by teenagers as the more recently introduced sports of football, baseball, and hockey. While northern games are often played by all ages and both sexes during community-wide celebrations such as Christmas and Easter, it is widely recognized that the very best northern games athletes are teenage boys and young adult men in their early twenties.

Recently, northern games have become international in character. Since the mid-1970s, pan-Arctic competitions have been held in different northern communities and are attended by the best Inuit athletes from Alaska, Canada, and Greenland. A number of Holman youths have had the opportunity to compete in these events and have even won medals in certain categories.

CHAPTER 6. GENDER PREFERENCE, SEXUALITY, AND MATE SELECTION

1. The draw-a-person data from Morocco are particularly interesting in this respect, since a significant number of informants made cross-sex choices in their initial drawings. When all the societies in the Harvard Adolescence Project were ordered from highest to lowest number of cross-sex choices, the Moroccan youths ranked highest while the Holman adolescents ranked lowest (Susan Davis, personal communication).

CHAPTER 7. SCHOOL, WORK, AND ASPIRATIONS

1. In the fall of 1984, the number of teachers at the Holman school was increased to five.

2. The Holman Education Committee's budget for the 1984–1985 school year was $18,000, compared to the school's supplies budget of $13,500.

3. The Special Committee on Education was organized in February 1980 by the Legislative Assembly of the Northwest Territories to investigate the problems and public concerns with education throughout the Northwest Territories. The committee initiated public hearings in thirty-four northern communities and conducted extensive interviews with school staff members. The committee's final report was submitted in March 1982 (Special Committee on Education 1982).

4. A 1985 communication with the principal of the Holman school states that the vast majority of students, both girls and boys, in grades 8 and 9 now apply to attend Sir John Franklin. This represents a significant increase from just three years ago when only a handful of students, all male, applied to high school.

5. Sir John Franklin High School operates two distinct tracks of instruction, one resulting in a high school diploma and the other resulting in a high school certificate. The course of study leading to the diploma is more rigorous and involves the successful completion of coursework in science, mathematics, English, foreign languages, and history. These students are predominantly the sons and daughters of non-native businessmen and government employees, all of whom are solidly middle class and education oriented. The certificate course, on the other hand, is much less rigorous, involving more vocational courses and fewer academic classes. Most high school certificates are awarded to native students whose academic preparation for high school prevents them from successful completion of the diploma program.

6. Recent data, however, suggest that homesickness may no longer be the primary "formal" reason for students leaving Sir John Franklin. Between 1982–1984, of all the students returned from Sir John Franklin to all settlements, 92 percent were for disciplinary reasons and the remainder were for home-

sickness. For the 1983–1984 academic year, Sir John Franklin returned six students for homesickness (one to Holman) and fifty-three for disciplinary reasons (two to Holman). According to the principal of the Holman school, from whom these data were obtained, these figures represent a reversal of those from just two to three years before, when the vast majority of students left school due to homesickness. These figures may be somewhat misleading since, in all probability, homesickness may be the primary cause of "disciplinary" problems. As a result, it is not surprising that many parents worry that their children may get into trouble in Yellowknife.

CHAPTER 8. REBELLION AND DEVIANCE IN ADOLESCENCE

1. In 1978, 37.09 percent of all deaths resulted from accidents, injuries, and violence; other causes were cardiovascular disease (20.19 percent), malignant neoplasms (12.68 percent), and lower respiratory ailments (11.74 percent) (*Report on Health Conditions in the N.W.T.* 1978, 13). It has been estimated that forty to fifty percent of the deaths falling into the first category involved, directly or indirectly, the consumption of alcohol (Finkler 1975, 24). Due to this alarming increase in alcohol abuse and concomitant law violations, many settlements have organized community plebiscites to restrict or completely ban the sale and importation of alcohol into their communities. By 1981 such community action resulted in the prohibition of alcohol in at least fourteen communities in the N.W.T., with an additional five communities instituting some form of alcohol restriction. Considering the grave problem that alcohol abuse poses for young Indians and Inuit in many areas, it is likely that similar plebiscites will result in restrictions or prohibitions in many other settlements in the N.W.T.

2. Holman residents are presently divided in their opinions regarding the establishment of a full-time detachment in the community. Supporters of such a move believe that the increase in alcohol use and subsequent law violations have made it desirable to have a full-time RCMP officer on duty. Others believe that the community is still small enough to manage its own affairs without a permanent detachment. Undoubtedly the establishment of a full-time RCMP post would result in an increase in law violations, since individuals would be more likely to be prosecuted for minor offenses that, at present, go unnoticed or unreported. Local residents are generally reluctant to bring complaints to the attention of the police. This is true not only in Holman, but in other areas of the Arctic as well (Clairmont 1962,1963; Finkler 1975). This unwillingness may be a function of two factors: persistence of the traditional tendency to forget disputes and forgive transgressions and lack of a resident RCMP on permanent duty in the settlement. A person wanting to file an immediate complaint against an assailant or thief may change his or her mind when the officer is in town. In one case, the victim of an assault called the Coppermine RCMP office to lodge a complaint, but then decided to withdraw it several days later when an officer arrived in town to investigate the matter.

REFERENCES

Abrahamson, G., P. J. Gillespie, D. J. McIntosh, P. J. Usher, and H. A. Williamson. 1963. *The Copper Eskimos: An Area Economic Survey.* Industrial Division, Department of Northern Affairs and National Resources, Ottawa.

Balikci, A. 1961. "Suicidal Behavior among the Netsilik Eskimos." In B. Blishen, ed., *Canadian Society: Sociological Perspectives*, article no. 35. Chicago: The Free Press of Glencoe.

————. 1970. *The Netsilik Eskimo.* Garden City, N.J.: Natural History Press.

Benedict, R. 1938. "Continuities and Discontinuities in Cultural Conditioning." *Psychiatry* 1:161–167.

Berman, M. L., K. Hansen, and I. L. Hellman. 1972. "Effect of Breastfeeding on Post-Partum Menstruation, Ovulation, and Pregnancy in Alaskan Eskimos." *American Journal of Obstetrics and Gynecology* 114:524–534.

Blackwood, L. 1981. "Alaska Native Fertility Trends, 1950–1978." *Demography* 18:173.

Blos, P. 1962. *On Adolescence.* New York: Free Press.

————. 1967. "The Second Individuation Process of Adolescence." In R. S. Eissley, ed., *Psychoanalytic Study of the Child.* Vol. 15. New York: International Universities Press.

Bowerman, C., and J. Kinch. 1959. "Changes in Family and Peer Orientation of Children between Fourth and Tenth Grade." *Social Forces* 37:206–211.

Briggs, J. 1968. *Utkuhikhalingmiut Eskimo Emotional Expression.* Northern Science Research Group, Department of Indian Affairs and Northern Development, Ottawa.

————. 1970. *Never in Anger.* Cambridge: Harvard University Press.

Brody, J., T. Overfield, and R. McAlister. 1965. "Draining Ears and Deafness among Alaskan Eskimos." Archives of Otolaryngology. 81:29.

Buliard, R. P. 1951. *Inuk.* New York: Farrar, Straus, and Young.

Burbank, V. N.d. *Three Young Girls: Female Adolescence in an Australian Aboriginal Community.* Book forthcoming in Adolescents in a Changing World series, Rutgers University Press.

Canada. Department of Local Government. 1971. *Settlement Councils: Some Notes for Secretary Managers*. Development Division, Department of Local Government, Government of the N.W.T., Yellowknife.

————. Department of Transport. 1970. *Climate of the Canadian Arctic*. Meteorological Branch, Department of Energy, Mines, and Resources, Ottawa.

Canada Yearbook. 1980–1981. Statistics Canada, Supply and Services, Ottawa.

Clairmont, D. H. 1962. *Notes on the Drinking Behavior of Eskimos and Indians in the Aklavik Area*. Northern Co-ordination and Research Centre, Ottawa.

————. 1963. *Deviance amongst Indians and Eskimos in Aklavik*. Northern Co-ordination and Research Centre, Ottawa.

Csikszentmihalyi, M., and R. Larson. 1984. *Being Adolescent: Conflict and Growth in the Teenage Years*. New York: Basic Books.

Damas, D. 1969. "Characteristics of Central Eskimo Band Structure." In David Damas, ed., *Contributions to Anthropology: Band Societies*. National Museums of Canada Bulletin No. 228, Ottawa.

————. 1972. "The Structure of Central Eskimo Associations." In Lee Guemple, ed., *Alliance in Eskimo Society*, pp. 40–55. Seattle: University of Washington Press.

Davis, S. 1983. "Sexual Maturation, Cultural Constraint, and the Concept of the Self." Paper read at 1983 American Anthropological Association Meetings, Chicago.

Delvoye, P., J. Delogne-Desnoeck, and C. Robyn. 1976. "Serum-Prolactin in Long-Lasting Lactation Amenorrhea." *Lancet* (August 7): 288–289.

DeVos, G. 1978. "Selective Permeability and Reference Group Sanctioning: Psychocultural Continuities in Role Degradation." In J. M. Yinger and S. J. Cutler, eds., *Major Social Issues: A Multidisciplinary View*, pp. 7–24. New York: Free Press.

Douvan, E. A., and J. Adelson. 1966. *The Adolescent Experience*. New York: John Wiley.

Dunphey, D. 1963. "The Social Structure of Urban Adolescent Peer Groups." *Sociometry* 26: 230–246.

Erikson, E. A. 1963. *Childhood and Society*. New York: Norton.

————. 1968. *Identity: Youth and Crisis*. New York: Norton.

Finkler, H. 1975. *Inuit and the Administration of Justice in the Northwest Territories: The Case of Frobisher Bay*. Department of Indian and Northern Affairs, Ottawa.

Foulks, E. 1974. *The Arctic Hysterias*. Seattle: University of Washington Press.

Franklin, J. 1928. *Narrative of a Second Expedition to the Shores of the Polar Sea in the Years 1819, 20, 21, and 22*. London: John Murray.

Freeman, M. A. 1978. *Life among the Qallunaat*. Edmonton: Hurtig.

Freud, S. 1949. *An Outline of Psychoanalysis*. New York: Norton.

Graburn, N. H. H. 1969. *Eskimos without Igloos*. New York: Little Brown.

Guemple, L., ed. 1971. *Alliance in Eskimo Society*. Seattle: University of Washington Press.

Hall, G. S. 1904. *Adolescence*. New York: Appleton and Co.

Hart, C. W. M. and A. R. Pilling. 1960. *The Tiwi of North Australia.* New York: Holt, Rinehart and Winston.

Hartup, W. W. 1983. "The Peer System," In P. H. Mussen, ed., *Carmichael's Manual of Child Psychology.* 4th ed., vol. 4. New York: John Wiley.

Hearne, S. 1958. *A Journey from Prince of Wales Fort in Hudson's Bay to the Northern Ocean, 1769–1770–1771–1772.* Ed. R. Grover. Toronto: Macmillan.

Hildes, J. A. and O. Schaefer. 1973. "Health of Igloolik Eskimos and Changes with Urbanization." *Journal of Human Biology* 2:241–246.

Hobart, C. W. 1970. "Some Consequences of Residential Schooling of Eskimos in the Canadian Arctic." *Arctic Anthropology* 6 (2):123–135.

Hobart, C. W., and C. S. Brandt. 1966. "Eskimo Education, Danish and Canadian: A Comparison." *Canadian Review of Sociology and Anthropology* 3(2):47–66.

Hoebel, E. A. 1954. *The Law of Primitive Man.* Cambridge: Harvard University Press.

Holm, G. 1914. "Ethnological Sketch of the Angmagssalik Eskimos." *Meddelelser om Gronland* 39.

Jenness, D. 1922. *The Life of the Copper Eskimos.* Report of the Canadian Arctic Expedition, 1913–1918, vol. 12, p. A. Ottawa.

Kippley, S. K., and J. F. Kippley. 1977. "The Relation between Breastfeeding and Amenorrhea: Report of a Survey." *Journal of Tropical Pediatrics* 23: 239–245.

Klengenberg, C. 1932. *Klengenberg of the Arctic: An Autobiography.* Ed. Tom MacInnes. London: Johnathan Cape.

Kohlberg, L. 1969. "Stage and Sequence: The Cognitive-Developmental Approach to Socialization." In D. A. Goslin, ed., *Handbook of Socialization Theory and Research.* Chicago: Rand-McNally.

———. 1976. "Moral Stages and Moralization: The Cognitive-Developmental Approach." In T. Lickona, ed., *Moral Development and Behavior.* New York: Holt, Rinehart and Winston.

Lewin, K. 1938. "Field Theory and Experiment in Social Psychology: Concepts and Methods." *American Journal of Sociology* 44:868–896.

Ling, D., R. McCoy, and E. Levinson. 1969. "The Incidence of Middle-Ear Disease and Its Educational Implications among Baffin Island Eskimo Children." *Canadian Journal of Public Health* 60:385.

McAlpine, P. J. and N. E. Simpson. 1975. "Fertility and Other Demographic Aspects of the Canadian Eskimo Communities of Igloolik and Hall Beach." *Human Biology* 48:113–138.

McGhee, R. 1972. *Copper Eskimo Prehistory.* Publications in Archeology, no. 2. National Museums of Canada, Ottawa.

Maynard, J. 1969. "Otitis Media in Alaskan Eskimo Children: An Epidemiological Review with Observations on Control." *Alaska Medicine* 11:93–97.

Mead, M. 1928. *Coming of Age in Samoa.* New York: Morrow.

Milan, F. A. 1978. "Demography and Population Parameters of the Present Inhabitants of North Alaska." In P. Jamison, S. Zegura, and F. A. Milan, eds., *Eskimos of Northwestern Alaska: A Biological Perspective*, pp. 222–232. Stroudsburg, Pa.: Dowden, Hutchinson, and Ross.

———, ed. 1980. *The Human Biology of Circumpolar Populations*. Cambridge: Cambridge University Press.

O'Neil, J. 1983. "Is It Cool To Be an Eskimo: A Study of Stress, Identity, Coping, and Health among Canadian Inuit Young Adult Men." Ph.D. diss., University of California, San Francisco.

Oswalt, W. 1979. *Eskimos and Explorers*. San Francisco: Chandler and Sharp.

Parsons, T. 1942. "Age and Sex in the Social Structure of the United States." *American Sociological Review* 7:604–616.

Piaget, J. 1965. *The Moral Judgement of the Child*. New York: Free Press.

Rasmussen, K. 1927. *Across Arctic America: Narrative of the Fifth Thule Expedition*. New York: G. P. Putnam's Sons.

———. 1932. *Intellectual Culture of the Copper Eskimos*. Report of the Fifth Thule Expedition, 1921–1924, vol. 1. Copenhagen.

Ratner, M. N.d. *Ethnographic Report on Adolescent Development in Baisoara, Romania*. Book forthcoming in Adolescents in a Changing World series, Rutgers University Press.

Reed, D., S. Struve, and J. Maynard. 1967. "Otitis Media and Hearing Deficiency among Eskimo Children: A Cohort Study." *American Journal of Public Health* 57:1657.

Report on Health Conditions in the N.W.T. 1978. Chief Medical and Health Officer, Government of the N.W.T., Yellowknife.

———. 1983. Chief Medical and Health Officer, Government of the N.W.T., Yellowknife.

Schaefer, O. 1959. "Medical Observations and Problems in Canadian Eskimos, Part II." *Canadian Medical Association Journal* 81:386–393.

———. 1971. "Otitis Media and Bottle-Feeding." *Canadian Journal of Public Health* 62:478–488.

———. 1973. "The Changing Health Picture in the Canadian North." *Canadian Journal of Opthamology* 8:196–204.

———. 1976. "Bottle-Feeding and Morbidity, Arctic Bay, April/76." Manuscript.

———. N.d. "The Impact of Culture on Breastfeeding Patterns." Manuscript.

Smith, T. G. 1973. "Management Research on the Eskimos Ringed Seal." *Canadian Geographic Journal* 86:118–125.

Special Committee on Education. 1982. *Learning: Tradition and Change in the Northwest Territories*. N.W.T. Legislative Assembly, Yellowknife.

Spencer, R. F. 1959. *The North Alaskan Eskimo: A Study in Ecology and Society*. New York: Dover.

Stefansson, V. 1913. *My Life with the Eskimo*. New York: Macmillan.

———. 1919. *The Stefansson-Anderson Arctic Expedition: Preliminary Ethnological Report*. Anthropological Papers of the American Museum of Natural History, vol. 14, p. 1. New York.

Sullivan, H. S. 1953. *The Interpersonal Theory of Psychiatry*. New York: Norton.

Tanner, J. M. 1978. *Fetus into Man: Physical Growth from Conception to Maturity.* Cambridge: Harvard University Press.

Usher, P. J. 1965. *Economic Basis and Resource Use of the Coppermine-Holman Region, N.W.T.* Ottawa: Department of Northern Affairs and National Resources.

Weyer, E. M. 1932. *The Eskimos.* New Haven: Yale University Press.

Whiting, J. W. M., V. K. Burbank, and M. S. Ratner. 1986. "The Duration of Maidenhood." In J. B. Lancaster and B. A. Hamburg, eds., *School Age Pregnancy and Parenthood.* Hawthorne, N.Y.: Aldine de Gruyter.

Whiting, J. W. M., I. L. Child, and W. W. Lambert. 1966. *Field Guide for the Study of Socialization.* Six Cultures Series, vol. 1. New York: John Wiley.

Whiting, J. W. M., K. Romney, B. B. Whiting, E. E. Maccoby, B. C. Ayres, H. Smith, and E. Lowell. 1953. *Field Manual for the Cross-Cultural Study of Child Rearing.* New York: Social Science Research Council.

Willmott, E. 1961. *The Eskimo Community at Port Harrison.* Northern Coordination and Research Centre, Department of Northern Affairs and National Resources, Ottawa.

Youniss, J. 1980. *Parents and Peers in Social Development.* Chicago: University of Chicago Press.

Index